The Gospels of Thomas and Mary Magdalene

The Gospels of Thomas and Mary Magdalene

Originally published by DISCUS Publishing, Anja Schäfer

2nd edition © 2023

Cover Illustration by Peter Holle

For permission requests send an email to info@discuspublishing.com.

Publisher's Website: https://discuspublishing.com

ISBN: 978-3-9817441-9-4

The Gospels of Thomas and Mary Magdalene

Dr. Raymond Keller

THE
GOSPELS OF JUDAS THOMAS AND MARY MAGDALENE,
AN ACCOUNT
WRITTEN BY THE DISCIPLES OF JESUS THE CHRIST,
THE FIRSTBORN IN THE FULLNESS OF TIME,
AND REVEALED TO THE INHABITANTS OF THE EARTH
THROUGH THE MINISTRY OF ANGELS
IN THESE LATTER DAYS

Wherefore it is an abridgment of the records of the General Assembly of the Church of the Firstborn in the Fullness of Time, and also of the Saints of the Lord Jesus the Christ in first century Egypt, India and the Islands of the Western Sea, written by way of commandment; and also by the Spirit of Prophesy and of Revelation, written and sealed and hid up in desert caves unto the Lord, that they might not be destroyed, to come forth by the gift and power of the Holy Ghost unto the interpreta-tion thereof; to come forth in due time by the way of the Gentiles.

Also, The Gospels of Judas Thomas, the twin brother of Our Lord and Savior Jesus the Christ; and Mary Magdalene, the beloved spouse of Jesus, the Christ, and mother of Our Lord's children, are provided herein; that they may show unto the inhabitants of the Earth in these Latter Days how great and marvelous things the Lord Jesus hath done for our ancestors and will yet accomplish on behalf of humankind; and that they may know the covenants of the Lord, that they are not cast off forever: And also to the convincing of all that Jesus is the Christ, the manifestation of the Eternal God, making Himself known unto all who believe and call out in His most holy name. And now, if there be any fault, it be by human error: wherefore condemn not the things of God, that ye may be found spotless at the Judgment seat of Christ, finding your place in the Pleroma of Celestial Light and the paradisiacal worlds without end.

By Raymond A. Keller, II, Ph.D., Author and Proprietor, with the divine assistance of the Seeress Annalee Skarin, Rev. Dr. Frank E. Stranges, and many other luminaries in the Celestial Hierarchy, revealed to the world at Mount Shasta, California, on Thursday, 26 August 2021, A.D.

DEDICATION

This inspired Morning Star Version of the Sacred Texts of the Gospels of Thomas and Mary Magdalene are dedicated to the following illumined ones, without whose assistance from both sides of the veil this work would not have been possible:

- Annalee Skarin (1899), Mormon prophetess and translated being, now known as Lady Encara
- Dr. Tatiana H. Irvin (1970-2019), descendant of Annalee Skarin, intuitive, metaphysician and teacher
- Dr. Frank E. Stranges (1927-2008), formerly of Van Nuys, California, Director, International Evangelism Crusade
- Robert Potter of the Promise Revealed, Mt. Shasta, California
- Omnec Onec, the Ambassador from Venus

Photo by Shareen Strauss, from 1 August 2018 edition of the Mt. Shasta News: Dr. Tatiana H. Irvin with Dr. Raymond Keller at Mt. Shasta, California, From Venus with Love Conference, 28 August 2018.

Table of Contents

Introduction by Robert Potter

Dear Brothers and Sisters,

It is with great humility and gratitude that I have accepted my brother Raymond Keller's request to write this introduction to the Gospel of Thomas. I am not a biblical scholar nor have I followed any religion in a secular framework. I am, however, a devout seeker of the truth who loves God with all my heart.

I admit that I am not perfect and still quite human, but aspiring to perfect devotion in my heart. For those that know me personally, I ask for you to look beyond my personal limitations in my Earthly life. My blemishes should not be associated with this revelation.

Realize that this is the first time ever that the true accounting of these gospels, events and records have ever been released to the world. These are faithfully reproduced in our modern understanding as they were written in their intended and complete form.

This Gospel of Thomas, inclusive of the Gospel of Mary Magdalene, was found at the Nag Hammadi site in the Egyptian desert in December of 1945 along with some other books collectively called the "Nag Hammadi Library." These texts were very fragmented with age and in a state of advanced decay. The original parchments now rest in the Coptic Museum in Cairo. They have been thought to have been written and dated from 100-245 A.D., according to some sources.

Until today these sacred texts have only been able to be partially interpreted by scholars because no complete record of these texts has ever been found. That these texts are even real is debated by many. It is possible, but doubtful, that these texts are in their complete form anywhere in the world, not even in the library beneath the Vatican. Even if these texts were there, they could not be as complete or as accurate as this version for this edition is a supernatural gift to the faithful through the Hierarchy of Light.

Divine Gift

The Gospel of Thomas in this present form is presented as a divine gift from the ministry of angels through their chosen messenger Raymond Keller. The Gospel of Thomas also includes the Acts of Thomas and the Gospel of the Young Jesus as well as the Gospel of Mary Magdalene.

I encourage you all to be at peace, tuning into the loving emanations from the heart of the Apostle Thomas and Mary Magdalene as they illumine us as to their unique relationship with Jesus, the Christ. For many, this spiritual understanding will prove more astounding than many of the miracles revealed herein. The Apostle Thomas and Mary Magdalene teach us that when we exercise our divine resolve, nothing shall be held back from us. Opening our eyes, hearts and minds to those miracles occurring in every moment of every day will serve us well when seeking a greater understanding of Christ's ministry and God's glory.

The magnificent and majestic beauty and order that we behold in all of nature throughout the universe leaves us breathless and clearly shows the intelligent design of our Creator. Certainly, our omnipotent and omnipresent God has a plan for each and every soul. But we must choose this plan to realize it in our life. It takes a humble spirit and pure heart to see this path to righteousness that we must choose of our own freewill.

Miracles

These miracles revealed herein, as performed by Jesus and Thomas, are meant to act as points of accentuation to the ministry of Christ and his message. These divine miracles have been imprinted on the hearts of the witnesses to facilitate a change in their way of thinking and acting and to assist them in setting aside their worldly ways of materialism, further to seek the eternal realms of light and life. The proud become humble; and the violent become peaceful through their own realization of the truths spoken of about the Master Jesus as Thomas revealed them through the course of his ministry.

The miracles in Thomas' ministry converted the witnesses of these supernatural events into the faithful who were baptized through the administrations of the disciples of Christ carried out by the power of the Holy Ghost. This gospel took place mostly in India shortly after Christ was resurrected. These miracles have served to keep the revelation of mankind's divinity as revealed through Christ intact for over 2,000 years. The Master said, "Greater things ye shall do." This is why the Acts of Thomas has no "AMEN" at the end, as the other books in the Bible. It means that the Acts are not complete nor will they ever be complete, as God's covenant is eternal and His acts will continue to be carried out by His servants on Earth forevermore.

Divine Personages Are Real

Mother Mary and Archangel Michael are real. The are many other such divine personages spoken about in the Bible and in many other texts all over the world throughout history. The administration of the heavenlies is vast and beyond comprehension to us in the material worlds. The details of exactly how the Avatars incarnate and are supported from the heavenly realms for their missions of revelation to the worlds they serve are still a mystery.

The point I make is to be aware that on a certain level human development is being managed and guided, because it is God's will that humankind know the truth. With this Gospel of Thomas, a more down to Earth explanation can be offered that will unveil the guidance mankind receives from the Hierarchy of Light, despite those who are aligned against God's will and working against such an impartation of revelation.

A Shibboleth Against Authorities

I must preface the revelation of how these texts were written, acting as a shibboleth before the fact, for my brother, who serves the Angel Force with absolute integrity and truth. Raymond has told me, "We are only postmen delivering a message. Therefore, we should not be offended by those who would defame us." Raymond will never offer to defend himself nor raise his voice in anyway or for any reason.... The angels have chosen well!

However, I must tell those of you who are about to read these pages, that this holy and precious record will stand wholly on its own merit. But in doing so, it will shine like a super nova and bring many into closer association with the Divine Providence of Almighty God.

Those of you with open minds and loving hearts are the true believers of the divine, One True Living God, and as such, you will know in your innermost hearts that this is an accurate account of Thomas and his life as it truly happened. As The Master would say, "Let those with ears hear."

Due to the nature of these revelations going against the accepted narrow and forever controlled narrative of the "Ecclesiastical Authorities," we can expect massive resistance to counter the truth and the promise of eternal life revealed in this work. Those ignorant priests who demand that their interpretation of the life of Christ and his disciples is the only version to be accepted are quite shallow and their teachings are bereft of life.

To those who will try denying the truth of this text, I must ask you to pause and think again and ponder this new revelation of Christ's ministry. Consider this: Does it not make sense that the ascended resurrected Master might see to it that some of his lost teachings be restored?

For those too stubborn to realize the purity of this Gospel of Thomas, and will try to sway people to their personal contrarian viewpoint, I will say it is wrong to do so. Christ was telling people throughout his ministry that there is no one between them and God and that God is within them; and furthermore, they have a direct connection to truth; and no priest, monk or rabbi is needed to commune with God.

Christ further proclaimed through the revelation of his life and in his teachings, that a great plethora of rules and laws imposed by the ecclesiastical authorities in the Sanhedrin were largely superfluous. This created animosity with the Sanhedrin, some of whom were jealous of Christ and his followers. So, I now deny the self-proclaimed authorities who will proclaim this Gospel of Thomas as false. This Gospel of Thomas will set the world of Christendom on fire.

For some, but not all of these "authorities" who need to be right and in control of other peoples' faith, this will be a fire of denial, anger and of confusion. But for the faithful followers of Christ who seek the truth of his life as a living example of the word of God, this Gospel of Thomas will further fan any spark of devotion into flames toward the One True Loving God. God lives and moves as a spirit throughout His Creation and exists in the center of everything. He exists in us, in our hearts as the Christ Consciousness.

In Christ's life his open proclamation of his Divine message cost him his life (which he chose to give willingly) at the hands of such spiritual authorities. Many likeminded "authorities" will rise in indignation and condemn this sacred text as blasphemous and untrue; they will seek to disparage my gentle and kind brother personally. This defamation will roll like water off a duck's back for my brother; and these cries to misdirect the faithful shall fail.

This holy text is not meant for such blind and profane eyes set in hearts of stone built on pride, entitlement and lack of discernment. They cannot recognize the power of Almighty God, nor the power of His omnipotent and omnipresent spirit. They are now, before they utter a word, rebuked.

This Gospel Is for You, the Faithful

This testament is for you the faithful, the meek, and it will only be revealed for the seekers of the whole truth. Those who will hear, will in their innermost heart know the reality of God and the Ascended Master Yehoshua ben Joseph. Drink slowly of this accounting of Christ's brother Thomas' life, and that of Jesus' wife Mary Magdalene, for there is much truth to be garnered in your understanding of just how Jesus the Christ lived. Imbibe the many and beautiful things as they are revealed in regard to the fusion of the very human life, and albeit divine expression of Christ's perfected love, his resurrection and Thomas' ministry.

This Gospel of Thomas is given at this time to buttress the faith in God and His angels' divine plan for the Earth and its inhabitants. God's creation is born of love. In the denser material world, in which we exist, freewill must reign. Throughout our life we make choices and we are tested through the temptations of flesh. We as souls must learn and choose to do His will according to His laws. Our limited perceptions materialistic views and apperceptions are many and we have forgotten the way to blessedness.

Our Choices Alone Will Transform the World

We can individually, one heart at a time, choose to do good and to do unto others as we would have others do unto us. Through our realization of the oneness of creation, we can expand our awareness of God's administration from the heavenly abodes, where other sentient life dwells. We are not alone in this universe. He has provided others with the charge of nurturing the inhabitants of the Earth into maturity.

Higher Realms-The Heavenlies-Life Eternal

In this Gospel of Thomas, it is directly revealed that there are other realms of light in the multiverse. In the multiverse the various dimensions and densities are infinite. We are not able to comprehend or explain the infinite with our limited human mind. However, with our mind and heart linked directly to God, we can know God and experience His Presence Love and Bliss.

This Gospel of Thomas is a declaration that there is a life after death beyond the gross material world. The heavenlies are populated with endless numbers of paradisiacal worlds populated by living, breathing, conscious beings. According to the transcriber of these gospels, Raymond Keller, "These beings in the higher dimensions do not need faith." When I asked him why they do not need faith, he said, "These beings exist in a type of perfected attunement without the need of faith because they live in a celestial realm, and everything hidden from our view is known to them.

"In their realm, which is made up of less-dense matter, they have more refined interactions and the actual experience of knowing and interacting within the presence of other divine beings personally. They know divine beings from actual experience. Therefore, they do not need faith since they have direct truth and experience."

"As Commander Valiant Thor, who acts a guardian in the Angel Force for Earth, and was commissioned directly by Jesus the Christ, has said, "We know the divine beings personally that you of the Earth only read about and speculate about." This too, is a quote from Valiant Thor revealed by the author of this book, Raymond Keller.

The Universal Space Family-Angels of the Lord

Our Heavenly Father has created a universe teeming with life. On those worlds adapted for human life, there exist many densities. The dwellers on these worlds have circumvented the limitations of time and space. They communicate and interact with each other; and in many ways they and their societies are similar to us and our own, respectively. A being from the higher realms can lower their vibration to visit the lower dimensions; but it is harder for the lower to go higher, unless the consciousness is augmented or sufficiently evolved.

"Wheels Within Wheels"

These space families seek to help us in the lower realms as we awaken to the truth long denied. Their presence on our world is increasing as humanity awakens to the Spirit of Truth that is pouring out on all flesh at this time. They are ever at the ready to support our growth in love and fostering harmonious relations with all life. Do not be distracted or dismayed or in denial just because they travel in multidimensional vehicles as described by the Prophet Ezekiel as "wheels within wheels," or as described by Moses as, "a pillar of cloud by day and a pillar of fire by night."

The angels' influence throughout recent history is benevolent yet hidden to allow humankind to be free to exercise its own discernment and to not interfere in the Earth's development.

The reality of our brothers and sisters from the stars nurturing our development through this time of transition and awakening to our cosmic destiny and divine heritage should not be marginalized by "silver spaceships and space suits." They are just other people full of love and concerned for their fellow beings.

We are not alone in the universe as the angels do attend us. Many are human and walk amongst us hidden from our awareness and sight. Reference is made to Hebrews 13:2: "Therefore, be kind to strangers, lest ye entertain angels unawares." The angels work without fanfare, silently serving and protecting the humans as much as possible behind the scenes to help the wayward children of Earth, created as embodiments of love, to return home. Just like the prodigal's son parable in the Bible, we will be welcomed home to our father's embrace.

Rejoice, God Has Cleared a Path!

We should rejoice that now we are witnesses to the culmination of the abomination on earth. "We wrestle not with flesh and blood but with principalities and powers." There is a concerted effort by those beings who are evil to destroy mankind and erase the awareness of our divine nature and the truth of God.

Rest assured their time is done now and we alone control our own destiny. It is true that at this time we still must unravel the Satanist system they created; and we must be vigilant and brave when dealing with those who would do us harm. We have been unwitting and ignorant of their depravity and corruption for a very long time. Soon Christ will declare "Enough" and his angels will administer divine justice.

Realize now, and know in your heart, that this is our chance to choose love. Know that we, now more than ever, have a clear choice. We can choose love now if we want to change our cosmic destiny. We are free to choose a path of compassion and forgiveness and act in direct service to those in need. We can correct our collective course as we have the power within us to bring peace to this world. We can, in our hearts, declare "We shall not participate in the folly of hateful division and separation and judgment of our fellow beings. We shall not participate in the orchestrated, malice-fueled destruction of our world."

Despite the chaos we currently see around us, through Christ and our faith in God's plan, we will be able to act as his instruments. We are individually bringing about, through devoted and selfless service, real and positive change. We are soldiers of peace and through our fiery hearts and willing hands, we will restore this beautiful world to the paradise it was meant to be.

We are together united as we clear a path to good works. We do no harm to others; we heal those who are ill; mend what is broken and we are rebuilding anew, like a Phoenix rising out of the ashes of the Old World.

The Emphasis on Spirit

This Gospel of Thomas is constantly urging us to follow the promptings of Spirit. The manifested glory of God can be seen all around us. In this Gospel of Thomas, are many examples of those who do not recognize the truth. Thomas in his ministry and through the miracles, brings many profane to find sanctity and the sacred in their lives.

Thomas emphasizes the obvious that we take nothing from this material world. It is the virtues of Loyalty, Honesty, Trust, Compassion, Continence, Courage, Charity, Temperance,

Perseverance and Faith that will allow us to enter heaven or the realms of Light.

Thomas and Christ both encourage us to not seek to satisfy the beastly nature of unsatiable appetite that can never be satiated. Rather, we are guided to adhere to the divine nature within us and put aside all manner of competition with each other. We are to live our respective lives as the sons and daughters of God, which is our rightful inheritance.

We can disagree; but we must act together as brothers and sisters in good works like charity and seeking to help our fellow beings. I myself pray fervently to devote each moment of my life as if it were my last and to the glorification of the God of Love and mercy while I am still on Earth.

The Challenge of the Hierarchy of Darkness

We must live by faith due to the situation the Earth is in at the present time. Now is the long-prophesized time of the Apocalypse, or end times, which in truth means "REVELATION." Be not afraid, stunned or shocked of the revelations of the whole truth; for now, all that was hidden shall be known. Gird your loins and arm yourself with the armor of truth and divine justice. Step forth into your knowledge and expand your thinking to embrace a broader view of the universe.

This is not the place or time to go into the details of Fallen Angels from the realms of light; but I will say that many have been cast from the realms of light into the lower and denser dimension of Earth. They have had their own time to choose love and redemption; and the time for them to repent is now over.

Thomas is confronted with these interdimensional demons, as was Christ during his ministry. These demons even challenge Thomas, saying in essence: "What are you doing here now? Our allotted time is not yet completed."

These encounters reveal that God has infinite patience; and even the wicked have a chance to turn away from evil and embrace God. The time of Judgement is now and these wicked ones will have their individual souls destroyed and recycled. The biblical scripture is brought to mind in the references to the "Lake of Fire." I suggest looking at the world's chaos and using discernment as to how this condition is possible, and the best way to avoid it.

This destruction of humanity is not caused by human mismanagement or ignorance; this is a concerted detailed plan by progenitors of destruction that could never succeed. For God is, was, and always will be; and the folly of evil always comes to an end. Research and study and you will find non-human influence tempting the people of Earth to ignore God and truth. This force is called Satan or the "adversary." The adversary takes many disguises; so be wary.

How this Gospel was Written

This Gospel was written by Thomas, a man inspired by God. Just like all of the Gospels, they are taken from written or verbal accounts of eyewitnesses who were present as the acts happened. To an extent this is true of this Gospel except that this particular Morning Star Version has a supernatural component.

The other Gospels may have or may not have been transcribed from earlier versions of originals. These also may have been altered from their intended description to not reveal the entire truth. There may have been unintended translational errors and other manner of faults to contribute to the incomplete revelation of all the Gospels. But thankfully, there are many Gospel accounts, from which many blank spaces might be filled insofar as the life of Jesus, the Christ, is concerned.

Supernatural Aspect of this Gospel

To understand the supernatural aspect of the writing of this Gospel of Thomas, I have laid a foundation in the paragraphs above to prepare the faithful who have known these hidden truths. In order to understand the guidance through the arc of time and to separate facts from myths, we must acknowledge the interdimensional Hierarchy of Light.

This Hierarchy of Light, God's administrators or association of divine personages, are all altruistic and benevolent. They are multi-dimensional and made up of women and men with many lifetimes of experience; and all have natural gifts we might consider superpowers. They convene in united universal councils with representatives from many worlds regularly. The grandeur and grace of the representatives in bursting with spiritual potency. These masters of many disciplines come together to consult in their agreed-upon parameters of interacting with regard to assisting or helping develop life on the multitudinous worlds. Research "Seraphin-Ophanim-Elohim" for further insight.

The Earth is a special case in their care for many reasons; but we are watched over more closely due to the fallen beings that now hold positions of influence on Earth for a short period time, that is just a little longer. We could go back to many interventions by these councils of light in the earth's history to see to it that the earth is not destroyed or that the true teaching of God is not erased or forgotten. But this is not the time to try and prove or explain these corrections in the course of human events.

Reflections on Mormonism

I will not debate or criticize the Mormon religion as it is today; other than to say that its origins stem from individuals sincerely seeking God's revealed truth; but whose ecclesiastical structure imposed upon them numerous unwarranted demands and a limited interpretation of their founder, Joseph Smith, Jr.'s teachings, after his death. This has nothing to do with the faithful who follow the true teachings of the founder of whatever religion is created. The divisions and infighting for spiritual supremacy between religions is pathetic, in my view, as we are all one people under God. To think that God would not make provisions for His children to learn the truths of His universe in multiple cultures and present the truth of love in various times is again to deny the power of God. The messages are the same; but for some reason, people need to always "be right" and, as a consequence, marginalize the beliefs of others.

Urimm and Thummin – The Seer and Interpreter

The Urim and Thummim are talked about in the Old Testament in regard to the Ark of The Covenant. They were given to the chosen messengers and used for guidance. They are said to be two objects that gave the messenger answers to questions. One was a stone that was said to be inlaid on the breastplate of Aaron, the brother of Moses. The messenger would face the Ark of the Covenant and a person would ask a question. The messenger facing the ark would see an answer in his mind to the question, and thereby apply an informed interpretation.

In this way the Hierarchy of Light was guiding limited human thinking to reestablishing a civilization after the flood. The teachings of love and light were lost and it was imperative that humanity be nurtured with direct contact that would not interfere with our development.

Joseph Smith – Urim and Thummim – Short Version

The founder of the Mormon religion, Joseph Smith, Jr., was visited by an angel named Moroni who encouraged him to go to a certain location and unearth some ancient tablets made of gold. He eventually did as he was asked and uncovered two objects that would allow him to interpret these tablets.

After he interpreted the plates amongst much controversy, he returned the plates to an unknown location. He started an association of followers that turned into a movement and now as we know it today, it is a worldwide religion. Joseph Smith, Jr., eventually was assassinated for his attempt to reaffirm the teachings of Christ that were lost. I strongly suggest you all research this history on your own.

Why this Gospel is Accurate

This gospel is accurate because Raymond Keller was given similar such Urim and Thummim by the primary guardians of Earth. This guardian angel force is from Venus and Raymond, being of pure heart and impeccable character, was entrusted with these tools.

He has faithfully completed his task to use this interdimensional tool to give an eyewitness accounting of the events as they truly happened.

The Seer Stone and Interpreter Explained

Raymond explained these tools to me and how he used them; and I felt it to be very important to reveal this information in this introduction. Raymond said he has one stone called the Seer and a pair of goggles called the interpreter. The process is that he places the Seer on his third eye and looks at the fragmented text through the goggles. He said these goggles are like the ones World War I pilots wore, at least in their outward appearance.

He says he is literally somehow transported mentally to the time and place that the event took place. He is in a type of bi-location signal that allows him to see into the Akashic Record, or Book of Life. For those unfamiliar with this term, I suggest you research it. I will say that all activities in the solar system are recorded and stored in crystals on the various worlds and can be resurrected through technology. Crystals grow for millions of years, and in some way, they are recording activities that can be accessed.

One of the most amazing things for me was to realize that with these tools the Seer and the Interpreter Raymond could actually look at an event again and again to observe the surroundings and perceive the thoughts and feeling of these historical characters.

The other wonderful thing that comes from this divine technology is that we get as close to the exact truth as it actually happened. I know Raymond's own viewpoint is inherent in the viewpoint as he describes the events. Please bear in mind the words from Thomas or Christ are as exactly as they happened and are written by Thomas.

When I consider the fluidity of the narrative and how easily Raymond has transcribed these events from so long ago, it is by far the easiest read and most realistic account of any of the other gospels, in my opinion. Raymond is a master scribe; and you will not even notice how seamlessly he fuses what was happening in each location with our own experiences in the contemporary age.

His eloquence and control of the English language is effortless. He has easily impressed upon our 21st century minds the events so we can envision, understand and believe this to be just as real as if he reported what happened yesterday. I have grown in my understanding of Christ through this Gospel of Thomas and I hope you will feel the same.

Rob Is Astounded

During the course of Raymond's preparing this book, I have been allowed to ask questions of him about this process and he has generously shared some insights with me. Naturally, I was astounded upon hearing about these gifts and asked so many questions I cannot remember them all or the answers right now; but he did say he was granted the license to interpret these in our modern vernacular of language and understanding. For instance, in the Gospel of Thomas, Raymond says "Jesus," but his name was Yehoshua or Joshua as it was pronounced at the time. Jesus comes from the Greek word IASOS which means "anointed one." He was called "Master" or "Rabboni" by most of the people during his ministry. I asked him why he said "Jesus" in the Gospel of Thomas, and Raymond replied, "Because this is how people know him today."

He also said in India at the time they could only pronounce Yesu; they could not articulate Joshua. So now I asked how Thomas, a Hebrew, could speak to the people of India in their native tongue. He explained that in the beginning, Thomas had an Indian merchant who served as an interpreter with him, but Raymond left much of that part out of the Gospel as it was unimportant to the overall message. After a time, Thomas could speak the language fluently enough that he did not need an interpreter.

I asked what the real Jesus looked like and suggested we hire a police sketch artist to allow him to reproduce the Master's likeness based on Raymond's description. This could not be allowed due to the security protocols of the Urim and Thummim. Therefore, Raymond contacted a talented artist, Daniel Gorman, who Raymond said has done an incredible job of reproducing these images.

The Urim and Thummim have now been returned to the Venusian guardians to be put back in their resting place for safekeeping. Raymond is constantly under surveillance and is protected from harm by any unstable people who might have had the inclination to take the Urim and Thummim, had this project been revealed prematurely.

Raymond also is an incredible researcher and he is a Biblical scholar. You will notice the in-depth references and annotations are impeccable and beyond reproach. The detail he provides lend great credibility of a truly remarkable character to the Gospel of Thomas.

In closing, I will address the fact that Raymond Keller is a physical contactee of the Venusians, our closest neighbors and celestial brothers and sisters. Raymond has a long history with our space family from Venus and he visited that planet for 10 weeks in 2012-2013. I strongly urge you to read all of his books as he is now finishing his eighth book on Venus and you will learn much of the space family who attended Christ and even walked with him during his ministry. Remember I said be not doubtful and to expand your thinking in regard to God's Ministry of Angels.

The guides and guardians have told me to tell everyone to have no fear, for God has not forsaken us. Continue in your good works and keep love in your hearts. Christ came to teach us to tap the spring of peace and to see God in everything; and as we act accordingly in all of our relationships, we will be granted life both happy and eternal.

May God Bless Us All,

Robert Potter
22 July 2021
Mt. Shasta, California

Dr. Raymond Keller "Cosmic Ray" and Robert Potter

Prophecy of the Coming Savior

Now we have entered into the last age prophesied by the Oracle at Cumae.[1]
This is the sign that the great cycle of periods is born anew.
Now returns the Maid, thus heralding the reign of Saturn:
Now from the Highest Realm of the Heavens a new generation comes down.
And with the birth of a humble boy in a distant land,
The iron race of Rome shall begin to give way,
To be supplanted by a gentler, golden one arising the world over.
Holy Diana, goddess of light, be gracious unto us;
For soon thine own Apollo will reign.

From the Caput IV of the *Eclogues*, written in 42 B.C.E. by Publius Vergilius Maro, a.k.a. the Roman poet "Virgil" (70 B.C.E.-19 B.C.E.)

---

1 Cumae was a Greek colony on the outskirts of Naples, Italy.

Gospel of the Young Jesus

Thomas is in awe as Jesus performs his first miracle.

Introduction

I, Judas Thomas, an Israelite philosopher and twin brother of Jesus, do hereby write this account of our Lord Jesus, also known as The Christ, for the benefit of the elect among the Gentiles, being numbered among the General Assembly and Church of the Firstborn, concerning his youth in Nazareth, some of that which he did after being born in our country. The beginning of the Master's story is as follows:

Chapter 1: The Sparrow

When the child Jesus and I were but seven years old, we were playing by the ford of a stream where the flowing waters formed into small, shallow eddies, making them pure. Along the bank, Jesus noticed a young sparrow splashing desperately, trying to keep afloat and make it back to safety on the shore. I said to Jesus, "I think the bird has a broken wing."

"Let's take a closer look and see what we can do to help the sparrow," said Jesus. At that, we held hands and stepped into the cold waters of the ford, whence Jesus retrieved the small bird. Looking at it closely, Jesus verified that a small portion of the bird's upper right wing appeared to be cracked. He then handed me the sparrow, sat down along the bank and made some soft mud out of the silt.

"Hand me the sparrow," said Jesus. I then turned it over to my twin brother, who cupped the bird in his left hand, gently moved the bone back into place, stroked its head and made a mud pack around the broken wing with his right hand. "Be at peace," he assured the sparrow.

"What is that going to do?" I inquired.

"I'm not sure," replied Jesus. "I just feel sorry for the poor, little bird."

When some other children of Nazareth noticed our activity, they came over to the streambank as well. As it was the Sabbath, however, all of this commotion attracted the attention of the local rabbi, named Annas, who rushed over to the edge of the ford to also see what was happening. "Don't you children have any common sense?" the rabbi yelled at all of the children.

Then he stormed over to the house of Joseph, the carpenter, our father. Pointing in the direction of the stream, the rabbi shouted at Joseph, "Look at your sons playing in the water. They have profaned the Sabbath!" he accused us.

The rabbi was pulling on my father's tunic, leading him to the streambank. When Joseph saw what was happening, he asked us, "Don't you two know that it is forbidden to play on the Sabbath?"

Jesus replied, "Father, I'm sorry. This bird was hurt and we were just trying to help it." He then clapped his hands and cried to the sparrow, "Be gone, little bird. Bird, fly home now." At that, the tiny sparrow took flight and went on its way, happily chirping.

Of course, after the rabbi informed the other Jewish elders in the synagogue, it wasn't too long before the legend of Jesus as a young miracle working healer spread out across the countryside. Our mother Mary had always suspected that such a day would come for Jesus, and she worried greatly over my dear brother.

Chapter 2: Guardian Angel

Now the son of Annas, the rabbi, was among the other children of Nazareth standing on the bank of the stream, along with our father Joseph. The boy was a few years older than Jesus and I; and as he was screaming at Jesus, calling him all manner of wicked names, I immediately began to suspect that he was going to charge into my brother and start a fight with him. This older boy snapped a branch from a willow tree overhanging the streambank. He pushed my brother down into the water and then began to stir up the mud at the bottom of the ford with it, messing up the pure waters.

Jesus, of course, became quite upset. Picking himself out of the ford, he said to the bully: "You should be ashamed of yourself, you irreverent oaf! What did the pools of the water do to harm you?"

Upon hearing this, I pushed the rabbi's son into a nearby thicket, trying to keep him from doing harm to my brother. Just as I was about to pounce upon the fallen lad, the rabbi and Joseph intervened and kept us apart. Joseph then took us home, as did the rabbi take his son back to their own house.

The next day, however, the older child developed a severe, irritating rash all over his body. His eyes were also inflamed. The rabbi brought his son to our house, accusing our father and asking him, "What kind of child do you have who does such things?" thinking that Jesus perchance had put a curse on him.

"Don't be ridiculous, Rabbi Annas," replied Joseph. "Your son fell into the thicket of oleander that grows along the bank. He probably rubbed his skin along its sap and is only suffering an allergic reaction."

The rabbi left our home in a huff, saying he didn't believe a word that Joseph was saying and swearing that Jesus was an evil spawn. Mother Mary put her arms around me and said, "Thank you, Thomas, for protecting Jesus. Continue to keep an eye on your brother; as I believe that God sent you to this world to be his guardian angel."

"I will, mother. I promise."

Chapter 3: Bully Seeks Revenge

Jesus and I had almost forgotten the incident; but apparently the son of Annas had not. Many months had already passed and one day, as Jesus and I were walking through the village, the same bully boy was coming down the center road toward us. Crossing over from the opposite side of the road, the bully purposely banged into Jesus' shoulder, laughing loudly. "Who is the oaf now, carpenter's son?" he mocked my brother.

Jesus emphatically scolded the brazen youth. "Stop what you are doing, before you regret it," said my brother.

"Let me handle this ruffian," I said to my brother, adding that, "You know that our mother wants me to watch over you."

"That will not be necessary, Thomas," replied Jesus. "Angels are watching over us at all times."

The ruffian proclaimed, "I'm not afraid of you, Jesus, or your brother, either." At that he picked up a stick; and as he raised it over his head about to strike my brother with it, he fell down and died right on the spot.

Jesus, having sympathy on the bully, said to me, "Thomas, you see that this boy does not understand what he is doing, what he is bringing down upon himself. Come, help me lift him up." At that, Jesus and I picked up the bully from the dust of the ground. Trembling and crying, he looked at us in amazement and ran straightaway home.

Some of the village folk who witnessed this event said of Jesus, "Where was this child born? For no one can threaten or raise a hand against him."

The rabbi Annas and his wife came to Joseph and blamed him, saying, "Since you have such a child, you cannot live in the village. Teach your son to bless and not to curse, for he may end up killing all of our children!"

Chapter 4: Joseph's Concern

Joseph called to Jesus separately and admonished him privately, "Why are you doing such things, my son? These townsfolk are bewildered and do not know what to make out of you. Nor do they know what they want to do with you, or our entire family; but already we are hearing spiteful words from some, and even suffering persecution from a few of the more zealous ones. And due to the ravings of that fanatical rabbi, business has certainly slackened off. If it weren't for the work that I've contracted with those along the caravan route or from the wealthy Greeks and Romans over in Sepphoris, I don't know how I could even keep on feeding all my children. Perhaps Thomas can help keep you out of trouble."

Jesus replied, "I know this, Father, and I am sorry that I have caused you so much concern. These incidents, however, are not being brought on by myself. It seems that there is a great power at work here well beyond my own, granted me from above."

"That's what your mother keeps telling me," Joseph affirmed, lovingly pinching Jesus cheek. "In any event," the carpenter reasserted, "our neighbors in Nazareth are disturbed and frightened. Everyone believes that everything you say is amazingly going to become a reality, one way or another, for good or bad."

Chapter 5: Itinerant Teacher

It came to pass that in the ensuing year, an itinerant teacher named Zachaeus was passing through Nazareth in a caravan heading north to Sepphoris. Requiring some repair to the axle of his wagon, he decided to stay over at our home while father replaced the broken beam and reset the wheels. Overhearing conversations that Joseph had with fellow Nazarenes, particularly concerning his remarkably wise son, Jesus, he approached my father and said to him, "You certainly have a bright child with a sharp mind. Come, let me have the opportunity of instructing Jesus in the reading and writing of Hebrew and Greek, that he may learn to properly address the elders, bring honor to his home and ancestors; and to improve his social standing with children his own age. He might also serve as a great help to you in your business, being a translator in negotiations or of documents."

Joseph, deeming the offer of Zachaeus to be very good, hired the teacher. The young Jesus was a quick learner. Jesus always had many questions for Zachaeus on numerous subjects, particularly concerning history, philosophy and religion; and at first, the teacher was able to provide the answers for most of my brother's inquiries. But within a few months, the student excelled the teacher in all aspects of learning, even to the point of instructing Zachaeus.

Then the day arrived when Zachaeus came to Joseph and said, "Woe is me! I am wretched and at a complete loss. I have put myself to shame, taking on this child, who now surpasses me in knowledge and understanding. I beg of you, brother Joseph, to terminate our contract. Though I am an old man, I have been befuddled by the child, who now teaches me."

"There is no problem, Zachaeus. I understand your dilemma and release you from the contract. Mary and I appreciate the time you have given to the teaching of our son Jesus. You are free to continue on to Sepphoris; and I will put a good word in for you with some of my noble clients there, if you like. Even the elders at synagogue are at a loss of words when it comes to discussing matters with the boy."

Zachaeus said, "Thank you, Joseph. I want you to know that you can be proud of your wonderful son. I do not know what kind of great teacher or leader he will become. I suspect he may be a divine being, perhaps an angel in disguise here upon the land. I just don't know what to say about this remarkable boy."

Chapter 6: Critics Rebuked

Our father Joseph, the supreme craftsman and artisan, was in frequent demand for many home improvement projects being undertaken by the diplomats and wealthy merchants in Sepphoris. Jesus and I would increasingly accompany Joseph on his trips to Sepphoris, being as how it was less than half a day's journey on the northern road up from Nazareth, to help him where we could in little ways. On one trip to the home of Aegeus, where Joseph was setting the tiles for a beautiful mosaic in the interior courtyard, Jesus was delighted to discover a large and wonderful collection of scrolls, to include some of the fables of

Aesop, many of the Greek and Roman sagas and various colorful stories from many other far-flung nations like Assyria, Egypt and India. Aegeus, seeing the interest that Jesus was showing in his library, allowed my brother to peruse the documents, provided he was careful in handling them. "Father, please let me read them. I will be careful and Thomas can help you with the mosaic."

Since I voiced no objections, Joseph replied to Jesus, "Very well, then. But be careful in handling them. I could never make enough money to replace even a single scroll, should you damage it in any way."

In the course of the next two months, Aegeus became very fond of Jesus, taking him under his wing, so to speak. Jesus was sad when Joseph had finished the tile work in the beautiful garden; but Aegeus invited my brother to visit him at any time and carry on their engaging discussions on all manner of subjects.

Meanwhile, in the synagogue at Nazareth, the young Jesus was frequently the topic of heated conversations among the elders. Jesus would frequently challenge the orthodoxy of Rabbi Annas and the quorum of elders assembled in the meetings. Jesus would speak of the abandonment of desires as the way to finding happiness, reincarnation, and the superiority of faith over belief. On the latter theme, Jesus explained that, "Belief merely acknowledges the future fulfillment of a righteous desire; but faith manifests the desired outcome in the here and now."

Rabbi Annas, speaking for most of the elders, declared, "Where does this boy get these unorthodox ideas, that border on paganism?"

But Jesus, who supported his contentions by citing Hebrew scriptures, rebuked the Rabbi and the others standing against him, "Your tree fails to bear good fruit, only vexations of the spirit, as far as I can see. I speak of the beauty of the worlds above, how it should be reflected here among us. And I speak not of my own authority; but the words I invoke are spoken for your benefit, given to me by the One whose Spirit empowers me."

While the rabbi was still angered, many in the quorum of elders began to reconsider their opinion of Jesus, speaking to him and Joseph privately and assuring them that they would not allow the rabbi to expel Jesus from among them. Joseph, on the other hand, felt that many of the elders were actually afraid of his son, fearing that Jesus might exercise a curse against them or their families if they continued in their persecutions. I think that Joseph preferred that Jesus just keep his opinions to himself, for the time being, to let the passion of the elders subside.

Chapter 7: Healing Ministry

Some days later, Jesus was playing on the flat rooftop of a neighbor's house. One of the children playing with him fell from the roof and died. When the other children saw what had happened, they ran away, leaving Jesus standing there all alone. When the parents of the child who had fallen returned home, they espied Jesus on the roof and began shouting at him, accusing Jesus of throwing their boy down. But Jesus said, "I certainly did not throw him down." The parents of the fallen boy did not believe Jesus, however, and began to verbally abuse him.

Jesus then leapt down from the roof and stood beside the child's corpse; and with a loud voice he cried out the fallen boy's name, issued a command and questioned him, "Zenon! Rise up and answer me: Did I throw you down?"

And straightaway Zenon rose up and said, "Not at all, Jesus. You did not throw me down; but you have raised me up!" When the boy's parents witnessed this, they glorified God for the sign that had occurred, thinking Jesus to be an angelic miracle worker and thanking him profusely.

A few days after the incident with Zenon, there was a young man who was splitting wood in a secluded spot. The axe slipped from his grip and split open the sole of his foot. He lost a lot of blood and was dying. There was a big disturbance and a crowd started to gather. The child Jesus also ran to the spot of the accident. Forcing his way through the crowd, Jesus grabbed the young man's foot that had been struck; and immediately it was healed. Then Jesus said to the young man, "Rise now. Continue to split the wood and remember what I have done for you."

The crowd, having seen this miracle and being awed by what a marvelous work Jesus had accomplished, greatly admired him and unanimously declared, "The Spirit of God certainly lives within this child!"

Chapter 8: Miracles at Home

On occasion, Jesus would carry out a miracle on behalf of our mother Mary or father Joseph. One of the earliest miracles that I recall took place when Jesus and I were just six years old. Then our mother gave Jesus a water jug and sent him to draw some water from the village well and bring it home. After obtaining the water, he was jostled by a crowd of women who were also trying to get some water from the well, and the water jug was shattered. Therefore, Jesus unfolded the cloak he was wearing and filled it with water, and brought it back to our mother without so much as leaking or spilling a drop. Our mother was delighted and kissed Jesus. She kept to herself this and many other wondrous deeds that Jesus did.

Besides being an able carpenter and craftsman, our father Joseph and our older half-brothers maintained a field of wheat a little way out from the village. When Jesus and I were in our eighth year, Joseph took us out to the field to watch him sow the wheat and thereby teach us how this is done. Jesus and I then each took a small portion of the field to sow the wheat, while Joseph and our half-brothers sowed the major part. When it came time for Joseph to harvest and thresh the grain, however, the small portion of land sowed by Jesus produced a hundred large bushels, far surpassing anyone else's in the family. Joseph then called for all the poor people of the village to come to the threshing floor and partitioned the wheat to all our neighbors that showed up; while Joseph kept the remaining wheat to later sell it in the marketplace.

Our father, being a carpenter, was often called upon to make plows and yokes for the farmers throughout the region. One day, however, he received an order from a certain rich man in Sepphoris to make a bed. But when the measurement for one of the beautiful crossbeams came out too short, Joseph did not know what to do. My brother Jesus then said to him, "Place the two pieces of wood on the floor and line them up from the middle to one end." Joseph did just as his son insisted. Then Jesus stood at the other end and grabbing the shorter board, stretched it out to make it the same length as the other.

Our father Joseph was amazed at what Jesus had done, embracing his son and giving him a kiss, declaring, "I am blessed that God has given me this child."

Chapter 9: The Snake Bite

Joseph had sent his oldest son James to bundle some wood and bring it to the house. Jesus went with James to the woodpile to see if he could be of help. While James was gathering the firewood, a snake slithered out from among the stack of wood and bit his right hand. James keeled over on the ground, screaming and in the throes of death. Jesus came up to him and breathed on the bite; and the pain immediately ceased. Jesus then turned his head in the direction of the snake, focusing an intense gaze on it. The snake stopped its sidewinding and menacingly raised its head, flicking its tongue and hissing at Jesus. Then it simply exploded from the inside out. There was nothing recognizable left of it but food for the birds. Straightaway James was returned to health.

Chapter 10: Raising a Dead Infant

After James' encounter with the snake in the woodpile, an infant in Nazareth became sick and died. The infant's mother was weeping loudly. When Jesus heard the outburst of sorrow and the disturbance, he ran up quickly and came upon the dead child. He gently touched the infant's breast and there seemed to be a white light shining forth from inside its chest. Jesus then spoke, "I say to you, young child, do not die, but live; and be with your mother." Straightaway the infant's eyes opened and the young child laughed. Then Jesus said to the child's mother, "Take him up now and give him some milk; and remember me."

When the crowd that had gathered there saw what had transpired, the people stood motionless, in total awe. Those in the crowd were in total agreement that Jesus was very special. "Truly this boy must be a holy one or an angel sent directly from God."

Chapter 11: Jesus at the Construction Site

There was a time that Joseph took Jesus to a construction site, where he was helping a fellow Nazarene build a house for his new family. There was a great commotion as Joseph's friend fell off some scaffolding and was lying down on the ground dead. Joseph called out to Jesus to come and look at his friend, to see what he might be able to do for him. Jesus saw the man lying motionless and took his hand. Then he said to him, "I say to you, O man, rise up and continue your work on this house." Immediately the man rose up, thanking the young boy profusely, and wanted to worship Jesus; but Joseph stopped him from doing so. "Worship no one but God," our father declared, "and to God be the glory."

Chapter 12: Sundry Teachers

When Jesus and I were in our tenth and eleventh years, our father's business was very good, so Joseph hired several wise men knowledgeable in Greek and Hebrew to serve as our teachers. None of these could match the knowledge possessed by Jesus, so none of them stayed in our father's employ for very long.

As there was a new rabbi at the synagogue friendly to our father, named Hananiah, Joseph approached him about teaching Jesus and I. "Bring the children to me at the school," said Hananiah, adding, "Yes, I have heard some rumors about Jesus; but I know that you are a good man, Joseph, and your children have always been well behaved in the synagogue."

Jesus went along gladly with Hananiah to the Hebrew school. I, on the other hand, preferred working with our father in the carpentry shop. Nevertheless, as Joseph wanted me to go to school, I was enrolled along with my brother.

Jesus entered the school with great confidence on the first day of classes. When he entered the classroom, he noticed a scroll lying on the reading desk and picked it up. But instead of reading the words in it, he laid it back down and ran his right hand over it. Then he began to speak through the gift and power of the Holy Spirit, teaching the law to the other students and the rabbi who were standing there. Suddenly, a great crowd gathered, standing near to Jesus. They were utterly amazed at his knowledge of the sacred scriptures, the great beauty of his teaching and his carefully crafted words. They were astounded that he could speak of such sacred things, though still a child, and the carpenter's son.

But when Joseph heard about Jesus debut at the school, he became frightened. He ran to the school, fearful of how Rabbi Hananiah might react to his most enlightened son. But Joseph's trepidation was unfounded, for the rabbi told him, "You should know, brother, that even though I took Jesus as a pupil, he is filled with great grace and wisdom unequaled among his peers. He is far ahead of all the other children. So now I kindly ask you, dear brother, to take him home. I will visit Jesus at home from time-to-time to tutor him in his Hebrew studies, though I suspect his knowledge may far surpass even my own."

Then Joseph took Jesus by the hand and walked him home, allowing me to continue my studies at the school under the tutelage of the good rabbi.

Chapter 13: Jesus at the Temple

When Jesus and I were in our twelfth year, our parents took us with them on their customary trip to Jerusalem, in a caravan, for the Feast of the Passover. After the Passover, we returned home. But somewhere on the road back to Nazareth, Jesus left the caravan. "I thought that Jesus was with you, Thomas. What happened to him?" asked Joseph.

I replied, "He said he was going back to Jerusalem, that he had to take care of something important there. That's all I know."

Therefore, it was after that first day back on the road that Joseph and Mary put me and the rest of my brothers and sisters under the supervision of James, to continue in the caravan to Nazareth. Then my parents returned to Jerusalem and began looking for Jesus among their relatives there. Naturally, they were quite upset at not being able to locate Jesus. On the second day they scoured the city and the market places, still unable to locate my brother; and on the third day they finally found Jesus, sitting in the temple in the midst of the teachers, both listening and asking them questions. Everyone was attending closely, amazed that a child could so astutely question the elders and teachers of Israel. Jesus even elucidated on sundry points of the Mosaic Law and the parables of the prophets.

When mother Mary came up to Jesus, she said, "Why have you done this to us, child? You can see how distressed we are, looking for you these past few days." Joseph sternly looked at his son, clearly being displeased.

Then Jesus replied with some questions of his own: "Why are you even looking for me? Don't you know by now that I must be with those who are about our Heavenly Father's business?"

Then the scribes and Pharisees asked of Mary, "Are you the mother of this child?"

She answered, "Yes, I am."

Then Nicodemus, speaking for the entire party of elders and teachers assembled, said to Mary, "You are certainly the most fortunate among women in Israel, for God has blessed the fruit of your womb. For we have never seen or heard of such glory, such virtue and wisdom." Then Nicodemus added from his own perspective, "I pray that God will grant me the years to behold the great destiny He has planned for your son."

With this being said, Jesus got up and Mary took her son by the hand and walked him out of the temple; and thenceforth the boy remained obedient to his parents. But his mother kept to herself all of these things that had happened in her heart; and Jesus grew in wisdom and stature and grace. To Him be the glory forever and ever. Amen.

The Gospel of Thomas

Jesus roasting a fish at campfire with his disciples.

Introduction

These are the esoteric teachings of Jesus, The Christ, spoken in the three-year period of his Judean ministry, as accurately conveyed by his twin brother, Didymus Judas Thomas.[2]

Chapter 1: Power over Death

Jesus declared that, "Whoever finds the true interpretation of these sayings will not experience death. Therefore, let the one who seeks knowledge of heavenly things continue in this manner until such time as they acquire it. No doubt, they will initially become troubled, finding the true meaning hard to accept, difficult to reconcile with the teachings of the religious authorities in Jerusalem. The puzzlement of the seeker will give way to an astonishment and a great wonder. The knowledge of the Kingdom far surpasses any knowing to be gained in this material world. The knowledge of the Kingdom imparts a power of the angels that far exceeds that of any powers and principalities of this world."[3]

Chapter 2: Kingdom of the Most High

Jesus explained that the seeker should not look for the Kingdom of God in the sky or under the waters. "Rather," he said, "the Kingdom is inside of you; and it is simultaneously outside of you. We may learn from the Greeks; for when you come to know yourselves, then you will

2 Herbert C. Merillat, "Introduction" in *Gnostic Apostle Thomas: "Twin" of Jesus?* (Hollywood, California: Gnostic Society Library, 1997): "In the Syriac-speaking culture of upper Mesopotamia and Syria the apostle was called Judas Thomas. Thomas (Tau'ma) means twin in Syriac, a form of the Aramaic which was the language of Jesus and his followers. And Didymus, a name by which the apostle is also called in the gospel of John, means twin in Greek. Perhaps some regarded the two as blood brothers. Perhaps the twinship was regarded as spiritual or symbolic. Sometimes, as in the Christian Gnostic systems, Thomas seems to be the this-worldly reflection or image of a divine savior-figure, an earthly body inhabited by a spirit like the Savior's. In any event Thomas became a focus of special reverence." See also Gnostic Society webpage, *http://gnosis.org/thomasbook/ch1.html* (Accessed 16 October 2020) and Bart D. Ehrman, *Lost Scriptures* (New York, New York: Oxford University Press, 2003), 19: "According to some early Christian legends, Thomas was Jesus' twin brother." Didymos is a variant spelling for Didymus in other parts of the Greek New Testament.

3 1 Corinthians 4:20 (KJV): "For the Kingdom of God is not in word, but in power."

become known. You will then realize that it is you who are the children of the Living God. But if you will not come to know yourselves, then it is you who inhabit the poverty of your own consciousness, being unaware of your divine access and potential, poor soul that you are."

Chapter 3: Primordial Spirit Overcomes Earthly Barriers

Jesus noted that an older man might gain illumination of the eternities when gazing upon an infant but seven days of age. "For many who are first will become last; and they will become one and the same," he taught his disciples on several occasions. This teaching was initially difficult for some of my brothers in the ministry to understand. Jesus clarified his remarks by emphasizing that the "Primordial Spirit of each soul transcends the varied aspects of human existence, superseding temporal impositions of age and sex."[4]

Chapter 4: Seeing with Spiritual Eyes

Jesus said, "Once you recognize what is fully within your sight, and that which has been hidden from you, then all will be manifest in plain view. There is nothing hidden which will not enter your awareness and become known to you."

Chapter 5: Conduct of Religious Rites

The disciples questioned Jesus about the conduct of certain religious observances: fasting, prayer, alms giving and dietary restrictions. Jesus replied, "Do none of these things that you perceive as burdensome, things that you are loathsome to do. For our Heavenly Father knows the intentions of your hearts. Rather, tell no lies. Be honest in all of your dealings that your Father in Heaven might be glorified. Remem-

4 Let us recall that in the *Acts of John* and the *Gospel of Judas* that Jesus did appear among his disciples as a little child. Also, as the Roman disciple Valentinus proclaimed, "A little newborn child was identical to the Divine Word."

ber, dear ones, that everything that is hidden will become manifest; and nothing covered will remain without being uncovered."

Chapter 6: Overcome Beastly Nature

Jesus spoke of a beastly nature in humankind, inhibiting, as it were, the growth of an individual's soul and terminating their spiritual progress, should one give in to it. The teacher explained that this beastly nature could best be compared to a roaming and roaring lion, ever hunting prey to devour. "Cursed is the person whom the lion consumes," said Jesus, "for the lion thereby possesses that unfortunate one." The lion is representative of Satan and the gullibility of humankind in succumbing to his temptations.[5]

Chapter 7: Prioritizing Concerns

Jesus said, "There was a man, a wise fisherman who cast his net into the sea and drew it up from the sea full of small fish. Among them, however, the wise fisherman found a fine, large fish. Thereupon, he threw all the small fish back into the sea and chose the large fish, without hesitation. Whoever has ears to hear, let them hear."

Chapter 8: Parable of the Sower

Jesus told his disciples a parable of the sower: "Now the sower went out, took a handful of seeds, and scattered them. Some fell on the road; but the birds came and gathered them up. Others fell on rock, did not take root in the soil and failed to produce ears. And yet others fell among the thorns, being choked thereby; and the worms ate them. Still others fell on good soil. These produced good fruit: some sixty per measure and others a hundred and twenty per measure." His disciples understood that the sower was the Kingdom proclaimer and the seeds were the words of hope.

---

5 1 Peter 5:8 (KJV): "Be sober, be vigilant; because your adversary the devil, as a roaring lion, walketh about, seeking whom he may devour."

Chapter 9: Tending to the Holy Fire

Speaking of his Holy Spirit, Jesus informed his disciples that, "I have cast fire upon the world; and see, I am guarding it until it blazes." By this, the teacher meant that his words were fire and that following his return to his celestial home, he would fan his active spirit on the Earth into a blazing illumination among his followers as they went forth to spread his kingdom message to every people and nation.[6]

Chapter 10: Vault of the Heavens

Jesus opined about the visible stars and their constellations in the vault of the heavens: "This heaven will pass away, as will the ones after it." Here he was referring to the temporal creation.

Chapter 11: On the Conditions of Death

Jesus continued, "In the eternities, the dead in spirit have no part. The spiritually awakened ones will never die. In mortality, you partake of what are dead animals, fruit and vegetables in order to live; but to dwell forever in the realms of light, you must partake of the word of God. His word is living manna. When Adam partook of the fruit of the Tree of Life, he obtained for himself and Eve a knowledge of the sure path that leads to eternal life and joy in the realms of light, collectively known as the Pleroma. When Adam disobeyed God, he was denied further access to the Tree of Life, whence he and his wife were banished from Paradise, blindly stumbling along many stony paths in this lone and dreary world. Through the word, we gain the requisite knowledge for our return to the Garden."

6 This is a prophecy of the Day of Pentecost as recorded in the *Acts of the Apostles*, Chapter 2, verses 1-5 (KJV) shown below: "And when the day of Pentecost was fully come, they were all with one accord in one place. And suddenly there came a sound from heaven as of a rushing mighty wind, and it filled all the house where they were sitting. And there appeared unto them cloven tongues like as of fire, and it sat upon each of them. And they were all filled with the Holy Ghost, and began to speak with other tongues, as the Spirit gave them utterance. And there were dwelling at Jerusalem Jews, devout men, out of every nation under heaven..."

Chapter 12: On Leadership

Then the disciples inquired of Jesus, "We know that you will one day depart from us. Who, then, is to be our leader?"

Jesus answered, "On that day, wherever you are, you are to go to my older brother James, the Righteous;[7] for it was for the sake of the goodly ones such as he that all the heavens and the Earth came into being."

Chapter 13: Comparisons Made to Jesus

Jesus said to his disciples, "Compare me to someone and tell me whom I am like."

Simon Peter said to him, "You are like a righteous angel."

Matthew said to him, "You are like a wise philosopher."

And I said to him, "Master, you are both a righteous angel and a wise philosopher, yet much more. My mouth is wholly incapable of saying whom you are like."

Then Jesus responded, "Thomas, I am not your master, for we are brothers and equals. Verily, you have become intoxicated from the bubbling spring which I have measured out to you, even above all the others. You have partaken from the spring of water that bubbles up to eternal life."[8]

My brother and I withdrew from the others, whereupon Jesus informed me of some of the deeper things and secrets of the Kingdom. When I returned to the encampment, the other disciples gathered round and inquired of me, "What did Jesus say to you, that he couldn't tell us?"

I answered them thusly: "If I tell you even one of the things which Jesus told me, you would pick up stones and throw them at me, thinking me a heretic. But fortunately, it will not come to this. Jesus and I know each other's hearts from birth; and what he told me must remain confidential between two brothers. For if our conversation did become

---

7 James was the carpenter Joseph's son by a previous marriage. See *Proto-Gospel of James* for account of the life of Mary leading up to the birth of Jesus.

8 John 4:14 (KJV): "But whosoever drinketh of the water that I shall give him shall never thirst; but the water that I shall give him shall be in him a well of water springing up into everlasting life." See also John 7:37-38.

known to you, and if you were to pick up stones against me, those very stones in your hands would emit fire and burn your flesh before you could ever hurl them in my direction."

Chapter 14: On the Work of Kingdom Proclaimers

The disciples were much concerned about fasting, prayer and alms giving, for these works were constantly emphasized by the rabbinical authorities, while Jesus seemed to pay these matters little heed. "Most of the rabbis will always find some fault with you in your conduct of these observances," said Jesus, adding that, "They will always find some excuse to condemn you, no matter what you do, for you are allied with me in announcing the good news of God's coming Kingdom."

"What actions, then, should we take?" they inquired.

"When you go into any land and walk about in the districts," explained Jesus, "if they receive you, eat what they will set before you and heal whomsoever is sick among them. And when it comes to the kind or food that you eat or whether you fast or not, disregard the criticism of those hypocritical rabbis. For what goes into your mouth will not defile you, but that which issues from your mouth, it is that which will defile you. Avoid disputations and quarrels with the religious authorities, for their days are soon concluding along with the wicked system of which they have part."

Chapter 15: Spiritual Fatherhood

Jesus informed his disciples, "In the world, all are born of a woman. But when you find one born again of the Spirit of God, to that one you should prostrate yourselves on your faces, for that one is rightly due homage. That one is your mentor and spiritual father."

Chapter 16: Family Dissention

Jesus said, "Perhaps there are many who think that it is peace which I have come to cast upon the world. But it is actually dissention which my message has stirred upon the Earth: fire, sword and war. For there will be five in a house where three will be against me and two for me, or three for me and two against. A father will be against his son, and the son against his father.[9] But those that have stood with me shall enjoy life eternal.

"For those that stand with me, these are the ones that receive of me that which no eye has seen and what no ear has heard and what no hand has touched, that which has never even occurred to the human mind."

Chapter 17: Fate of the Disciples

The disciples, having firmly decided to stay with Jesus, requested of him, "'Tell us how our end will be."

Jesus replied, "Have you discovered, then, the beginning, that you now look for the end? For where the beginning is, there the end will be. Blessed are you for standing with me in the beginning, for I tell you that while your Earthly ministry will come to an end, you will live on into the realms of light with me. You will not experience death."

Chapter 18: Preexistence of the Human Spirit

Jesus enlightened his disciples with the teaching that, "Blessed is the one who comes to the realization that their spirit came into being long before it took up habitation in a human soul."

There is great power in the teachings of Jesus. He further explained that, "Those who become my disciples and take my words to heart will acquire access to the Holy Spirit such that even the stones at your feet will become as bread to you.[10] All the powers of heaven will be at your command to aid you in the ministry of preaching the coming Kingdom of God.

"For there are five trees for you in Paradise that remain undisturbed throughout the year; their leaves never fall. The one exercising wisdom

9 Micah 7: 6-7 (KJV): "For the son dishonoureth the father, the daughter riseth up against her mother, the daughter in law against her mother-in-law; a man's enemies are the men of his own house. Therefore, I will look unto the Lord; I will wait for the God of my salvation: my God will hear me."

10 Here Jesus is pointing out that the spiritual adept can literally turn stones into loaves of bread. See Matthew 4:3 (KJV) and Luke 4:3 (KJV), where the devil tempts Jesus to break his fasting and end his hunger by exercising this power, also proving his divinity in the process.

will acquaint themselves with these trees, for thereby they will never experience death."[11]

Chapter 19: Heaven Already Here

The disciples inquired of Jesus, "Can you tell us what the Kingdom of Heaven is like?"

He said to them, "It is like a mustard seed. It is the smallest of all seeds. But when it falls on tilled soil, it produces a great plant and becomes a shelter for the birds of the sky."

On many occasions did the Master speak to us in this manner. We understood that the Kingdom was already among us, in the hearts of the people. One day the Kingdom of Heaven would conquer the whole world and everyone would recognize their Everlasting King, the Son of David.

Chapter 20: True Disciples as Children

Then Mariamne,[12] a disciple of Jesus' older brother James, asked the Master, "Whom are your disciples like?"

---

11 These five trees exhibit the spiritual properties of the unfailing "tree of life" mentioned by the Apostle John in Revelation 22.2. They are five in number because they are seen as the spiritual counterparts to the five natural senses: hearing/understanding, sight/revelation, touch/empathy, taste/access to spiritual gifts, powers and smell/discernment of spirits. The natural powers are intensely magnified when operative from a spiritual plane, or higher dimension of consciousness. In the Gnostic *Pistis Sophia*, beginning in the first chapter, there are repeated mentions of the "five trees" made available to the seekers of spiritual gifts in the "Treasury of Light." These become like unto the angels, the illuminated ones. Only those partaking of the fruit of these trees can step out of the cycle of death and reincarnation, avoiding physical death by becoming translated beings. The Apostle John was one so blessed. See John 21:20-23 (KJV): "Then Peter, turning about, seeth the disciple whom Jesus loved following; which also leaned on his breast at supper, and said, Lord, which is he that betrayeth thee? Peter seeing him saith to Jesus, Lord, and what shall this man do? Jesus saith unto him, If I will that he tarry till I come, what is that to thee? follow thou me. Then went this saying abroad among the brethren, that that disciple should not die: yet Jesus said not unto him, He shall not die; but, If I will that he tarry till I come, what is that to thee?"

12 Mariamne was a member of the inner circle of a pre-Naassenes sect that followed closely the teachings of Jesus' older half-brother, James, sometimes called "The Just." James preached that those called by the Anointed One ("The Christ"), and who garnered the knowledge requisite to transcend the dominion of matter (the material world), could become one of the "elect"of God and even be translated into a spiritual being of light and lifted into the heavens without tasting of physical death.

Jesus explained that, "They are like children[13] who have settled in a field which is not theirs. When the owner of the field returns to it, he will say, 'Let me have back my field.' Then will the children remove all of their clothing, ridding themselves of all vestiges of the material world, and hand back the field to the one demanding it; for their task is done and they are ready to leave.

"Therefore, I say, if the owner of a house knows when the thief is coming, he will begin his watch before he (the thief) comes and will not let him dig through into his house to carry away his goods. You must be on guard against the world and the wiles of the devil and his minions. Arm yourselves with great strength lest the robbers find a way to come to you; for the difficulty which you expect will surely materialize. Let there be among you one of understanding; for when the grain is ripened, the thief shall come with his sickle in hand and reap it. Whoever has ears to hear, let them hear what I am saying."

"This is a hard saying for us, Master," said Mariamne.

Jesus then explained to her that, "The field is the world with all of its travail and you the children, both the called and elect, need to occupy it for yet a short time until the Master returns. Always be on guard, for the devil is waiting to steal all that you produce in the field on behalf of its rightful owner, to whom you are servants all."

Chapter 21: Suckling Infants

Jesus pointed out some suckling infants to his disciples. Then he said, "These infants being suckled are like those who enter the Kingdom."

Then his disciples inquired of him, "Shall we then, as children, enter the Kingdom?"

Jesus said to them, "When you make the two one, and when you make the inside like the outside and the outside like the inside, and the above like the below, and when you make the male and the female one and the same, so that the male not be male nor the female be female; and when you fashion eyes in place of an eye, and a hand in place of a

13 Matthew 18:3 (KJV): "Verily, I say unto you, Except ye be converted, and become as little children, ye shall not enter into the kingdom of heaven."

hand, and foot in place of a foot, and a likeness in place of a likeness; then you will enter the Kingdom.[14]

"I choose you, one out of a thousand, and two out of ten thousand, and they stand as a single one."[15]

Chapter 22: Jesus in the Secret Place

The disciples of Jesus wanted to know the place where he was coming from. "Show us the place where you are, since it is needful for us to seek it," they said to the Master.

Jesus replied, "Whoever has ears, let them hear. There is a divine light in the hearts and minds of the illuminated ones. It is a light that brings radiance to the entire world. If the light in that one burns out, then those around the other one also shall find themselves in darkness."

Chapter 23: Brotherly Love

Then Jesus taught his disciples about true love for a brother:[16] "Love your brother like your own soul; and guard him like the pupil of your eye.

14 *Second Clement* 12:2-6 (J. B. Lightfoot's translation): "For the Lord Himself, being asked by a certain person when his kingdom would come, said, When the two shall be one, and the outside as the inside, and the male with the female, neither male or female. Now the two are one, when we speak truth among ourselves, and in two bodies there shall be one soul without dissimulation. And by the outside as the inside He meaneth this: by the inside he meaneth the soul and by the outside the body. Therefore, in like manner as they body appeareth, so also let thy soul be manifest by its good works. And by the male with the female, neither male nor female, he meaneth this; that a brother seeing a sister should have no thought of her as a female, and that a sister seeing a brother should not have any thought of him as a male.

These things if ye do, saith He, the kingdom of my father shall come." See Peter Kirby, *Early Christian Writings*, 2020: http://www.earlychristianwritings.com/text/2clement-lightfoot.html (Accessed 21 October 2020). This is a clear reference to the teachings of the Gnostic school of Christianity at Alexandria, Egypt, where Jesus was said to have taught his disciples that the "two become one" through the obliteration of all Earthly differences and distinctions; and that just like little children, the true entrants into the Kingdom of God are found without an overpowering sexual awareness or exhibition of shame in their sexuality.

15 Matthew 22:14 (KJV): "For many are called, but few are chosen." With our incarnation on Earth, we have accepted the call to enroll as students in the School of Life. The chosen ones, albeit few, are the graduates of this school. We are one in constituting the body of the school's alumni.

16 The use of the masculine form "brother" does not exclude the equal application of these principles to female disciples. Note the following from Michael D. Marlowe, "Gender Neutral

"You see the mote in your brother's eye, but you do not see the beam in your own eye. When you cast the beam out of your own eye, then you will see clearly to cast the mote from your brother's eye."[17]

The Master desired all of his disciples to treat one another as family. To put aside criticism of a brother will foster cooperation. To gain victory over one's own vices is to conquer the lures of the material world and to live in the transcendental power of God.[18]

Chapter 24: Religious Observances

With respect to religious observances, Jesus taught that, "If you do not fast with regards the world, you will not find the Kingdom; and if you do not observe the Sabbath as a Sabbath, you will not see the Father."[19]

Here the Master speaks of his disciples abstaining from the world and all of its temptations. Verily, one must interact with the world on a daily basis; but fasting from the world means abstaining from all of the material goods that the world has to offer, the material goods that

---

Bible Controversy," Bible Researcher website (2001, revised January 2005), http://www.bible-researcher.com/inclusive.html (Accessed 5 November 2020): "The Hebrew and Greek texts of the Bible often use generic masculine nouns (*adam* and *anthropos*, both meaning "man") and generic masculine pronouns in a gender-inclusive sense, in reference to persons of unspecified gender. In the Epistles, believers in general are addressed as *adelphoi*, "brethren." Such usages are not merely figments of "sexist" English translations; they are a normal feature of the original languages, just as they are normal in English and many other languages. In most cases the inclusive intent of the writer is obvious from the context, and when the intent is not inclusive, this is also obvious enough from the context. The interpreter must not proceed mechanically with the idea that every occurrence of *adam* and *anthropos* is to be understood in a gender-inclusive sense, because the Bible for the most part records the names and actions of men, uses male examples, assumes a male audience, and in general focuses on men and their concerns while leaving women in the background. This feature of the text is obviously related to the cultural situation and expectations of the original authors and recipients, and so any movement to disguise it in translation runs up against the academic qualms already being expressed by theologian Bruce Metzger: "How far is it feasible to eradicate from an ancient text those features that belong to the patriarchal culture in which its narratives had their origin?" See Bruce Metzger, "Trials of the Translator," *Theology Today* 33/1 (April 1976), pp. 98-99. Metzger also mentions that "such problems.... are currently being considered by the Revised Standard Version Bible Committee."

17 Matthew 7:3-5 (KJV): "And why beholdest thou the mote that is in thy brother's eye, but considerest not the beam that is in thine own eye? Or how wilt thou say to thy brother, Let me pull out the mote out of thine eye; and, behold, a beam is in thine own eye? Thou hypocrite, first cast out the beam out of thine own eye; and then shalt thou see clearly to cast out the mote out of thy brother's eye."

18 The spiritual principles for the functioning of Christians as one body are outlined by Paul the Apostle in 1 Corinthians 12 (KJV).

19 1 John 2:15 (KJV): "Love not the world, neither the things that are in the world. If any man love the world, the love of the Father is not in him."

evoke a snaring of your heart and diversion of your full attention on the words of life and salvation. This is inclusive of the Sabbath, which on a higher order of spirituality should be attended to all seven days of the week. The Father of Lights gave humankind the Sabbath for his people to approach the heavenly throne with a totality of their hearts and minds, setting aside all other worldly concerns. One in the way of salvation will keep this attitude ever present in their heart and mind, not just on the Sabbath or high holy days.

Chapter 25: Spiritual Yearning

Then Jesus said, "I took my place among humankind, dwelling in their midst and appearing in a body of flesh, as you see me now. I found the inhabitants of this world intoxicated by all of its material and sensual lures. There were none of them thirsty for the spiritual knowledge I came to share. And I became afflicted for the sons and daughters of Adam's race, for the blindness of their hearts. For it is through the heart that one truly sees.[20] And these are the ones who remain sightless with respect to spiritual matters. These are the ones who came empty into the world, yet will leave this world no better off than they entered. Their only hope lies in shaking off their intoxication with the wine of this world; for then they will see the light of hope and speedily repent."

Chapter 26: Priority of Spirit

"Of course," Jesus noted, "one has to marvel how it is that something as wondrous as the Spirit has taken up residence in the fleshly body. It is not the Spirit that has come into being because of the body, but the body that has come into existence as a vehicle to convey the Spirit in its journey through this material world. I stand truly amazed at how this great wealth of Spirit, descending from the Realm of Perpetual Light, has accommodated to its home in this world of dire inequity and poverty, albeit on a temporary basis."[21]

20 1 Kings 8:61 (KJV): "Let your heart therefore be perfect with the Lord our God, to walk in his statutes, and to keep his commandments, as at this day."

21 Hebrews 13:14 (KJV): "For here we have no continuing city, but we seek the one to come."

Chapter 27: Omnipresence of God

Jesus said, "In any group of three or more, one is likely to find a variety of opinions concerning the existence of various gods, all divine to greater or lesser degrees. And where there is but one individual who believes in the One Supreme God of the Universe, I am with that one. The Spirit of the Almighty One permeates each individual soul and all of creation."[22]

Chapter 28: Rejected Prophets

Then Jesus sadly took note that, "No prophet is accepted in his own village;" and "No physician heals those who know him."

Here the Master referred to the rejection and outright hostile reception that he and the disciples received in our boyhood home of Nazareth. After being upset by his interpretation of the sacred scrolls of Isaiah[23] in the synagogue, the elders challenged Jesus to cure the local crippled and sick ones as he had previously done in Capernaum. After refusing to reduce his spiritual gifts to a sideshow, the elders encouraged the people to stone the "son of the carpenter" and cast him and his band of apostate disciples out of the village.[24]

Chapter 29: The High City

Jesus said, "A city built on a high mountain and fortified cannot fall, nor can it be hidden."[25]

---

22 John 4:24 (KJV): "God is a Spirit: and they that worship him must worship him in spirit and in truth." See also Romans 1:20 (KJV): "For the invisible things of him from the creation of the world are clearly seen, being understood by the things that are made, even his eternal power and Godhead; so that they are without excuse." and Psalms 14:1 (KJV): "The fool hath said in his heart, There is no God." Thomas indicates Jesus' awareness that most individuals can easily recognize the hand of the Divine in nature itself.

23 See Isaiah 61:1-2 (KJV), for scripture quoted by Jesus.

24 A parallel account is found in Luke 4:14-30 (KJV).

25 Matthew 5:14-16 (KJV): "Ye are the light of the world. A city that is set on an hill cannot be hid. Neither do men light a candle, and put it under a bushel, but on a candlestick; and it giveth light unto all that are in the house. Let your light so shine before men, that they may see your good works, and glorify your Father which is in heaven."

The disciples understood that they, and the followers of the Anointed One (The Christ), were indeed the inhabitants of this strong city. Fortified with the good news of the Kingdom, the light of this marvelous city could never be hidden from the truth-seeking masses of the world.

Chapter 30: Sharing the Light

Then Jesus continued to speak, "Preach from your housetops that which you have heard from me. For no one lights a lamp and puts it under a bushel; nor does that one put it in a hiding place; but rather, sets it on a lampstand so that all may see its light."

The Master entrusted the good news of God's Kingdom to his disciples; for he knew that we would go forth boldly to proclaim it to the world at large that all might rejoice thereby.

Blind Cannot Lead the Blind

Jesus explained that, "If a blind man leads a blind man, they will both fall into a pit."[26]

The student can only learn and progress from the tutelage of a true master.

Chapter 31: House of the Strong Man

Jesus said, in the context of his disciples going against the strongholds of Satan, that, "It is not possible for anyone to enter the house of a strong man and take it by force unless that one binds his hands. Then that one will be able to ransack his house."[27]

The binding of Satan can only be accomplished through the power of Holy Spirit. Only then will demonic influence be cast out and the captive set free.

---

26 Matthew 15:15 (KJV): "Let them alone: they be blind leaders of the blind. And if the blind lead the blind, both shall fall into the ditch." Here Jesus was referring to the Pharisees, who had some knowledge of the Jewish law, but not enough to teach others to the point of spiritual illumination and salvation. The law was not sufficient, unto itself, to save anyone.

27 Matthew 3:27 (KJV): "No man can enter into a strong man's house, and spoil his goods, except he will first bind the strong man; and then he will spoil his house."

Chapter 32: On Material Needs

Jesus told his disciples, preparatory to their going forth into the world to proclaim the Kingdom message, "Do not be concerned from morning until evening about what you will wear."[28]

Jesus wanted us to ever be aware that God knows what his people stand in need of and is faithful to supply. Therefore, we should not be overly concerned about material things.

Chapter 33: Truly Seeing the Lord

The disciples inquired of Jesus, "When will you become revealed to us and when shall we truly see you in your divine presence?"

Jesus answered, "When you disrobe without being ashamed and take up your garments and place them under your feet like little children and tread on them, then you will see the Son of the Living One, and you will not be afraid."[29]

Here the Master reveals that his true, divine presence could have been viewed by his disciples at any time. Becoming as little children and looking upon Jesus through the eyes of innocence, the disciples become as Father Adam who, being naked in Paradise, was not ashamed.

Chapter 34: Words of Jesus

Jesus said, "Many times have you desired to hear these words which I am saying to you, and you have no one else to hear them from. There will be days when you will look for me and will not find me.[30]

28 For a more detailed response from the Master Jesus, please see Luke 12:22-31 (KJV).

29 In reference to the *Gospel of the Egyptians*, fragment 5: "This is why Cassian indicates that when Salome asked when the things that she had asked about would become known, the Lord replied, 'When you trample on the shameful garment and when the two become one and the male with the female is neither male nor female.' The first thing to note, then is that we do not find this saying in the four Gospels handed down to us, but in the *Gospel* according to the Egyptians." -Clement of Alexandria, *Miscellanies*. Clement may possibly be denoting the primordial state of androgyny in which the sexes are not differentiated.

30 John 7:34 (KJV): "Ye shall seek me, and shall not find me: and where I am, thither ye cannot come." Jesus alerted his disciples that the day was fast approaching when he would return to his celestial abode.

"The Pharisees and the scribes have kept the keys of knowledge from you, hiding them from your understanding. They themselves have failed to comprehend these keys; and they desire that no one else enter into this knowledge before them, barring the way to all who seek after further illumination. You, however, should become wise as serpents and innocent as doves, guarding in your hearts the truths I have taught you until the time that the light of revelation comes upon the world."

Chapter 35: Grapevines

Jesus stated that, "Any grapevine planted outside of my Father is unsound. It will be pulled up by its roots and destroyed."[31]

Chapter 36: Useful Knowledge

Jesus said, "Is it not fitting for all who have acquired some knowledge of things above to also better come to a knowledge of themselves? For those who lack knowledge of their true, divine nature, their time in this world may seem dull and futile. On the other hand, the ones who truly know themselves will live with holy purpose, being happy with all that God has blessed them with."[32]

---

31 John 15:1-8 (KJV): "I am the true vine, and My Father is the vinedresser. Every branch in Me that does not bear fruit He takes away; and every branch that bears fruit He prunes, that it may bear more fruit. You are already clean because of the word which I have spoken to you. Abide in Me, and I in you. As the branch cannot bear fruit of itself, unless it abides in the vine, neither can you, unless you abide in Me.

"I am the vine; you are the branches. He who abides in Me, and I in him, bears much fruit; for without Me you can do nothing. If anyone does not abide in Me, he is cast out as a branch and is withered; and they gather them and throw them into the fire, and they are burned. If you abide in Me, and My words abide in you, you will ask what you desire, and it shall be done for you. By this My Father is glorified, that you bear much fruit; so you will be My disciples."

One might infer from these words of the Master that the systems of organized religion built apart from the words of Jesus are doomed to failure. Jesus abides in the believer when his words are cherished in the heart.

32 *Gospel of Philip* 105: "Is it not fitting for all who have all this also to know themselves? But some, if they do not know themselves, will not enjoy what they have. The others, who have come to know themselves, will enjoy them (their possessions)."

The *Gospel of Philip* was among the documents discovered at the Nag Hammadi site in Upper Egypt in 1945. Unlike the self-contained sayings of Jesus as found in the *Gospel of Thomas*, the Gospel of Philip excerpts some of these sayings of Jesus from multiple sacred books to offer the

Chapter 37: "Passers-By"

Jesus instructed his disciples to, "Become passers-by."

You cannot remain in this world forever; for it is but a bridge. Do not become too attached to this world; for one day you must cross over that bridge to enter into the realms of light.[33]

Chapter 38: Identity of Jesus

Then his disciples inquired of him, "Who are you, that you should say these things to us?"

Jesus answered them, "You do not realize who I am from what I say to you; but you have become like most of the Jews; for these are the ones that either love the tree and hate its fruit, or love the fruit and hate the tree, not realizing that the tree and its fruit are inseparable.[34]

"Whoever blasphemes against the Father will be forgiven; and whoever blasphemes against the Son will be forgiven; but whosoever blasphemes against the Holy Spirit will not be forgiven, either on Earth or in the heavenly realms."[35]

---

seeker mystical reflections based on the Gnostic tradition prevalent in the third century of the Common Era.

Thomas O. Lambdin in James Robinson, *Nag Hammadi Library in English*, 3rd edition, (Leiden, Netherlands: E. J. Brill, 1988), translates this verse from the *Gospel of Thomas* as follows: "Whoever has something in his hand will receive more, and whoever has nothing will be deprived of even the little he has." The Gnostic interpretation of it as found in the *Gospel of Philip*, in the opinion of this author, more accurately reflects the spiritual intent of the Master. In an esoteric context, however, one might surmise that the possessions "in hand," may well go beyond the material plane of existence.

33 A very similar saying attributed to Jesus is preserved in the form of an Arabic inscription at the site of a mosque at Fatehpur-Sikri, India. Apparently, it was once taught to the inhabitants of India by Thomas when Jesus sent him there on his apostolic journey.

34 Luke 6:43-44 (KJV): "For a good tree bringeth not forth corrupt fruit; neither doth a corrupt tree bring forth good fruit. For every tree is known by his own fruit. For of thorns men do not gather figs, nor of a bramble bush gather they grapes."

35 Mark 3:28-29 (KJV): "Verily I say unto you, All sins shall be forgiven unto the sons of men, and blasphemies wherewith soever they shall blaspheme: But he that shall blaspheme against the Holy Ghost hath never forgiveness, but is in danger of eternal damnation." God is a divine Spirit and all abiding therein are sanctified and empowered from above.

Chapter 39: Prevailing Heart

Jesus said, "Grapes are not harvested from thorns, nor are figs gathered from thistles, for they do not produce fruit. A good person brings forth good from their storehouse; and an evil person brings forth evil things from their evil storehouse, which is situated in their heart, and therefore says evil things. For out of the abundance of the heart a person brings forth either good or evil things."[36]

Chapter 40: John the Baptist

On the mission of our cousin John, called the Baptist, Jesus said, "Among those born of women, from Father Adam until John the Baptist, there is no one so superior to John the Baptist that his eyes should not be lowered before him. Yet, I have declared that whichever one of you comes to be as a child will be acquainted with the Kingdom and will become superior to John."[37]

Chapter 41: Undivided Loyalty

Jesus said, "It is impossible for one to mount two horses or to stretch two bows. And it is impossible for a servant to serve two masters; otherwise, that individual will honor the one and treat the other contemptuously. No one can drink old wine and then immediately desire to drink new wine. And new wine is not put into old wineskins, lest they burst. Nor is old wine put into a new wineskin, lest it spoil it. And old patch is not sewn into a new garment because a tear would result."[38]

---

36 Luke 6:45 (KJV): "A good man out of the good treasure of his heart bringeth forth that which is good; and an evil man out of the evil treasure of his heart bringeth forth that which is evil: for of the abundance of the heart his mouth speaketh." Clearly, our motivations hinge upon the inclinations of our heart.

37 Luke 7:28 (KJV): "For I say to you, among those born of women there is not a greater prophet than John the Baptist; but he who is least in the kingdom of God is greater than he."

38 Matthew 6:24 (KJV): "No one can serve two masters; for either he will hate the one and love the other, or else he will be loyal to the one and despise the other. You cannot serve God and mammon." The Gnostic interpretation of this scripture is that the true follower of Christ will not let the religious doctrines and laws of the past encumber their journey to spiritual enlightenment.

Chapter 42: Seek Peace

Jesus stressed the importance of keeping peace in the home. The Master explained, "If two make peace with each other in this one house, they will say to the mountain, 'Move away,' and it will move away."[39]

Chapter 43: "Solitary and Elect"

Jesus further enlightened his disciples, declaring that, "Blessed are the solitary and elect; for you will find the Kingdom. For you are from it; and to it you will return."[40]

Jesus said, "If they ask you, 'Where do you come from?', reply thusly: 'We come from the Light,[41] the place where the Light came into being on its own accord and established itself, becoming manifest through the image of the Elohim.'

"If they say to you, 'Is it you?', say "We are its children; and we are the elect of the Living Father.'[42]

"And if they ask you, 'What is the sign of the Father in you?', say to them, "It is movement and ultimately resting in the assurance of having found my place in unification with God and his will.'"

Upon hearing these words, the disciples wanted to know when such a repose would come about, and when they should expect the end of the world. To this, the Master replied that, "What you look forward to has already come; but you do not recognize it."[43]

---

39 Matthew 5: 9 (KJV): "Blessed are the peacemakers: for they shall be called the children of God." Striving for agreement and becoming of one mind on various matters can be quite empowering, enabling the peacemaker to assume their rightful place as a child of the Living God by adoption.

40 This is one of the most important verses in the *Gospel of Thomas*, for Jesus declares that those who are drawn to follow him are counted among the "solitary" and the "elect," that they were predestined from before they were even born on the Earth plane to become disciples of the Master. They are no more from this world than Jesus himself is (John 17:16). They are one as Jesus and the Father are one (John 17:23). Where Jesus is, they will also be found (John 17:24).

41 Genesis 1:3 (KJV): "Then God said, 'Let there be light'; and there was light." Light was the first emanation from the Pleroma to penetrate the darkness of the material universe.

42 James 1:17 (KJV): "Every good gift and every perfect gift is from above, and cometh down from the Father of Lights, with whom is no variableness, neither shadow of turning."

43 Luke 17:20-21 (KJV): "And when he was demanded of the Pharisees, when the kingdom of God should come, he answered them and said, The kingdom of God cometh not with observation: Neither shall they say, Lo here! or, lo there! for, behold, the kingdom of God is within you." With the Kingdom being there all along, it only takes some measure of self-realization to arrive at an understanding that you are already inhabiting it.

Chapter 44: Words of the Prophets

Jesus' disciples said to him, "Twenty-four prophets spoke in Israel; and all of them have spoken through you."

Then Jesus replied, "It is well that you have recognized the words of truth spoken by the prophets of Israel. But you have omitted the one living in your presence, having spoken only of the dead."

Chapter 45: On Circumcision

Jesus' disciples asked him, "Is circumcision beneficial or not?"

Jesus answered, "If there were any benefit in it, their father would beget them already circumcised from their mother. Rather, the true circumcision in spirit has become completely profitable."[44]

Chapter 46: The Poor

Jesus said, "Blessed are the poor, for theirs is the Kingdom of Heaven."[45]

---

44 Jeremiah 4:1-4 (KJV): "If thou wilt return, O Israel, saith the Lord, return unto me: and if thou wilt put away thine abominations out of my sight, then shalt thou not remove. And thou shalt swear, The Lord liveth, in truth, in judgment, and in righteousness; and the nations shall bless themselves in him, and in him shall they glory. For thus saith the Lord to the men of Judah and Jerusalem, Break up your fallow ground, and sow not among thorns. Circumcise yourselves to the Lord, and take away the foreskins of your heart, ye men of Judah and inhabitants of Jerusalem: lest my fury come forth like fire, and burn that none can quench it, because of the evil of your doings." It is clear from this passage that the need for circumcision in the heart is the plain teaching of the Lord as revealed through his prophet Jeremiah, who was sent to preach to the covenant community of Israel and call the people to repent and turn from their idolatry made manifest through their refusal to recognize God's rightful ownership of them. In these verses, Jeremiah reminds the people that they cannot rightfully trust in the mark of circumcision for covenant blessings; rather, they have to experience the inner reality of a circumcised heart that the circumcision in their flesh only signifies. The Lord's covenant of salvation for his elect has always been a covenant of the heart. Your attention is also invited to the Apostle Paul's interpretation of this passage in Romans 2:25-29 (KJV): "For circumcision verily profiteth, if thou keep the law: but if thou be a breaker of the law, thy circumcision is made uncircumcision. Therefore if the uncircumcision keep the righteousness of the law, shall not his uncircumcision be counted for circumcision? And shall not uncircumcision which is by nature, if it fulfil the law, judge thee, who by the letter and circumcision dost transgress the law? For he is not a Jew, which is one outwardly; neither is that circumcision, which is outward in the flesh: But he is a Jew, which is one inwardly; and circumcision is that of the heart, in the spirit, and not in the letter; whose praise is not of men, but of God."

45 Matthew 5:3 (KJV): "Blessed are the poor in spirit: for theirs is the kingdom of heaven." Thomas' version appears to be an assimilation of Matthew 5:3, in the tradition of the Coptic

Chapter 47: Taking up the Cross

Jesus explained a hard doctrine to his potential disciples: "Whoever does not set aside his father and mother cannot become a disciple to me. And whoever does not set aside his brothers and sisters and take up his cross in my way will not be worthy of me."[46]

Many found this doctrine too difficult to follow and departed from the way of the Master. Others continued with Jesus, each vowing: "I have left father and mother and brother and sister. I have become a stranger for the sake of your name. I have taken up my cross, and I have followed you. I have left the things of the body for the sake of the things of the Spirit. I have disregarded the glory of the world for the sake of your glory that does not pass away."[47]

Chapter 48: Assessment of the World

Jesus said, "Whoever has come to understand this world with its exploiting systems eventually arrives at the realization that all of its ways lead only to death. By contrast, the souls dwelling on the worlds above, being animated by the Spirit, enjoy life eternal."[48]

---

churches. Jesus has always sided with the poor, not because they are righteous, but because they are suffering. The Master has always stood in solidarity with the poor, as well as the hungry, imprisoned, persecuted and sick ones among us.

46 Luke 14:26-27 (KJV): "If any man come to me, and hate not his father, and mother, and wife, and children, and brethren, and sisters, yea, and his own life also, he cannot be my disciple. And whosoever doth not bear his cross, and come after me, cannot be my disciple." The practicing of an ascetic philosophy is common in many cultures among those seeking redemption, salvation or a higher degree of spirituality. Ascetism, where the simple is sufficient, frugality is stressed and bliss is found within, is seen in the ancient theologies as a journey towards spiritual transformation. In the Buddhist tradition, the Indian Prince Gautama Siddhartha (the Buddha) left his family and riches behind, literally all his material possessions, when he went in search of all things spiritual. As both Jesus and Thomas had traveled in India, they were no doubt aware of the history of the enlightened Buddha.

47 *Manichaean Psalm Book* 175:25-30. This quote comes from a third century Common Era Coptic text partially based on the *Acts of Thomas.*

48 This is a paraphrase of the *Manichaean Kephalaia*, XLVII 120:31-121:2. This document, partially based on the writings of the Apostle Thomas, is a Coptic text written sometime in the mid-third century of the Common Era by the Persian prophet Mani, expounding a universal religion consolidating the teachings of Buddha, Zoroaster and Jesus.

Chapter 49: Harvest of Souls

Of the Kingdom of the Father, Jesus explained that, "It is like a man who had good seed. His enemy came by night and sowed weeds among the good seed. The man did not allow them to pull up the weeds. He said to those urging him to do this, 'I fear that you will go intending to pull up the weeds and pull up the wheat along with them.' For on the day of the harvest, the weeds will be plainly visible; and they will be pulled up and burned."[49]

Chapter 50: Worthy Strivings

Jesus exclaimed, "Blessed is the one who has labored diligently in the search for truth and wisdom, and thereby found life."

Chapter 51: Seek the Living One

Jesus instructed the spiritual pilgrim to, "Seek after the Living One while you are yet alive, lest you die and be unable to do so."[50]

Chapter 52: The Samaritan's Lamb

While Jesus was traveling with his disciples, they met a man from Samaria carrying a lamb. Jesus said, "See that tied-up lamb. What do you think about it?"

Then Peter replied, "He has the lamb tied up so that he might kill it and eat it later."

The disciples asked for clarification on this story, and Jesus replied, "Take care, my friends, lest you are likewise tied up in such manner that your spirit will be killed and reduced to nothing by someone else; for only the truly free have life. Let this be a lesson for you on your

49 This verse is a retelling of Matthew 13:24-30 (KJV).

50 John 7:33-34 (KJV): "Then said Jesus unto them, Yet a little while am I with you, and then I go unto him that sent me. Ye shall seek me, and shall not find me: and where I am, thither ye cannot come."

journey through life. You yourselves need seek a place of safety and rest,[51] lest you become corpses and are eaten."

Chapter 53: In the House of Salome

While the disciples and some of the women who followed after them were gathered in the house of Salome at Galilee, anticipating their journey to Jerusalem, Peter and James had been the first ones to recline at the dining couch while Salome and Mary Magdalene continued in the kitchen preparing the meal. Then Jesus pointed out that, "Death can come at any time. Two can be resting on a bed, enjoying their meal, as these men, when all of a sudden one will die for no obvious reason and the other will live."[52]

Salome, hearing these words, ran out into the dining area and demanded of Jesus, "Who are you, sir, really, that you have come to my home and my couch to partake of my food, and say such things?"

Then Jesus calmly explained to her, "I am one that exists from the undivided, given some gifts to share with the inhabitants of this lost world from the Father of Lights."

Salome replied, "Forgive me, Master Jesus; then I remain your disciple."

Jesus continued to speak, adding that, "All is well, Salome. If the physical body is destroyed, the undivided light that dwells within will carry that one into the eternities; whereas the soul whose attention is distracted by the lures of this world is thereby divided and will be filled with darkness."

---

51 Only by maintaining freedom from religious systems and embracing the true words of Christ to work out one's own salvation will the spiritual pilgrim avoid the snares of the devil and all his minions. See 2 Timothy 3:16-17 (KJV): "All scripture is given by inspiration of God, and is profitable for doctrine, for reproof, for correction, for instruction in righteousness: That the man of God may be perfect, thoroughly furnished unto all good works;" and Philippians 2:12 (KJV): "Wherefore, my beloved, as ye have always obeyed, not as in my presence only, but now much more in my absence, work out your own salvation with fear and trembling."

52 Mark 15:40-41 (KJV): "There were also women looking on afar off: among whom was Mary Magdalene, and Mary the mother of James the less and of Joses, and Salome; (Who also, when he was in Galilee, followed him, and ministered unto him;) and many other women which came up with him unto Jerusalem."

Chapter 54: Being Worthy

Jesus said, "It is to those whose souls are focused on the light, hence worthy of my mysteries, that I reveal them. Do not, therefore, let your left hand know what your right hand is doing."[53]

Chapter 55: Act While the Sun Shines

The Master, desiring to point out the fleeting nature of life in the material world, told his disciples the parable of the rich man:

"There was a rich man who had an exceedingly great amount of money. He said, 'I shall put my money to use so that I may sow, reap, plant and fill my storehouse to the roof with produce, with the result that I shall lack nothing.' Such were his intentions; but that same night, he died. Let the one who has ears hear what I am saying."[54]

Chapter 56: Dinner Invitations

Then Jesus related another parable, saying: "A man had received visitors. And when he had prepared the dinner, he sent his servant to invite the guests. He went to the first one and said to him, 'My master invites you.'

"He said, 'I have claims against some merchants. They are coming this evening. I must go and give them my orders. I ask to be excused from the dinner.'

"He went to another and said to him, 'My master has invited you.'

---

53 Your attention is invited to 1 Corinthians 2:14 (KJV): "But the natural man receiveth not the things of the Spirit of God: for they are foolishness unto him: neither can he know them, because they are spiritually discerned." While Matthew 6:3 (KJV), encourages secrecy in generous giving, here the "right hand/left hand" analogy refers to guarding esoteric knowledge within the privileged confines of the teacher-student relationship. By this statement, not made to be cruel, the Master meant that the sacred doctrines taught by him in the inner circle of the disciples should not be shared with the unappreciative and unworthy masses.

54 For a parallel version, see Luke 12:13-21 (KJV). In these verses, Jesus emphasizes that those who are "rich toward God," rather than "laying up treasures" for themselves, are the more prudent, for their quest is spiritual rather than material. Nikos Kazantzakis summed up the Gnostic philosophy of Jesus quite nicely: "My principal anguish and the source of all my joys and sorrows from my youth onward has been the incessant, merciless battle between the spirit and the flesh."

"He said to him, 'I have just bought a house and am required for the day. I shall not have any spare time.'

"Still, he went to another and said to him, 'My master invites you.'

"He said to him, 'My friend is going to get married; and I am to prepare the banquet. I shall not be able to come. I ask to be excused from the dinner.'

"And yet he went to another and said to him, 'My master invites you.'

"But even this last one had an excuse not to attend, for he replied to him, 'I have just bought a farm; and I am on my way to collect the rent. I shall not be able to come. I ask to be excused.'

"At this, the servant returned and said to his master, 'Those whom you invited to the dinner have asked to be excused.'

"The master said to his servant, 'Go outside to the streets and bring back those whom you happen to meet, so that they may dine.'

"I tell you this, businessmen and merchants will not enter the places of my Father."[55]

Chapter 57: Owner of the Vineyard

Then Jesus told his disciples another parable, that of a good man who owned a vineyard. "He leased it to tenant farmers so that they might

55 For a parallel version, see Luke 14:15-24 (KJV). Those that are preoccupied with the financial and other concerns of this world will miss out on partaking of the celestial glories, which will be passed on to others. When Dante Alighieri's beloved Beatrice guided him to the Third Sphere of Heaven (the planet Venus), she introduced him to Cunizza da Romano and Folco of Marseilles. Both of these pointed out Rahab, the prostitute who hid in her inn the two Israelite spies sent by Joshua to carry out a reconnaissance mission in Jericho prior to launching an attack on it (Joshua 2:1-24, KJV), as a typical resident of that celestial realm. Cunizza lived in the 13th century, was married four times, and was the mistress of the poet Sordello, who appears in *Purgatorio* (Purgatory). Cunizza is portrayed as an erotically passionate yet warm-hearted figure, in contrast to her cruel despot of a brother, Ezzelino, who shows up in *Inferno* (Hell). Folco was a 12th-century poet who later became a bishop. He was said to have been an amorous figure when young. Folco explains to Dante that the souls in Heaven do not brood over their earthly sins, instead they are praising God's providential reordering and transformation of those characteristics that occasioned sin on Earth. As for Rahab, she is lauded in the *New Testament* as one who, despite her previous life of ill-repute, served as an outstanding example of a saintly individual who lived by faith (Hebrews 11:31, KJV) and was esteemed righteous for her good works (James 2:25, KJV). Rahab also appears in the genealogy of Jesus (Matthew 1:1-16, with special attention to verse 5, KJV), which many find surprising not only because of her occupation, but also because she was a Canaanite, a people frequently at war with Israel. Interestingly, many of the ecclesiastical, financial, military and political leaders deemed corrupt by Dante (1265-1321 C.E.) during his day, are not found anywhere in the heavenly spheres, or even Purgatory, where they would still find a chance for redemption, for they had their rewards on Earth.

work it and thereby he might collect the produce from them," said Jesus, adding that, "He sent his servant so that the tenants might give him the produce of the vineyard. They seized his servant and beat him, all but killing him. The servant went back and informed his master, whereupon the master said, 'Perhaps they did not recognize you as my servant.'

"Then he sent another servant; but the tenants beat this one as well. Then the owner sent his own son, and declared, 'Perhaps they will show respect to my son.'

"But because the tenants knew him to be the heir to the vineyard, they seized him and killed him. Let the one who has ears hear."[56]

Chapter 58: Rejected Stone

Jesus said, "Show me the stone which the builders have rejected. That one is the cornerstone."[57]

---

56 Mark 12:1-9 (KJV): "And he began to speak unto them by parables. A certain man planted a vineyard, and set an hedge about it, and digged a place for the winefat, and built a tower, and let it out to husbandmen, and went into a far country. And at the season he sent to the husbandmen a servant, that he might receive from the husbandmen of the fruit of the vineyard. And they caught him, and beat him, and sent him away empty. And again he sent unto them another servant; and at him they cast stones, and wounded him in the head, and sent him away shamefully handled. And again he sent another; and him they killed, and many others; beating some, and killing some. Having yet therefore one son, his wellbeloved, he sent him also last unto them, saying, They will reverence my son. But those husbandmen said among themselves, This is the heir; come, let us kill him, and the inheritance shall be ours.' And they took him, and killed him, and cast him out of the vineyard. What shall therefore the lord of the vineyard do? he will come and destroy the husbandmen, and will give the vineyard unto others." The meaning of this parable is made clear in Mark's version. The owner of the vineyard is Jesus' Heavenly Father. The servants represent the prophets sent to Israel from God who had been rejected or killed throughout that nation's long history, and the husbandmen, or tenants, signify the religious leaders of Israel who seek to control the people by claiming exclusive spiritual authority. The Son, of course, is Jesus; and the predicted vengeance of God wreaked upon Israel was fulfilled with the Roman invasion that ultimately came to pass in 70 C.E., the destruction of the city and the temple and the diaspora of the remnant. And the others to whom the vineyard would be given are the gentiles.

57 Mark 12:10-12 (KJV) provides a continuation of the parable referenced in the above footnote. King David's predicted stone (Psalm 118:22, KJV) was the message of Jesus and his disciples. It is clear that the religious leaders in Israel found these allusions in the statements of Jesus in Mark 12:1-12 a direct threat to their rule.

Chapter 59: On Knowing

Jesus declared, "If one knows the mysteries of the universe but does not know themselves, then that one has failed to gain an understanding of all that matters in their material existence."

Chapter 60: Persecution

Jesus averred that, "Blessed are you when you are hated and persecuted. Whoever has persecuted you will find no place in the Kingdom of Heaven."[58]

In the same line of thought, Jesus continued, "Blessed are those of a pure heart that have suffered persecution, for these ones have truly come to know the Father, and are known by Him.[59] And blessed are the hungry, for they shall be fed."[60]

Chapter 61: Salvation

Jesus remarked, "Finding the divine spark within you and bringing it forth to manifest good works in this world is that which will save you and carry you over into the eternities. The soul without it is dead already, lost to the darkness."[61]

---

58 Luke 6:22-23 (KJV): "Blessed are ye, when men shall hate you, and when they shall separate you from their company, and shall reproach you, and cast out your name as evil, for the Son of man's sake. Rejoice ye in that day, and leap for joy: for, behold, your reward is great in heaven: for in the like manner did their fathers unto the prophets."

59 Matthew 5:8 (KJV): "Blessed are the pure in heart: for they shall see God."

60 Luke 6:21 (KJV): "Blessed are ye that hunger now: for ye shall be filled. Blessed are ye that weep now: for ye shall laugh."

61 The latter-day prophetess Annalee Skarin wrote the following in Chapter XX, "Oil for the Lamps of Israel," in her classic book of divine revelation, *Ye Are Gods* (Camarillo, California: DeVorss and Company, 1952; original volume self-published in 1948): "The very voice of the scriptures thunders forth a warning to the world that the wicked shall be cast out into outer darkness, and our minds will shiver and pass on, ignoring the warning- while we have all been living in outer darkness- in the very darkness of our physical minds and thoughts. We have groped through our mortal consciousness of dark perception, wallowed in our earthly conditions, been ruled by the flesh- tossed and churned by the mental storms of hurt, pride, fears, worries, vanities, bigotry, confusion, ego, anger, selfishness, greed and jealousies. Outer darkness? Yes, the outer darkness of the flesh- and this will continue to be our abiding place until we are willing to return to our Father's house and partake of the warmth and the light that awaits us there.

Chapter 62: The Temple No Longer God's House

Jesus, upon visiting Jerusalem and recognizing that the priestly class had corrupted the temple through their abominable administrations of it and collaboration with the Roman occupation, declared to his disciples that, "The day will soon come when God shall permit the destruction of this structure and no one will be able to rebuild it; for it has ceased to function as His house."[62]

Chapter 63: Jesus Not an Arbitrator of Disputes

A certain man approached Jesus and said to him, "Tell my brothers to include me in the division of my father's property and possessions."

"'The kingdom of heaven is within you,' Son of man- how far you will have to journey from your particular place in outer darkness to that glorious realm of peace and light that you might fulfill your own ultimate glory will depend on you- what you desire to accept and fulfill- and the vision you hold in your heart- for 'Faith promises all things- and fulfills all things.' According to your faith be it unto you."

62 Acts 6:12-14 (KJV): "And they stirred up the people, and the elders, and the scribes, and came upon him, and caught him, and brought him to the council, And set up false witnesses, which said, This man ceaseth not to speak blasphemous words against this holy place, and the law: For we have heard him say, that this Jesus of Nazareth shall destroy this place, and shall change the customs which Moses delivered us." The Master spoke not against the temple, but condemned the corrupt priests who mismanaged it. Entrusted by God with the temple's proper administration, the priests had failed in all of their duties and responsibilities. Therefore, God would allow for it to be taken away from them with its destruction by a Roman legion in 70 C.E.

The great reformer Martin Luther also pointed out that all believers are inherently part of a royal priesthood in Christ Jesus, thereby eliminating the need for any priestly class. In 1 Peter 2:5-9 (KJV) we understand that all believers are "living stones" building up a "spiritual house," a holy priesthood, to offer up "spiritual sacrifices" acceptable to God through Jesus Christ: "But you are a chosen generation, a royal priesthood, a holy nation, His own special people, that you may proclaim the praises of Him who called you out of darkness into His marvelous light." Old Testament priests were chosen by God, not self-appointed; and they were chosen for a purpose: to serve God with their lives by offering up sacrifices. The priesthood served as a picture or "type" of the coming ministry of Jesus Christ--a picture that was then no longer needed once His sacrifice on the cross was completed. When the thick temple veil that covered the doorway to the Holy of Holies was torn in two by God at the time of Christ's death (Matthew 27:51, KJV), God was indicating that the Old Testament priesthood was no longer necessary. Now people could come directly to God through the great High Priest, Jesus Christ (Hebrews 4:14-16, KJV). There are now no Earthly mediators between God and man as existed in the Old Testament priesthood (1 Timothy 2:5, KJV). This is a truly revolutionary concept for the Christian, who has no need of king or priest but Jesus.

He said to him, "O man, I have not come into the world to arbitrate family disputes. Guard against greed in all its forms; for an abundance of wealth cannot guarantee eternal life."[63]

Then Jesus directed the man's attention to the disciples surrounding him. "These dear ones have given up all to follow me. If you ask any one of them, that one will tell you that I am a teacher, not an arbitrator."

Chapter 64: Great Harvest

Jesus said, "The harvest is great but the laborers are few. Beseech the lord, therefore, to send out laborers to the harvest."[64]

Chapter 65: Venture for Illumination

Jesus remarked, "There are many on the cusp of finding illumination, but they are not willing to risk everything, including their lives, to find it.[65] Indeed, there are many who stand at the door of divine knowledge, but unwilling to rid themselves of the burdensome rituals and traditions imposed upon them by the pretentious religious authorities, they fail to pass through this portal that leads to freedom from the material world by unification with God through the Holy Spirit."

Chapter 66: The Pearl

Jesus said, "The Kingdom of the Father is like unto a merchant with a consignment of goods who discovered a precious pearl therein. This merchant was shrewd. He sold all of the merchandise, but reserved the pearl for himself, which he purchased from his commission garnered from the sale of the other merchandise. You, also, needs seek after and

63 A similar but more extended teaching is found in Luke 12:13-21 (KJV).

64 This seems to be a paraphrase of Matthew 9:38 (KJV).

65 Matthew 16:25 (KJV): "For whosoever will save his life shall lose it: and whosoever will lose his life for my sake shall find it."

hold onto the unfailing and enduring treasure that cannot be devoured by moths or destroyed by worms."[66]

Chapter 67: Motivated by the Holy Spirit

Jesus, when the Holy Spirit was upon him, proclaimed, "It is I who am the Light which is above them all.[67] It is I, now speaking, the very One that encompasses the all; for it is through me that all has come forth; and it is unto me that the all did extend. Split a piece of wood and I am there. Lift up the stone and you will find me there."[68]

Chapter 68: Jesus in the Judean Desert

Many pilgrims had flocked to the Judean Desert. Jesus inquired of them, "Why have you come out into the desert? To see a reed shaken by the wind? Or to see a man clothed in fine garments like unto your kings and great men? Verily, upon them are the finest of garments; yet they are unable to discern the truth."[69]

Then a woman stepped out from the crowd and said to him, "Blessed is the womb which bore you and the breasts which nourished you."

To this, the Master replied, "Blessed are those who have heard the Word of the Father[70] and have truly kept it. For there will be days when each of you will come to say, 'Blessed is the womb which has not conceived and the breasts which have not given milk.'"[71]

---

66 Luke 12:33-34 (KJV): "Sell your possessions and give to the poor. Provide purses for yourselves that will not wear out, a treasure in heaven that will never fail, where no thief comes near and no moth destroys. For where your treasure is, there your heart will be also."

67 The reader's attention is invited to Hebrews, Chapter 1 (KJV), for an understanding of the position and power of Jesus, The Christ, with respect to the angels and all of creation.

68 The Greco-Roman author Lucian of Samosata (125-180 C.E.) found agreement with the 6th century B.C.E. Greek philosopher Hermotimus that, "God is not in heaven but rather permeates all things, such as pieces of wood and stones and animals, even the most insignificant (Lucian in *Hermotimus* 81)."

69 Thomas indicates that Jesus is carrying on the ministry of his cousin John, called the "Baptist." See Luke 7:24-30 (KJV).

70 Thomas recognizes that Jesus is a true prophet and serves as a mouthpiece for God on Earth.

71 Jesus was alluding to times of tribulation to come upon Israel, most likely the Roman Legion's destroying Jerusalem in 70 C.E. and the subsequent diaspora of the Jewish people.

Chapter 69: Proper View of the World

Jesus said, "The material world is dead to the things of God. Those whose hearts incline toward the Spirit shall overcome the world."[72]

Chapter 70: Wise Rulers

Jesus said, "Let him who has grown rich in wisdom be king; and let him who possesses power, yet lacks the wisdom to wield it for the good of all, renounce it."[73]

Chapter 71: Risk and Reward

Jesus said, "The one who is near me risks their life; for many in authority wish nothing more than to hunt down and kill me and all my disciples. On the other hand, the one who is far from me is far from the Kingdom."

Chapter 72: Lights Within

Jesus said, "There is a light in each individual; but their physical body conceals it from the eyes of the world. There is an image of the Father, but those in the material world cannot fully perceive it for it is concealed by the perpetual emanations of a divine light."[74]

---

72 James 4:4 (KJV): "Ye adulterers and adulteresses, know ye not that the friendship of the world is enmity with God? whosoever therefore will be a friend of the world is the enemy of God."

73 James 1:5 (KJV): "If any of you lack wisdom, let him ask of God, that giveth to all men liberally, and upbraideth not; and it shall be given him."

74 2 Corinthians 4:4-6 (KJV): "In whom the god of this world hath blinded the minds of them which believe not, lest the light of the glorious gospel of Christ, who is the image of God, should shine unto them. For we preach not ourselves, but Christ Jesus the Lord; and ourselves your servants for Jesus' sake. For God, who commanded the light to shine out of darkness, hath shined in our hearts, to give the light of the knowledge of the glory of God in the face of Jesus Christ."

Chapter 73: Body Celestial

Jesus spoke of the new body awaiting elect souls in the celestial realms: "When you behold your true self as a child of light created in the likeness of the Father of Lights, you will surely rejoice. In the celestial body you shall never die, nor be required to return to the material world. Be patient and endure for but a little time.[75] Adam was created from an unsurpassed power and placed in a world of endless abundance; but this first of men failed you through his disobedience to God, hence bringing corruption and death unto his descendants. Had he remained faithful to his Creator you would have no need to experience death."[76]

Chapter 74: No Place to Rest

Jesus said, "Foxes have their holes and the birds have their nests, but the son of man has no place to lay his head and rest."[77]

The Master was explaining the challenges and hardships one would face upon becoming a disciple.

Chapter 75: Physical vs. Spiritual Body

Jesus said, "Don't become obsessed with your physical body, which came into this world through the womb of woman. Let not your soul become dependent on satisfying the needs of your physical body at the expense of attending to spirit."[78]

---

75 Genesis 1:26-28 (KJV) highlights the creation of humankind in the image and likeness of God.

76 In Genesis 3:17-19 (KJV), God explains to Adam the consequences of his disobedience.

77 Luke 9:57-62 (KJV) places this saying of Jesus in a fuller context.

78 Galatians 5:16-18 (KJV): "This I say then, Walk in the Spirit, and ye shall not fulfil the lust of the flesh. For the flesh lusteth against the Spirit, and the Spirit against the flesh: and these are contrary the one to the other: so that ye cannot do the things that ye would. But if ye be led of the Spirit, ye are not under the law."

Chapter 76: Heavenly Assistance

Jesus spoke of heavenly ministrations: "The angels and prophets will come to you, bestowing all that you need to successfully carry out the work I have already assigned you.[79] And you, too, should render unto these celestial emissaries every measure of kindness and all that they require.[80] You have been sent out into the world as harvesters of souls; but these souls belong to God. The angels will escort these souls to their homes prepared for them in the celestial realms."

Chapter 77: Futility of Keeping Up Appearances

Jesus, when confronting the Pharisees for the pompous manner in which they carried out a certain religious observance, asked them, "Why do you wash the outside of the cup? Do you not realize that he who made the inside is the same who made the outside?"[81]

Chapter 78: Finding Rest in Jesus

Jesus, ever mindful of the endless religious laws and ordinances imposed upon the people by the Jewish authorities, addressed a crowd which had gathered to hear him: "Come unto me, for my yoke is easy and my lordship is mild; and you will find repose for yourselves."[82]

Chapter 79: Conspiring Religionists

Some of the Pharisees approached Jesus, asking him, "Tell us who you are so that we may believe in you."

Jesus, not wanting to fall into the snare these religionists had set for him, declared, "You seem to have no difficulty in reading the face of the

79 Psalms 91:11 (KJV): "For he shall give his angels charge over thee, to keep thee in all thy ways."

80 Hebrews 13:2 (KJV): "Be not forgetful to entertain strangers: for thereby some have entertained angels unawares."

81 For a parallel scripture, see Luke 11:39-41 (KJV).

82 For a parallel scripture, see Matthew 11:25-30 (KJV).

sky and thereby determining when the rains will fall to the earth; but you cannot recognize the one who is now before you. You do not have a clue. You do not even know what to make out of this moment.[83]

"If you seek for the answer, you will find it.

"I want you to know that I was prepared to answer some of the questions you previously asked of me. I had my reasons for not answering your questions at that time; but I came here today willing to answer those very questions.[84] But now you have not asked those questions, so I have nothing to say more of those matters."

Jesus, hoping his disciples would learn something from this encounter, then turned to them and provided the following guidance, "Do not give what is holy to dogs, lest they take it away with them to a dung heap. And do not cast pearls before swine, lest they trample them under their feet, turn again and rend you."[85]

Chapter 80: Disciples Rewarded

Then the Master addressed those who truly sought for spiritual illumination: "Insofar as I have chosen you, it is indeed my Father's pleasure to give you whatsoever you ask for. Therefore, seek and you shall find. Knock and you shall be granted entry."[86]

Chapter 81: Money Management

Jesus said, "If you have money beyond meeting your basic needs, do not lend it at interest, whence it shall vex your soul. Rather, give it to one in need and do not expect to get it back. You shall be amply re-

83 For a parallel scripture, see Luke 12:54-56 (KJV).

84 See Matthew 7:7-11 (KJV) for similar comments.

85 Matthew 7:6 (KJV): "Give not that which is holy unto the dogs, neither cast ye your pearls before swine, lest they trample them under their feet, and turn again and rend you."

86 John 15:16-17 (KJV) provides further insight. Also pay close attention to Jeremiah 1:5 (KJV), where the call and election made sure of the prophet is explained: "Before I formed thee in the belly I knew thee; and before thou camest forth out of the womb I sanctified thee, and I ordained thee a prophet unto the nations."

paid many times over and abundantly rewarded in the Kingdom of my Father."[87]

Chapter 82: "Kingdom of the Father"

Jesus desired for his disciples to understand the true nature of his Father's Kingdom.

The Master declared, "The Kingdom of the Father is like a certain woman. She took a little leaven, concealed it in some dough, and made it into large loaves. Let the one who has ears hear.[88]

"The Kingdom of the Father is like a certain woman carrying a jar full of meal. While she was walking on the road, still at some distance from home, and unbeknownst to her, the handle of the jar broke and the meal spilled out behind her onto the road. When she arrived at her house, she set down the jar and found it empty.[89]

"The Kingdom of the Father is like a Zealot who wanted desperately to kill a powerful man who collaborated with the Roman occupiers. In his own house, he drew his sword and stuck it into the wall, wanting to find out whether his hand was strong enough so that he could follow through in this contemplated action. Having satisfied himself on this account, he then went on to slay the powerful man."[90]

---

87 Matthew 5:42 (KJV): "Give to him that asketh thee, and from him that would borrow of thee turn not thou away."

88 Matthew 13:35 (KJV): "That it might be fulfilled which was spoken by the prophet, saying, I will open my mouth in parables; I will utter things which have been kept secret from the foundation of the world." The saving doctrine of the Kingdom is hidden from everyday view; but once it becomes incorporated into the hearts of the believers, it produces a large and wondrous spiritual body.

89 In the second parable, the Master is pointing out that revealed knowledge of sacred things should not be taken for granted. Inattention to these spiritual teachings could cause the seeker of the Kingdom to gradually lose the inner Light of Christ altogether. Being empty of the Light, they can in no ways enter into the Kingdom of the Father.

90 The closest parallel is Luke 14:31 (KJV). The phraseology in Thomas indicates that it is the older section insofar as the reference to a political assassin was probably edited out by the Greek physician Luke who was somewhat more sympathetic to the Romans and did not want to bring down Roman persecution against the emerging sect of the followers of the Way. In the last parable of the Kingdom, one comes to understand that preparation is required before embarking on a dangerous mission that might even cost one's life to carry out. It may also indicate some degree of force needing to be exercised before the Kingdom can be established, thereby taking it by force. Section 32 in this same *Gospel of Thomas* explains that such an attack against the forces of evil can only be carried out under the auspices of the Holy Spirit.

Chapter 83: True Family

The disciples came up to Jesus and informed him, "Some of your brothers, sisters and mother are standing outside."

Then Jesus said to them, "Those who do the will of my Father are my brothers, sisters and mother. It is they who will enter the Kingdom of my Father."[91]

Chapter 84: "Born again unto life eternal"

Jesus said, "Verily, we have a mother and father who gave us our life in this world; but one needs turn to our Father and Mother in Heaven if we seek to be born again unto life eternal."[92]

Chapter 85: Give Caesar His Due

Once again, the religious authorities in Jerusalem sent spies to the public discourses of the Master Jesus to see if they could catch him in pronouncing harsh words against the emperor or urging the people not to pay the taxes assessed upon them. To this end they showed Jesus a gold coin and said to him, "Caesar's men are demanding taxes from us."

Jesus said to them, "Then give Caesar what belongs to Caesar; give God what belongs to God; and give me what is mine."[93]

---

91 For parallel versions see Matthew 12:46-50 (KJV) and Luke 8:19-21 (KJV). The word "brethren" in these verses also includes sisters of Jesus. See Mark 6:3 (KJV) and Matthew 13:55-56 for the references to Jesus' unnamed sisters. According to Epiphanius (310–403, C.E.), the bishop of Salamis, Cyprus at the end of the 4th century who gained a reputation as a strong defender of orthodoxy and was best known for composing the *Panarion*, a very large compendium of the heresies up to his own time, full of quotations that are often the only surviving fragments of suppressed Gnostic texts, it was alleged that Jesus had at least four brothers and two sisters.

92 John 3:3 (KJV): "Jesus answered (Nicodemus) and said unto him, Verily, verily, I say unto thee, Except a man be born again, he cannot see the kingdom of God."

93 For a parallel version see Luke 20:20-26 (KJV). The comment made by Jesus to give him what is rightly his may be a demand for recognition and respect as a teacher in Israel.

Chapter 86: Pharisees Critiqued

The Master had some harsh words for certain religious authorities in Israel who would not recognize the truth of his words, nor permit the people to hear the words of life that he desired to impart to them: "Woe to the Pharisees! For they are like a dog sleeping in the manger of oxen. The dog can cannot eat the grain of the oxen, nor by his barking does he let the oxen eat."[94]

Chapter 87: Fortify your Domain

Jesus said to his disciples, "Fortunate is the man who knows where the brigands will cross over onto his property, for he will get up and muster his forces to fortify and defend his domain, being well-armed before the invasion commences."[95]

Chapter 88: Spiritual Unification with the Father

The disciples came to Jesus, wishing to fast and pray with him. "Come," said Peter, "Let us pray today and let us fast."

Jesus replied, "What is the sin that I have committed, or wherein have I been defeated? But when the bridegroom leaves the bridal chamber, then let them fast and pray."[96]

---

94 Jesus was quoting a variant of a Greek fable attributed to Aesop (620-524 B.C.E.). As originally told, the fable had a barking dog in the stable that would hinder the donkey from eating.

95 See Section 20, *Gospel of Thomas* and Luke 12:39-40 (KJV) for a parallel version. As Section 20 indicates the benefit of knowing the time that a raid may occur, Section 88 demonstrates an awareness on the part of the owner of the weak points along his property line and within his home that need fortification. The latter-day prophetess Annalee Skarin frequently stated that the manifestation of any attitude outside of gratitude, love and the praise of God in one's life would only lend itself to darkness and rob one of the blessings that flow from the Light of Christ that emanates within you. This is fully explained all throughout her book, *Secrets of Eternity* (Marina del Rey, California: DeVorss and Company, 1960). This seems a most excellent bulwark against the wiles of the devil.

96 In Mark 2:18-22 (KJV), the meaning of this section is clarified. Jesus, having already attained to a state of spiritual unification with the Father, had no need of prayer or fasting. As long as Jesus was with his disciples, a greater spiritual enlightenment would accrue to them from listening to and taking in his profound teachings. Once he returned to the Father, however, the disciples could once again continue in prayer and fasting in their quest for spiritual enrichment.

Chapter 89: Original Sin

Jesus spoke to the disciples concerning their birth to parents in the material world. "It is the estimation of the angels that all born of a mother and father in this world are no more regarded than the child of a harlot, for all are equally born in corruption and needs be redeemed through being born again of the Spirit."[97]

Chapter 90: Power from On High

Jesus said, "When you unite with the Father, you can bring down the powers of Heaven. And when you tell a mountain to move away, it certainly will."[98]

Chapter 91: The Lost Sheep

Jesus said, "The Kingdom is like a shepherd who had a hundred sheep. One of them, the largest, went astray. He left the ninety-nine and looked for that one until he found it. Having gone to all of that trouble, the shepherd said to that sheep, 'I certainly care for you, even more than the ninety-nine.'"[99]

Chapter 92: Drink of the "Water of Life"

The Master would often speak of his words as the "water of life." Jesus explained this to his disciples: "My words are the water of life. He who imbibes them will become like me. I shall become a part of him, too; and all things that are hidden will be revealed unto him as well."[100]

97 John 8:39-47 (KJV) denotes that those identified as spiritually reborn are the ones who manifest the works of the Father. See Section 85, which reinforces this doctrine.

98 For a parallel scripture, see Matthew 17:19-20 (KJV).

99 For a parallel scripture, see Luke 15:3-7 (KJV).

100 Revelation 22:17 (KJV) provides further illumination.

Chapter 93: Hidden Treasure

Jesus said, "The kingdom resembles a man who possessed a hidden treasure in his field, without being aware of it. Upon his death, he bequeathed the field to his son. The son also did not know about the hidden treasure. After assuming ownership of the field, the son sold it. The purchaser of the field then started to plow it and discovered the treasure, whence he began to lend out money at interest to whomever he wished, thus multiplying his riches."[101]

Chapter 94: Renouncing the World

Jesus said, "Whoever finds the world and becomes rich, let him renounce the world."[102]

Chapter 95: Fate of the Enlightened

When speaking of the end of life in the material world, the Master explained, "At that time, the heavens and the Earth will roll up as a scroll in your presence.[103] And from your dying material body will emerge your indestructible spirit."[104]

---

101 Jesus was quoting a variant of a Greek fable attributed to Aesop (620-524 B.C.E.). In the original fable, the owner of the field on his deathbed tells his sons that there is buried treasure somewhere on the property, motivating them to plow the entire field looking for it. Although they do not find it, the very process of tilling all the land was conducive to later providing the sons with an unusually abundant harvest. The moral of the story is that hard work pays off handsomely. In Jesus' version, the Master desires for us to know that the bounty of the Kingdom resides within. We should not, therefore, sell out to the world, before embarking on a search for this treasure. And in the diligent search for the treasure, we shall surely find it, either in a great abundance of wealth or through the spiritual riches that come through illumination; for in the very process of seeking for this, we find it. If we do not even try, we should not be surprised when the treasure falls into the hands of another, to do with it as they wish. Knowledge is power; and this especially applies to esoteric or occult (previously hidden) knowledge.

102 Matthew 19:24 (KJV): "And again I say unto you, It is easier for a camel to go through the eye of a needle, than for a rich man to enter into the kingdom of God."

103 Isaiah 34:4 (KJV): "And all the host of heaven shall be dissolved, and the heavens shall be rolled together as a scroll: and all their host shall fall down, as the leaf falleth off from the vine, and as a falling fig from the fig tree."

104 1 Corinthians 15:35-42 (KJV): "But some *man* will say, How are the dead raised up? and with what body do they come? *Thou* fool, that which thou sowest is not quickened, except it die: And that which thou sowest, thou sowest not that body that shall be, but bare *grain*, it may chance of wheat, or of some other grain: But God giveth it a body as it hath pleased him, and

Clearly, Jesus was teaching us that the world and all that is in it can never be worthy enough for the one who has attained enlightenment, touching, as it were, the Light of Christ that dwells in every human heart.

Chapter 96: False Dependence

From the teachings of the Master, the disciples came to understand that an individual soul was constituted of the fleshly body and the spirit. Keeping this in mind, Jesus informed us: "Woe to the flesh that depends on the soul; and woe to the soul that depends on the flesh."[105]

The spirit is linked to the soul for its duration on the material plane. Unlinking the spirit from the soul, thus leaving the flesh behind, is what sets it free.

Chapter 97: Thy Kingdom Come

The disciples inquired of the Master, "When will the Kingdom come?"

Jesus replied, "It will not get here any sooner by waiting for its arrival. It will not be a matter of simply saying, 'Here it is;' or 'There it is.' Rather, the Kingdom of the Father is spread out over the entirety of the Earth; but there be few who actually see it."[106]

---

to every seed his own body. All flesh *is* not the same flesh: but *there is* one *kind of* flesh of men, another flesh of beasts, another of fishes, *and* another of birds. *There are* also celestial bodies, and bodies terrestrial: but the glory of the celestial *is* one, and the *glory* of the terrestrial *is* another. *There is* one glory of the sun, and another glory of the moon, and another glory of the stars: for *one* star differeth from *another* star in glory. So also *is* the resurrection of the dead. It is sown in corruption; it is raised in incorruption: It is sown in dishonour; it is raised in glory: it is sown in weakness; it is raised in power: It is sown a natural body; it is raised a spiritual body."

105 Genesis 2:7 (KJV): "And the LORD God formed man *of* the dust of the ground, and breathed into his nostrils the breath of life; and man became a living soul." From this scripture, we learn that the human soul is "God-breathed." God breathed His spirit into Adam, whom He created from the elements of the Earth.

106 Luke 17:20-21 (KJV): "And when he was demanded of the Pharisees, when the kingdom of God should come, he answered them and said, The kingdom of God cometh not with observation: Neither shall they say, Lo here! or, lo there! for, behold, the kingdom of God is within you."

Chapter 98: Peter's Dispute with Mary Magdalene

Simon Peter urged the other disciples to expel Mary Magdalene from their band, saying, "We should ask Mary to leave us, for women have no part in the work of the brethren, let alone fellowship."

Jesus, overhearing this remark, said to Peter, "Have no qualms about Mary, for I have found her worthy of the work. Know ye not that the Father created man and woman in His image, 'male and female created He them.'[107] Like yourself, Mary possesses a living spirit. All spirits that enter the Kingdom of Heaven are equal in the eyes of the Father of Lights."

107 Genesis 1:27 (KJV): "So God created man in his own image, in the image of God created he him; male and female created he them."

The Acts of Thomas

Thomas before the Indian King and Queen

Chapter 1: Origins of the Calling

The Sun had already set and I, Judas Thomas, also called Didymus, being the twin brother of Jesus, and the other apostles were all gathered in Jerusalem. We came together to portion out the regions of the world, in accordance with the last instructions given us by the Master Jesus, in order that each one of us might go into the region that fell to him by lot. And by this lot, the nation of India fell to me, a land to which I did not want to go. "I am too weak of body to make such a journey," I protested to Simon Peter, the chief of the apostles, further asking him, "How can I, being a Hebrew, go among the Indians to proclaim the truth?"

And while Peter was considering my petition to stay behind in Jerusalem amongst our own people, the Master Jesus appeared in our midst. "Fear not, Thomas, to go away to India and preach the word of truth there, for my grace is with you."

Knowing of some of Jesus' own difficult experiences in India during his youth that he had previously revealed to me, I still objected to embarking on this journey. I therefore addressed Jesus: "Dear brother, wherever else you wish to send me I will go; but I am not going to the Indians."

Chapter 2: Arrangements for the Journey

The Master tarried with us through the night; and on the following day it happened that a merchant named Abban, who had come from India, was present in the city, being dispatched there by Gundaphorus, a king of that far country. As Jesus and I were walking in the market at noon, the Master caught sight of Abban, immediately identifying him as Indian by his distinctive clothing, walked over to him and asked him in the language of the Indians, "Do you wish to contract the services of a carpenter?"

He replied, "Yes, I certainly do. My king Gundaphorus sent me here to bring a carpenter to him, to do some work in the royal court."

Then Jesus said, "That is good, for I would like you to consider contracting with me for my brother Judas Thomas' service, insofar as I can understand your tongue and we can reach an equitable agreement."

After reaching a consensus concerning the terms of my service, Jesus called me over for the purpose of introducing me to Abban and explaining the terms of the contract, this being that he would be paid the sum of three pounds of uncoined silver now and that I would be placed in the custody of Abban until the work in the king's court had been completed, after which time I would be joined to a caravan and could return to Jerusalem. Jesus explained that the silver would be given to Joseph of Arimathea, a wealthy member of our mother's family, who was safeguarding Jesus' spouse and children.

For our mother's sake, I agreed to these terms and my brother wrote it up in a contract with Abban which read as follows: "I, Jesus, son of the carpenter Joseph of Nazareth, declare that I have sold the services of my brother, Judas Thomas by name, to you, Abban, a merchant of Gundaphorus, king of the Indians, for such time as my brother completes the assigned work in the court of your king. You, Abban, agree to take care of my brother's food, shelter and health needs; and upon completion of the carpentry work, you, Abban, agree to return my brother back to his family here in Jerusalem."

Jesus signed the bill, as did Abban. Then Jesus turned me over to the custody of the Indian merchant. Abban looked at me closely, and then likewise scrutinized the face of Jesus, while questioning me, "Is this really your master? You look like twins!"

"We are;" I replied, "and yes, he is my Lord for he was the firstborn from our mother's womb."

"Very well," said Abban, "I have bought your services from him. I shall allow you one day to gather your clothes and tools, for we leave on the morrow."

Upon hearing this, I held my peace as it was the wish of my brother that I should go to India with this merchant.

Chapter 3: Contracting with the Merchant

On the following morning, Jesus and I came together for prayer. In my prayers, I asked our Heavenly Father for the assurance that what I was about to do was in accordance with His will. A great calm came over my entire being and I turned to my brother, saying to him, "I will go wherever you wish, O Lord Jesus. Let your will be done; for I am assured that the words you speak are given to you from the Father Above."

Jesus embraced me and said, "Let your worth be acknowledged at all times, Thomas, as you go with my grace to whatever lands the Father directs your steps."

Then we both proceeded to meet up with Abban in the market district for me to continue on with him in his journey, for he was headed north to the port of Caesarea on the coastal plane, whence we would continue on by boat to the Delta of Egypt and from there to the trading center of Andropolis. Jesus helped Abban and I in packing our luggage on the camels.

A few days later, after spending the night in Caesarea resting at an inn, Abban and I carried our luggage onto the boat and took our seats. Once at sea and away from the noise and commotion of the caravan, the merchant and I shared the time in getting to know each other. "Specifically," Abban asked me, "what kind of work do you know, Thomas?"

I replied, "I work in wood, ploughs and yokes and boats' oars and masts and small blocks. I also work in stone, pillars and temples and palaces."

Abban wanted to know where I learned such great craftsmanship and I said, "My father Joseph taught me these skills in Sepphoris, the cultural center not far from my home village of Nazareth in the Galilee district. We completed many projects for the Greeks and Romans resident there."

"We certainly need such a workman as you, Thomas," declared the merchant.

As we enjoyed a fair wind, we sailed cheerfully until at last coming to Andropolis, a royal city of the Ptolemy dynasty in Roman occupied Egypt.

Chapter 4: Arrival in Andropolis

Disembarking from the boat, Abban and I proceeded into the city. And behold, the sounds of flute players, water organs and trumpets echoed round about us. And then I inquired of a passerby, "What festival is it in this city?" And the inhabitant of Andropolis answered, "The gods have brought you to this city to keep festival here. For the king has an only daughter and now he is going to give her to a husband in marriage. And the king has sent forth heralds to proclaim everywhere in the city limits that all are to come to the marriage, the rich and the poor, the bond and the free, strangers, royal subjects and citizens of the empire. But if anyone should refuse and not come to the marriage, that one is answerable to the king."

Then Abban turned to me and said, "Let us go there." And having obtained lodging at an inn and rested a little, we went to the wedding. Seeing the guests reclining, Abban and I likewise reclined in their midst. Recognizing that we were strangers, all eyes turned in our direction. Being a merchant, Abban felt it best that we split up; and he went to recline at another place in the great hall.

Chapter 5: At the Wedding Feast

And while the guests were eating and drinking, I tasted nothing. Then some of those about me, asked, "Why have you come here, neither eating or drinking?"

And then I answered them, saying, "For something greater than food or even drink have I come here, that I might accomplish the will of the king who sent me. As the heralds of your king must proclaim his wishes, they will be liable to the judgement of their king if they fail to do so. And even so, I am liable to my king."

When they had dined and drunk, and crowns and perfumes had been brought, each took perfume, and one anointed his face, another his beard and others different parts of the body. Then I anointed the crown of my head, and put a little ointment in my nostrils, and dropped it also in my ears and applied it to my teeth; and carefully I anointed the parts round about my heart. And the crown that was brought to me, wreathed with myrtle and other flowers, I placed upon my head, and took a branch of reed in my hand and held it. And the flute girl, holding her flute in her hand, went round about us all; and when she came to the place where I was, she stood over my head for a long time. She singled me out for her attentions, being that this flute girl was a Hebrew by race.

Chapter 6: Song of Thomas

Humbled by the attention of the flute girl, my eyes were fixed upon the ground, when one of the cup bearers stretched forth his hand and struck me. Raising my eyes, I looked upon the face of the man who struck me, and said, "My God will forgive you for this in the world to come; but in this world, He will manifest His wonders; and I shall soon see that very hand that struck me dragged along the street by dogs."

Then I proceeded to sing the following song:

"The maiden is the daughter of the light,
On whom rests the majestic splendor of kings.
Delightful is the sight of her.
Resplendent with brilliant beauty,
Her garments are like spring flowers
Sending forth fragrance.
On the crown of her head the king is seated,
Feeding with his own ambrosia those who live under him.
Truth rests upon her head.
Joy she shows forth with her feet.
Her mouth is opened, and becomingly.
Thirty and two are they who praise her.
Her tongue is like a door curtain,
Drawn back for those who go in.
Made by the First Creator,
Her two hands point and make secret signs predicting the chorus of the blessed ages.
Her fingers show the gates of the city.
Her chamber is bright.
Breathing forth scent from balsam and every perfume,
Sending forth a sweet smell of myrrh and herbs.
Within are strewn myrtle branches and all manner of sweet-smelling flowers.
The portal is adorned with reeds.

Chapter 7: Song Continues

She is surrounded by her groomsmen, seven in number.
Chosen by herself;
Her bridesmaids are seven,
Whom dance before her.
Twelve in number are they who minister before her
And are at her bidding.
Their gaze is attentively directed at the bridegroom,
That they be enlightened by his sight,
And be forever with him in that everlasting joy,
And sit down at that wedding to which the princes assemble,

And abide at the supper of which the eternal ones are deemed worthy,
And don royal garments, and be dressed in splendid robes,
That both may rejoice and exult
And praise the Father of all,
Whose majestic light they have received
And have been enlightened by the sight of their Lord,
Whose ambrosial food they received,
Of which there is no deficiency,
And drank also of the wine,
Which brings to them neither thirst nor desire,
And they praised and glorified with the Living Spirit
The Father of Truth and the Mother of Wisdom."

Chapter 8: Attention of the Flute Girl

Upon finishing my song, the eyes of all present in the hall were upon me. I kept silence. Thereupon, many reported that they had noticed my form change, as though my face, in some way, was emitting an intense light. The attendees, for the most part, did not understand my words, insofar as I am a Hebrew and sang the song in the Hebrew language. The flute girl, being of the Hebrew race, was among the few present who did understand me. To take the attention away from me, she moved apart from me and began to play her flute for other guests; but she repeatedly looked back and gazed at me. There was an unspoken communication between us. She loved me as one belonging to her race, traveling in a far country.

When the flute girl had finished her flute playing, she sat down opposite me. She looked steadily at me and said, "From the moment my eyes first beheld you, I knew in my heart that there is something very special about you. I see that you are beautiful in appearance, above all in attendance here. You have the face of an angel."

I truly felt a great affinity for that flute girl; but realizing that I could not stay there and must move on with Abban to fulfill the desires of my brother and family, I cast my eyes upon the ground, not looking at the girl or anyone else, just biding my time until I could excuse myself, meet up with Abban and depart the hall. The flute girl returned to her duties.

As I was previously singing, however, the cupbearer who struck me had himself left the hall, drawing some water from a fountain on the outskirts of the city. There happened to be a wild lion that entered Andropolis in the vicinity of the fountain which attacked the cupbearer there, killing him instantly, tearing his limbs asunder and leaving his body in that place. It was then that dogs immediately seized his limbs, among them a huge black dog, which grasped his right hand in its mouth and brought it to the place of the banquet.

Chapter 9: Fate of the Cupbearer

When the startled guests saw it, they were frightened and inquired who was absent. And when it became known that it was the hand of the cupbearer that struck me, the flute girl broke her flute in half and threw it away, coming to stand by my side and declare to all, "This man is either an angel or God's apostle. For I heard him say in Hebrew to the cupbearer, 'I shall soon see the hand that struck me dragged about by dogs.' This you have now seen. For just as he said, so also it has come to pass."

Some of the guests believed her, and some not. But when the king heard the words of the flute girl, he came up to me and said, "Rise up and go with me; and pray for my daughter. For she is my only child and today I give her away in marriage." Despite my hesitance, as I was sure that Abban had other plans for me, the king took me away against my will to the bridal chamber, that I might pray for his daughter and the bridegroom.

Chapter 10: Blessing of Thomas on the Newlyweds

It was then that I did as the king commanded. Entering the bridal chamber, I rose upon my feet and began to pray:

"My Lord and my God Who accompanies his servants, Guide and Leader of those who believe in Him, Refuge and Repose of the Afflicted, Hope of the Poor and Deliverer of the Captives, Physician of the souls laid low by disease, and Savior of Every Creature Who gives life to the world and strengthens the souls, it is You Who knows the future and will accomplish it through us. You, Lord Who reveals hidden mysteries and declares the secret words, You, Lord, are the Planter of the

Good Tree and by Your hand all good works are produced. You, Lord, are in all and come through all. Jesus Christ, the Son of Compassion and Perfect Savior, Christ, Son of the Living God, the Undaunted Power which has overthrown the enemy, the Voice, heard by the rulers, which shook all their powers, Messenger sent from on high who went down even to Hades, Who also having opened the doors, brought out from there those who had been shut in for many ages in the treasuries of darkness and showed them the way that leads up on High; I beseech You, Lord Jesus, offering You supplication for these young persons, that You may do to them that which helps, benefits and is profitable for them." I then laid my hands upon their heads and proclaimed, "The Lord be with you."

I then left the chamber and proceeded to rendezvous with Abban that we might continue on our journey.

Chapter 11: Appearance of Jesus

Then the king requested the groomsmen and others present to depart the bridal chamber. After all of those in the groom's party had departed, the chamber doors were shut that the groom might bring the bride unto himself. An intense light filled the chamber, momentarily blinding the eyes of the groom. There were no windows in the bridal chamber, so the groom was puzzled as to the source of this blinding light. When his vision cleared, he saw a man with the appearance of Judas Thomas, the apostle who had recently blessed them before he departed, standing next to the bed. The groom questioned this man, whom he had presumed to be the apostle. "Did you not go out before them all? And how is it that you are here now?"

And the kindly man spoke, "I am not Judas Thomas. I am his brother Jesus." Then the Lord sat down on the bed and ordered the groom and his bride to sit down on some couches. Thereupon, the Lord Jesus began to speak to them.

Chapter 12: Jesus Instructs the Newlyweds

The Master Jesus instructed them in this manner: "Remember, my children, what my brother said to you; and to whom he commended you. Be assured that if you refrain from sexual intercourse with any but your spouse, you become as temples, pure and holy, also being released from afflictions and troubles, both known and unknown; and you will not be embroiled in the cares of life and of quarrelsome children caught up in dissention with the both of you, and each other. But if it comes to pass that you have children outside of the bonds of marriage, for their sakes you will become grasping and avaricious, plundering orphans and deceiving widows; and by doing this, you subject yourselves to the most grievous punishments. For without proper guidance and a strong and accepting family environment, most of such children become unprofitable, being possessed of a contentious spirit, some openly and others secretly. For if your children see no love between the two of you, they will become as good for nothing, doing unprofitable and even abominable works. For they, following your bad example, will be detected in all manner of unchastity and adultery or in murder or in theft; and by all these, you will become afflicted. But if you obey and preserve your souls pure to God, there will be born to you living children of the light, obedient to you and hence, untouched by these hurtful things. And you will be without care, spending a happy and untroubled life, free from guilt and care and looking forward to receiving the blessings that come from that incorruptible and true marriage. Ultimately, you will enter undefiled, and hence qualified, into that celestial bridal chamber that is filled with immortality and perpetual light."

And when the young couple heard these words, they believed my brother, taking his wisdom to heart. They gave themselves over to the Lord Jesus, promising to restrain their lusts and to behave themselves circumspectly, one with another, in the bounds that Jesus had set. Then the Master Jesus departed, bidding them farewell. "I extend my grace to you always,"[108] said Jesus.

Chapter 13: Search for Thomas

At the break of dawn on the following day, when the king went to check on the newlyweds and heard their account of the alleged visit of Thomas' twin brother Jesus to the newlyweds' bridal chamber, he became irate, thinking a deception was being carried out on him and his family. He therefore commanded those of his servants standing near him to search the entire city and to go and seize Thomas and bring him

108 See 1 Corinthians 16:23 (KJV): "The grace of our Lord Jesus Christ be with you."

back to his house. Not taking into account the righteous instructions that were imparted to his daughter and her groom, the king declared, "For I led that sorcerer with my own hands into my home and told him to pray for my most unfortunate daughter. I know not the intent of the foolish trick perpetrated by Thomas, but whoever shall find him and bring him to me, I shall give to him whatsoever he asks of me."

The servants departed the house of the king and thoroughly went round about Andropolis seeking Thomas. They even went into the inn where Abban and Thomas had been staying, and there found the Jewish flute-playing girl weeping and in distress because the apostle and his companion had not taken her with them on their journey. "They did not confide in me where they were going," she informed the servants of the king. The flute girl also had no knowledge of any twin brother of Thomas accompanying the two travelers.

Abban, at Thomas' request, had paid for the girl's lodging for one month's time. "Now I have found great repose here," she told the king's servants." After the passing of fourteen days and having no success in finding the so-called "apostle," however, they did at least come to discover that Thomas and Abban had departed the city by a southern route on the morning following the wedding party, heading to a port on the Arabian side of the Erythraean Sea where they could sail out of the gulf and eastward to the cities of India.

Chapter 14: Apostle Meets the Indian King

When I came into the cities of India with Abban the merchant, Abban went to greet King Gundaphorus of the House of Suren in the province of Drangiana and told him about me, the one with the carpentry skills whom he had brought with him. And the king was glad and ordered me to appear before him. When I had come in, the king said to me, "What trade do you know?"

Then I answered the king, "I know those trades of the carpenter and the house builder."

The king said to me, "What work in wood do you know, and what in stone?"

"In wood, ploughs, yokes, balances, pulleys; as well as ships and oars and masts. In stone, I work with monuments, temples and royal palaces," I replied.

The king continued with his questioning. "Will you then build me a palace?"

"Yes," I declared, adding that, "I shall build it and finish it; for because of this I have come here, to build and do carpentry work."

Chapter 15: At the Work Site

The king garnered a good impression of me and bid me follow him to the gates of the city. On our way to the gates, King Gundaphorus began to discuss with me his plans for the construction of the palace and particularly, how its foundations should be laid. When we arrived at the site where the work of building was to be carried out, the king proudly proclaimed, "Here is where I wish the structure to be!"

Then I answered the king, "Yes, I perceive that this place is suitable for building; for there is an abundance of wood and water here."

Upon hearing my affirmation, King Gundaphorus proclaimed, "Then, by all means, begin at once."

However, I had a certain hesitation on commencing the project. "I am sorry, King Gundaphorus; but I cannot start so soon."

"Oh," he replied, "Well, when can you?"

I assertedly answered him, "I shall begin in November and finish in April."

My reply surprised the king. He replied that, "Every building is built in the summer; but how is it that you can build and finish a palace in the winter?"

"But in this manner, it must be accomplished," said I, adding that, "for it is impossible through any other way."

"I have a good feeling about you," mused the king. "Since you have resolved upon this course of action, draw up a plan for me denoting how the work of building my palace shall be done, since I shall return here after some time."

"But do not go yet, King Gundaphorus; for I have something to show you."

Ergo, given the assurance of the king and the go ahead for the project, I picked up a reed and measured the designated plot, marking out its boundaries. The doors were to be set towards the rising of the Sun, in order to face the light. The windows would be situated toward the west, whence cometh the winds. The bakehouse would be located to the south; and the pipes, necessary to carry water into and out of the palace, would be installed toward the north, close to the more abundant and fresh supply.

The king was more than satisfied with my enthusiasm for the work and cursory recommendations for the layout of the building. "You are truly a craftsman of the highest order, Judas Thomas; and it is fitting that you should find yourself in the service of a king." He then left me with a tidy sum of silver to begin the project and departed the site, promising to send me a full work crew in the next few days.

Chapter 16: Tending the Poor

At the appointed times, the king sent coined silver and other necessities as required by me and my workmen for the completion of the task of building his palace. As I was in the process of setting apart various sums for the respective tasks of meting out pay for the workers and purchasing fine, hardened wood for the interior, however, the voice of my brother Jesus came to me audibly, instructing me to, "Take everything of the funds and divide it, going about in the cities and surrounding villages, distributing to the poor and needy, and bestowing alms, and provide them relief, declaring, 'The king surely knows that he will receive a royal recompense; but the poor must needs be refreshed, as their condition requires it.'"

Insofar as my brother has always been right in all that he has commanded me, I did as he said. Continuing to distribute food and other needed items for the benefit of the poor among the area's local inhabitants, my heart was gladdened that I was able to alleviate some of their more dire circumstances. When I expressed my concern of what King Gundaphorus might do to me and my work crew when they discovered how little progress we had actually made at the site, and what I had done with the king's monetary allotments for the construction of his palace, Jesus communicated again, in an audible voice, but heard only inside my head, "Do not be afraid, Thomas, for all will go well with thee. Simply inform the king that your brother has come to visit you and has – as a fellow craftsman– been assisting you in the work of building the palace. Tell him that thanks to the arrival of your brother, the palace is essentially complete. The only thing missing is the installation of the roof."

I then sent a runner to the king's court with this message. King Gundaphorus, in turn, dispatched his own messenger with instructions for me. "As the palace is now built, then let it be roofed."

I, Thomas, therefore continued to minister unto the inhabitants of the region, teaching them the principles of the gospel of Jesus Christ, refreshing the afflicted and declaring unto them, "The Lord Jesus the Nazarene has dispensed this food for you, as he gives to all in need. For he is the supporter of orphans and the nourisher of widows. He provides rest and repose to all of those who are afflicted."

At night I would pray thusly: "I thank you, Lord, in every respect, that you died for but a short time that I may live in you forever; and that you have placed me in these circumstances whereby you might deliver souls through me."

Chapter 17: King Checks on Progress of the Work

After some time, King Gundaphorus, returning from an inspection of the defensive fortifications of Drangiana, inquired of his friends and satraps (crown representatives) with respect to the palace which Judas, surnamed Thomas, had built for him. "He has neither built a palace, nor did he do anything of that which he promised to do. Rather, he goes about in the cities and villages, and if he has anything, he gives it to the poor and teaches of a new god, all the while healing the sick, driving out demons and performing many miracles. Frankly, our king, we think him to be some kind of magician; but his acts of compassion and the cures done by him as a free gift, along with his simplicity and gentleness and fidelity, show that he is a just man, or an apostle of this new god of whom he preaches. For he is continually fasting and praying; and he eats only bread with salt and his only drink is water. He wears but one coat, whether in or out of season, and appears to take nothing from anyone, but gives to others from what little he seems to have," said one of the satraps.

King Gundaphorus came to ask this chief satrap, "Has he made any treasonous statements about me or my family?"

"No, good king, he has credited you with the sharing of this wealth and the people rejoice in your name."

Upon hearing this, King Gundaphorus was somewhat befuddled, hitting his face with his hands and shaking his head for nearly a minute. Then the king declared unto the satrap, "I shall hold off on making any executive decision until I can go to the worksite and assay the situation there for myself."

Chapter 18: King Angered

Prior to leaving for the worksite, King Gundaphorus summoned me and the merchant Abban, who brought me to India, to stand before him and answer questions concerning the building of his palace. Upon our arrival in the home of the satrap, where the king was dwelling as his honored guest, the satrap escorted us into the presence of the king.

"Have you built the palace yet?" immediately inquired King Gundaphorus.

"Yes, I have built it," I respectfully replied.

"When shall we go to inspect it?" asked the king.

"Now," I hesitatingly declared, "you cannot see it. But you shall see it when you depart this life."

Much as I expected, upon hearing my response to his question, the king became quite angry and ordered both Abban and I to be cast into prison. King Gunaphorus gave instructions to the satrap that as soon as his property that I had dispensed to the needy ones had been recovered, that both I and Abban should be executed. Naturally, Abban was quite upset as well. "Fear nothing," I assured him, "but believe only in the god who is preached by me; and you shall be freed from this world and obtain life in the world to come."

Chapter 19: Manner of Death Determined

After the royal caravan arrived back in the capital city, King Gundaphorus considered by what manner of death he should order my and Abban's execution; whereupon he decided that we should both be flogged and then burned with fire.

However, on that very night, the king's brother, Prince Gad, fell both severely depressed and ill. Calling the king to his chamber, the prince said to him, "Brother and king, I commend to you my house and my children, for I have been grieved on account of the insult that has befallen you. And lo, I am dying; and if you do not proceed against the life of that magician, you will give my soul no rest in Hades."

Then the king said to his brother, "I've spent the whole night considering by what death I should kill him; and I have decided to flog him and burn him with fire, along with that merchant who brought him to our land."

Chapter 20: Gad Falls Dead

While they were talking, the soul of Gad, his brother, departed; and the king mourned for Gad exceedingly, because he loved him dearly. King Gundaphorus then ordered that his brother's body be prepared for burial in the most-costly royal robe.

While the king was making the arrangements for the royal burial ceremony of Gad, angels descended from the invisible realms to receive the soul of Gad, whence they took him up to heaven and showed him the great variety of mansions and palaces there. Then one of the angels in the heavenly escorting contingent asked Gad, "In which of these edifices do you wish to dwell?"

Gad was greatly impressed with a white marbled palace of exquisite and unparalleled beauty. "That one is fit for a king's habitation. As I am a but a prince, however, I would be satisfied to dwell in but one of that palace's lower chambers."

Then the angel sadly replied, "In this building, Gad, you cannot dwell."

"Why not?" Gad inquired.

"This palace is the one that the Christian named Thomas has built for your brother, the king," said the angel, adding that, "It is reserved unto him."

Upon hearing the guiding angel's reply, Gad made a most unusual request. "I entreat you, O heavenly being, allow me to return to the land of the living and go to my brother, that I may purchase this beautiful palace from him. For my brother has no idea of just how wonderful this edifice is, and he shall surely sell it to me."

Chapter 21: Gad Returns to Earth

It came to pass that the angels conferred one with another to consider the request of Gad. After coming to a decision, the chief angel and guide approached Gad and informed him, "It has been decided. Gad, we shall allow you to return to Earth to do as you have said."

As the king's attendants were dressing the body of Gad in his burial robe, the soul of Gad returned to inhabit his physical body, thereby reanimating it, and much to the surprise of all in the room. Then Gad leapt to his feet and demanded of all those standing startled around him, "Call my brother to me, immediately! I must needs make a special request of him."

Straightaway they went to impart the good news to King Gundaphorus, seated in his throne room, declaring unto him, "Your brother has become alive again!" Then the astonished king arose and with the great multitude that was in the throne room, followed the messengers proceeding to the presence of Gad, the brother of the king and prince of the realm. Upon entering the room where Gad had resurrected, the stupefied king approached his brother's bed, momentarily unable to speak, being so stunned as he was to see him once again.

Wasting no time, Gad was the first to speak. "It is so good to see you again, dearest brother. From where my soul has traveled, I know and am convinced, brother Gundaphorus, that if anyone had asked of you the half of your kingdom, you would give it, for my sake. Wherefore, I entreat you, to grant just one favor; nay, I beg of you that you sell to me that which I ask from you."

And King Gundaphorus answered and said, "And what is it that you wish me to sell to you?"

And Gad replied, "Assure me by an oath that you will grant it to me;" and the king so swore to him.

"Whatever of my possessions that you ask, I will give it to you," emphatically stated King Gundaphorus in the presence of all in the room.

Then Gad said to his brother, "Sell me the palace which you have in heaven."

The king, somewhat perplexed by this request, replied, "A palace in heaven, from whence cometh this to me?"

Gad explained, "It is the Christian Thomas who built it for you, the man whom you now hold in prison, the one whom the merchant brought to our land, having purchased him from a certain Jesus, a god disguising himself as a Hebrew prophet. I am talking about that Hebrew slave whom you wished to punish, after having suffered a seeming deception from him, and on whose account, I also was grieved and died, but now have come alive again."

Chapter 22: Royal House Honors the Apostle

Seeing his brother return from some heavenly realm, King Gundaphorus was convinced that Prince Gad's words concerning the eternal benefits that were conferred and destined upon him were real. "That palace I cannot sell you, dear brother; but I pray to be permitted to enter it and to dwell there, being deemed worthy to be counted among the inhabitants of that mystic realm. But if you really wish to buy such a palace, behold, the man is alive and will surely build you an even better one than that."

Then the king immediately sent his chief satrap to bring me and the merchant that accompanied me out of the prison. And after the satrap brought us to stand before King Gundaphorus, his majesty spoke to me in this manner, "I entreat you, as a man entreating the servant of God, to pray for me; and I ask you, whose servant you are, to pardon me and to overlook what I have done to you or intended to do; and that I may become worthy to be a dweller of that house for which I, indeed, have done nothing; but which you, laboring alone, have built for me with the help of the grace of your god; and that I may also become a servant and serve this god, whom you preach."

Gad, the king's brother, next spoke up. "I also entreat you and supplicate before your god that I may become worthy of this service and become a partaker of even a portion of that which was shown me by the angels."

"Blessed be the name of the Lord Jesus Christ," I proclaimed to the royal persons of the House of Suren. "All that you have asked, and more, shall be granted unto you by His graces, for He is the King of Angels and the Lord of Countless Worlds."

Chapter 23: Thanks Be to Jesus

Being filled with joy, I prostrated myself upon the ground and raised my hands to the heavens, declaring with a loud voice:

"I praise thee, O Lord Jesus, that thou hast revealed thy truth unto these men; for thou only art the God of Truth, and none other, and thou art He that knows all things that are unknown to most that dwell upon the land. Thou, Lord, art He that in all things shows compassion and sparest men. For men, by reason of the error that is in them, have overlooked thee; but thou hast not overlooked them. And now at my supplication and request, do thou receive the king and his brother and join them unto thy fold, cleansing them with thy washing and anointing them with thine oil, thereby ridding them of the error that has ensnared them. And do keep them also from the wolves, bearing them into thy pleasant meadows. And give them drink out of thine immortal fountain, which is neither fouled nor dries up; for they entreat and supplicate thee and desire to become thy servants and ministers. Yea, for this they are content even to be persecuted of thine enemies, and for thy sake to be hated of them and to be mocked and to die, like as thou for our sake didst suffer all manner of injustices, that thou might preserve us, thou that art Lord and verily the Good Shepherd. And do thou grant them to have confidence in thee alone, and the succor that cometh of thee and the hope of their salvation which they look for from thee alone; and that they may be grounded in thy mysteries and receive the perfect good of thy graces and gifts, and flourish in thy ministry and come to perfection in thy Father, the Source of All Goodness and Light."

Chapter 24: Christian Seal Bestowed

Being therefore wholly moved by my words spoken and my acts carried out on behalf of my brother Jesus, the Anointed One of Israel, both King Gundaphorus and Gad his brother followed me, not departing from my side. The king and his brother aided me in my ministrations to the people and even dispatched his satraps to the far corners of his kingdom to continue the great work of giving unto all in need and refreshing all that might require such assistance. And they besought me, in my capacity as an apostle of the Lord Jesus, that they also might henceforth receive the seal of the Word of God, petitioning me thusly: "Seeing that our souls are at leisure and eager toward God, give thou us the seal, for we have heard thee say of the god whom thou dost preach about, that He knows his own sheep by his true seal."

Then I said unto my new Christian friends, "Verily, I also rejoice and entreat you to receive this seal, and to partake with me first in this memorial feast of bread and wine and blessing of the Lord, and to be made perfect therein. For this Jesus Christ whom I preach is the Lord and God of all, and He is the Father of Truth, in whom I have taught you to believe." And following the common table, I commanded them to prepare themselves for baptism as a sign of their repentance from sin and acceptance of Jesus Christ as their Lord and Savior, for this is the true sign of the faith.

Then King Gundaphorus ordered that the pool of his palace be drained, cleaned and refilled, and that no one be allowed to enter into the waters therein for a period of seven days, and that in the interim period that oil be brought so that many lights may be lit for a baptismal ceremony to be conducted at night. When these seven days were done, on the eighth day he, his brother Gad and I should enter into the bath by night that I might baptize them in the name of God the Father, His Son Jesus, the Christ; and the Holy Ghost whom Jesus hath sent to be the Comforter unto all of his pilgrim church on the Earth.

Chapter 25: Baptism of the King and Prince

At the appointed time I appeared at the pool, stepping into its warm water and sealing King Gundaphorus and Prince Gad with the true sign of faith through baptism by immersion for the remission of their sins, just as the Lord Jesus commanded me and his other disciples to do. And the Lord was revealed unto them by His own voice speaking out of the night sky: "Peace be unto you, brethren." And they heard his voice only, but his likeness they saw not; for they had not yet received the added sealing of the baptism by fire, or to say, the baptism of the Holy Ghost. And then I, Judas Thomas, the apostle, took the oil and poured it upon their heads and anointed and christened them, declaring:

> Come, thou Holy Name of the Christ that is above every name.
> Come, thou Power of the Most-High, and the compassion that is perfect.
> Come, gift of the Most-High Holy Ghost.
> Come, compassionate Mother.
> Come, communion of the Father.
> Come, She that reveals the hidden mysteries.
> Come, Mother of the Seven Houses, that thy rest may be in the eighth house.
> Come, elder of the five members, mind, thought, reflection, consideration and reason. Communicate with these young men.

Come, Holy Ghost, and cleanse their reins and their heart, and give them the added seal, in the name of the Father and the Son and the Holy Ghost.

And when they were sealed, there appeared unto them a beautiful young man out of the darkness holding a lighted torch, so that their lamps became dim at the approach of the light thereof. And he went forth and was no more seen of them. And then I said unto Jesus, thinking that he had sent one of his angels: "Thy light, O Lord, is not to be contained by us; and we are not able to bear it, for it is too great for our sight."

When the dawn came and it was morning, I once again broke bread and made them partakers of the Communion of the Saints in Christ. And they were glad and rejoiced. And many others also, believing, were added to the Church of the Firstborn throughout the Parthian region of India and the provincial kingdom of Drangania, and came into the refuge of my brother and most beloved Savior.

Chapter 26: Three Sources of Iniquity

I, Judas Thomas, in fulfillment of my calling as an apostle of the Lord Jesus Christ, ceased not to preach unto all who were willing to hear me:

"Ye men and women, boys and girls, young men and maidens, strong men and aged, whether bond or free, abstain from intercourse outside the bonds of marriage, and covetousness, and gluttony; for it is from these three that all manner of iniquity cometh about. For intercourse with other than one's spouse blinds the mind and darkens the eyes of the soul, and is an impediment to the life of the body, turning one's whole being unto weakness and casting the whole body into sickness. And greed puts the soul into fear and shame. Being within the body, it seizes upon the goods of others, and causes that soul to remain under fear until that one brings about a restoration of others' goods to their owners. And the service of the belly, or to say gluttony, casts the soul into many diverting thoughts and cares and vexations. Let not this one waste their body on the fruitless pursuit of attempting to fulfill self-appetites, which shall never be sated.

"If, then, ye be rid of these, ye become free of care and grief and fear, and the Holy Ghost abides with you. Then ye shall find rest in the Lord Jesus Christ, taking no thought for the morrow, for the morrow shall take thought for the things of itself. Remember also that word of Him of whom I spoke: 'Look at the ravens and see the fowls of the heaven, that they neither sow nor reap nor gather into barns, and God provides amply unto them. Then how much more unto you, O ye of little faith?'[109]

"But look ye for His coming and have your hope in Him and believe on His name. For He is the judge of the quick and dead, and He giveth to every one according to their deeds; and at His coming and His latter appearing, no man hath any word of excuse when he is to be judged by Him, as though he had not heard. For His heralds, a vast contingent of angels surrounding our world, do proclaim from its four cardinal directions, 'Repent ye, therefore, and believe the promise and receive the yoke of meekness and the light burden, that ye may live and not die. These things get, these keep! Come forth of the darkness that the light may receive you! Come unto Him that is indeed good, that ye may receive grace of Him and implant His sign in your souls.'"

Chapter 27: Compassion and Mercy

And after I had thus spoken, some of them that stood by said, "Good teacher, your wisdom has provided us with a great boon. Now let us honor and bless you as a true servant of the Most-High God."

Replying to these generous souls, I declared, "I have not come to take from you, dear brothers and sisters in the Lord Jesus, the Christ. Rather, I have come to this land as your ministering servant." Then I placed my hands on the heads of each individual separately and blessed them all. Taking bread and oil and herbs and salt, I distributed these to all of the assembled saints. As the Sun was going down, I prepared to break my fast and join my Christian friends in eating with them.

And when night fell, I quickly went to sleep. The Lord Himself then came and stood above my head, waking me in the middle of the night. "Thomas," he said, "It is good that you have blessed my people in India; and I am well pleased. Now rise early and after the prayer at daybreak, go by the eastern road two miles and there will I show thee my glory; for by thy going, many shall take refuge with me; and thou shalt reveal to them the nature and power of the enemy, that they may be forewarned and prepared to face the tribulations to come."

109 Matthew 6:25-34 (KJV) includes the entire discourse.

At the break of day, I gathered all the brothers and sisters in the camp and informed them, "Children, the Lord would accomplish somewhat by me today; but let us pray, and entreat of Him that we may have no impediment toward Him; but that as at all times, so now also it may be done according to His desire and will by us."

Thus, having spoken, I laid my hands on them and blessed them, and broke the One Loaf,[110] distributing to each and saying: "Let this bread be unto you for compassion and mercy, and not unto judgement and retribution."

And those assembled declared in one voice, "Amen!"

Chapter 28: Young Man Found Dead

I, Thomas, an apostle of the Lord Jesus, the Christ, went forth to go where the Master had bidden me. As I came near to the second milestone and had turned a little out of the way, I saw the body of a comely youth lying dead on the ground, and said, "Lord, is it for this that thou hast brought me forth, to come hither that I might behold this sight? Thy will, therefore, be done as Thou desires."

And I began to pray and to say, "O Lord, the Judge of the Quick and the Dead, of the quick that stand by and the dead that lie here, and Master and Father of all things; and Father not only of the souls that are in bodies but of them that have gone forth of them, for of all the souls Thou art Lord and Judge; come Thou at this hour wherein I call upon Thee and show forth Thy glory upon him that lieth here."

Then I turned myself unto them that followed me and said, "This thing is not come to pass without cause, but the enemy hath effected it and brought it about that he may assault us thereby; and see ye that he hath not made use of another sort, nor wrought through any other creature save that which is his subject."

Chapter 29: Perpetrator Revealed

And after I had spoken this, a great serpent emerged out of the darkness of a cave, beating with his head and shaking his tail upon the

110 1 Corinthians 10:17 (KJV): "For we being many are one bread, and one body: for we are all partakers of that one bread."

ground, and declaring with a loud voice unto me, "I will tell before thee the cause wherefore I slew this man, since thou art come hither for that end, to reprove my works."

And I replied, "Yea, say on."

And the serpent continued, "There is a certain beautiful woman in this village over against us; and as she passed by my cave, I saw her and was enamored of her; and I followed her and kept watch upon her; whereby I found this youth kissing her, and he had intercourse with her and did other shameful acts with her that for me, it makes it easy to declare them before thee,[111] for I know that thou art the twin brother of the Christ and are always fighting against the sinful nature of all humankind. But because I would not affright her, I slew him not at that time, but waited for him till he passed by in the evening and smote and slew him, and especially because he adventured to do this upon the Lord's Day."

Chapter 30: Serpent Race

Knowing somewhat of the other worlds spoken of by my brother and wishing to confirm my suspicions, I inquired of the serpent being, "Tell me of what seed and of what race thou art."

And he said unto me: "I am a reptile of the reptile nature you associate with the constellation of Orion, a noxious son of the noxious father, in the tradition of Nimrod, the Mighty Hunter,[112] of him that hurt and

111 In Hebrew, the name "Satan" signifies an accuser of humankind. See Revelation 12:10 (KJV): "And I heard a loud voice saying in heaven, Now is come salvation, and strength, and the kingdom of our God, and the power of his Christ: for the accuser of our brethren is cast down, which accused them before our God day and night."

112 Nimrod was a Biblical figure described as a king in the land of *Shinar* (*Mesopotamia*). According to the *Book of Genesis* and *Books of Chronicles*, he was the son of *Cush*. The *Bible* states in Genesis 10:8-10 (KJV) that, "A*nd Cush begat Nimrod: he began to be a mighty one in the Earth.* "*He was a mighty hunter before the LORD: wherefore it is said, Even as Nimrod the mighty hunter before the LORD.* "*And the beginning of his kingdom was Babel, and Erech, and Accad, and Calneh, in the land of Shinar.*" Extra-biblical traditions associating him with the *Tower of Babel* led to his reputation as a king who was rebellious against God. In the apocalyptic Christian tradition, Nimrod has come to represent the corrupt world system of things. Historians have failed to match Nimrod with historically attested figures. Nimrod may not represent any one personage known to history and various authors have identified him with several real and fictional figures of Mesopotamian antiquity, including the Mesopotamian god *Ninurta* or a conflation of two Akkadian kings: *Sargon*'s grandson *Naram-Sin* (2254–2218, B.C.E.), and *Tukulti-Ninurta I* (1243–1207, B.C.E.), believed to be a descendant of the god Ninurta, probably one of the Biblical Nephilim as described in Genesis 3. Several ruins of the Near East are named after him.

smote the four angels[113] sent from Barbelo[114] which stood upright, guarding the four cardinal points of your known world since times long past, those appointed to their posts by the Ancient of Days. I am the very son of him that sits on a throne presiding over all the Earth,[115] to whose inhabitants owe their very existence.

"I am son to him that reigns over this sphere;[116] and I am kin to him that is outside the ocean, whose tail is set in his own mouth.[117] I am the one that entered through the great barrier, breaking into Paradise and spoke with your Mother Eve the things which my father bade me speak unto her. I am he that kindled and inflamed Cain to kill his own brother, and on mine account did thorns and thistles grow up in the earth. I am he that was responsible for some of the angels being cast down from above and binding them in lusts after women, that children born of the Earth might come of them and I might work my will in them. I am he that hardened Pharaoh's heart that he should slay the children of Israel and enslave them with the yoke of cruelty. I am he that caused the multitude to err in the wilderness when they made the golden calf. I am he that inflamed Herod and enkindled Caiaphas unto false accusation of a lie before Pilate; for this was fitting to me. I am he that stirred up Judas and bribed him to deliver up the Christ, your brother. I am he that inhabits and holds sway over the depths of Tartarus;[118] but

---

113 Spiritual emanations from the mind of the Celestial Queen taking on a physical appearance while on the Earth plane. All spiritual creations begin as thoughts, or emanations of the Divine, and then take physical form once condensing in the material universe.

114 The directing orb in the star system in closest orbit to the Kolob, or Great Central Sun of the Milky Way galaxy, approximately 50,000 light years from the Earth and barely seen with the most powerful of telescopes through nebula surrounding the constellation of Sagittarius.

115 2 Corinthians 4:4 (KJV): "In whom the god of this world (Satan) hath blinded the minds of them which believe not, lest the light of the glorious gospel of Christ, who is the image of God, should shine unto them."

116 Revelation 1:6 (KJV): "And hath made us kings and priests unto God and his Father; to Him be glory and dominion for ever and ever. Amen." Just as a hierarchy exists among the gods in the celestial realms, a hierarchy exists in the realms in outer darkness.

117 *The* ouroboros or uroboros is an ancient symbol depicting *a serpent* or dragon eating *its* own tail. In Gnosticism, *a serpent* biting *its tail* symbolized eternity and *the* soul of *the* world. *The* Gnostic Pistis Sophia (c. 400, C.E.) describes *the* ouroboros as *a* twelve-part dragon surrounding *the* world with *its tail in its mouth.*

118 There was a great battle for the control of the Earth between the gods known as the Titans and the Olympians. The gods of Olympus eventually triumphed. Kronos, the god of time, and many of the other Titans were banished to Tartarus, though Prometheus, Epimetheus, and female Titans such as Metis were spared. According to Pindar, Kronos later earned Zeus' forgiveness and was released from Tartarus to become ruler of Elysium. Another Titan, Atlas, was sentenced

the Son of God hath wronged me, against my will, choosing certain ones and taking them that were once his own from me. I am kin to him that is to come from the east, unto whom also power is given to do what he will upon the surface of the Earth."

Chapter 31: Commanding the Devil

And when that serpent had spoken these things in the hearing of all the people, I lifted up my voice on high and said, "Cease thou henceforth, O most shameless one, and be put to confusion and die wholly, for the end of thy destruction is come, and dare not to tell of what thou hast done by them that have become subject unto thee. And I charge thee in the name of that Jesus who until now contends with you for those that are his own, that thou suck out thy venom which thou hast put into this man, and draw it forth and take it from him."

But the serpent replied, "Not yet is the end of our time come,[119] as thou hast said. Wherefore, why are you compelling me to take back that which I have put into this man,[120] and to die before my time, insofar as mine own father, when he shall draw forth and suck out that which he hath cast into the creation, then shall his end come?"[121]

And then I answered the sly serpent, "Show, then, now the nature of thy father."

With this command, the serpent came near and set his mouth upon the wound of the young man and sucked forth the gall out of it. Little by little, the color of the young man which was as purple, became white; but the serpent swelled up. And when the serpent had drawn up all the gall into himself, the young man leapt up and stood, and ran and fell down at my feet. But the serpent, being swelled up, burst and died,

to hold the sky on his shoulders to prevent it from resuming its primordial embrace with the Earth. Other gods could be sentenced to Tartarus as well. *Apollo* is a prime example, although Zeus freed him, too. The Hecatonchires became guards of Tartarus' prisoners.

119 Other-worldly beings often speak from a collective consciousness. The reader's attention is invited to Mark 5:9 (KJV): "And he asked him, 'What is thy name?' And he answered, saying, 'My name is Legion: for we are many.'" In this case, the collective consciousness of the entity was reflected in the speech of one possessed. Such may also be noted in the speech of walk-ins or the channeling of mediums.

120 1 Peter 5:8 (KJV): "Be sober, be vigilant; because your adversary the devil walks about like a roaring lion, seeking whom he may devour."

121 In the Hindu tradition, the venom of the serpent may be representative of a polluting and suppressive force that shuts down the prana, or life force, of the human victims.

and his venom and gall were shed forth. However, in the place where his venom was shed, the ground cracked open and there came to be a great gulf; and that serpent was swallowed up therein.

And then I said unto my new Christian friends, King Gundaphorus and his brother, Prince Gad, "Take workmen and fill up that place, and lay foundations and build houses upon them, that it may be a dwelling-place for strangers."

Chapter 32: Young Man's Eyes Opened to Spirit Realm

But the youth, sobbing and weeping many tears, said unto me, "Wherein have I sinned against thee? I know that thou art a man, and much more than a mere mortal, that hast two forms, the physical that now stands before me, and a spiritual body of vast supernatural power, for wheresoever thou wilt, there thou art found, and art restrained of no man; as I have beheld you on the other side of the veil doing many great works for the spirits of those trapped in that realm of the dead.[122]

"For I saw one who appeared to be your angelic counterpart, standing by thee and saying unto thee, 'I have many wonders to show forth by thy means and I have great works to accomplish by thee, for which thou shalt receive a reward; and thou shalt make many to live, and they shall be in rest in perpetual light as children of God.

"Do thou then," saith the angel, speaking unto thee of me, "quicken this youth that hath been stricken of the enemy and be at all times his overseer."

"Well, therefore, art thou come hither, and well shalt thou depart again unto that angel, and yet that spiritual being never shall leave thee at any time. But I am become without care or reproach: and he hath enlightened me from the care of the night and I am at rest from the toil of the day: and I am set free from him that provoked me to do thus, sinning against Him that taught me to do contrary thereto: and I have lost him that is the kinsman of the night that compelled me to sin by his own deeds, and have found Him that is of the light, and is my kins-

122 The young man, not knowing that Jesus and Thomas are twin brothers, assumed that Jesus was the angelic aspect, or oversoul, of the apostle. Such supernatural beings, in the Hindu tradition, were understood to possess the power of bilocation; hence the lad's interpretation of the events is understandable in the context of the given circumstances.

man. I have lost him that darkens and blinds his own subjects that they may not know what they do and, being ashamed at their own works, may depart from the Angel of the Lord, and their works come to an end; and have found Him whose works are light and His deeds truth, which if a man doeth he has no need for repentance. And I have left him with whom lying abides, and before whom darkness proceeds as a veil, and behind him follows shame, shameless in indolence; and I have found Him that shows me fair things that I may take hold on them, even the Son of the Truth that is akin unto concord, who scatters away the mist and enlightens all of His own creation, and heals the wounds thereof and overthrows the enemies thereof. But I beseech thee, O man of God, cause me to behold Him again, and to see Him that is now become hidden from me, that I may also hear His voice whereof I am not able to express the wonder, for it belongs not to the nature of this physical body, but a world of spirit and filled with the most powerful of angels, of which I presume He is their Commander, of whom all the other angels that abide there do love greatly, yet fear and obey."

Chapter 33: Need for Repentance

And then I answered him, "If thou depart from these things that thou hast received knowledge of, as thou hast said, and if thou know who it is that hath wrought this in thee, and learn and become a hearer of Him whom now in thy fervent love thou seek; thou shalt both see Him and be with Him forever; and in His rest shalt thou rest, and shalt be in His joy. But if thou be slackly disposed toward Him and turn again unto thy former deeds, and leave that beauty and that bright countenance which now was showed thee, and forget the shining of His light which now thou desire, not only wilt thou be bereaved of this life but also of that which is to come and thou wilt depart unto him whom thou said thou had lost, and will not any more behold Him whom thou said thou had found."[123]

123 Acts 3:19 (KJV): "Repent ye therefore, and be converted, that your sins may be blotted out, when the times of refreshing shall come from the presence of the Lord."

Chapter 34: Superiority of the Spirit

And after I had said this, I entered into the city holding the hand of that youth, and saying unto him:

"These things which thou hast seen, my child, are but a few of the many glories of which God hath, for He doth not give us good tidings concerning these things that are seen, but greater things than these doth He promise us;[124] but so long as we are in the body, we are not able to speak and show forth those marvels which he shall give unto our souls. If we say that He giveth us light, it is this which is seen, and we have it: and if we say it of wealth, which is and appears in the world, we name it, and we need it not, for it hath been said, 'Hardly shall a rich man enter into the kingdom of heaven;[125] and if we speak of apparel of raiment that are luxurious in this life whereby the wealthy are clad, it is named; and it hath been said they that wear soft raiment are in the houses of kings. And if of costly banquets, concerning these we have received a commandment to beware of them, not to be weighed down with many concerns thereof. With reveling and drunkenness and cares of this life – speaking of things that are – and it hath been said to take no thought for your life, what ye shall eat or what ye shall drink, neither for your body, what ye shall put on, for the soul is more than the meat and the body than the raiment.[126] And of rest, if we speak of this temporal rest, a judgement is appointed for this also. But we speak of the worlds which are above, of gods and angels, of watchers and holy ones of the immortal, ambrosial food and the drink of the true vine, of raiment that endures and grows not old, of things which the physical eye hath not seen nor physical ear heard, neither have they entered into the heart of sinful men, the things which the Almighty God hath prepared for them that love Him.'

"Of these things do we converse and of these do we bring good tidings. Do thou therefore also believe on Him that thou mayest live, and put thy trust in Him, and thou shalt not die. For He is not persuaded with gifts, that thou shouldest offer them to Him, neither is he in

124 1 Corinthians 2:9 (KJV): "But as it is written, Eye hath not seen, nor ear heard, neither have entered into the heart of man, the things which God hath prepared for them that love him."

125 Matthew 19:24 (KJV): "And again I say unto you, It is easier for a camel to go through the eye of a needle, than for a rich man to enter into the kingdom of God."

126 For a complete discourse by Jesus as to the cares of this world, the reader's attention is invited to Matthew 6:25-33 (KJV).

need of sacrifices, that thou shouldest sacrifice unto him.[127] But look thou unto Him, and he will not overlook thee; and turn unto Him, and he will not forsake thee. For His comeliness and His beauty will make thee wholly desirous to love Him: and indeed, He permits thee not to turn thyself away."

Chapter 35: Jesus as Harbor on a Troubled Sea

And when I, Thomas, had said these things unto that youth, a great multitude joined themselves unto us. And I looked and beheld this throng raising themselves on high that they might see me and the resurrected boy, and they were going up into the high places. Therefore, I spoke to them in this manner:

"Ye that are come unto the Assembly of Christ, the Firstborn of Creation, and would believe on Jesus, take example hereby, and see that if ye be not lifted up, ye cannot see me who am little, and are not able to spy me out who am like unto you. If, then, ye cannot see me who am like you unless ye lift yourselves up a little from the earth, how can ye see him that dwelleth in the heights of glory and now is found in the depth, unless ye first lift yourselves up out of your former conversation, and your unprofitable deeds, and your desires that abide not, and the wealth that is left here, and the possessions of Earth that grow old, and the raiment that corrupts, and the beauty that waxes old and vanishes away, and yet more out of the whole body wherein all these things are stored up, and which grow old and becometh dust, returning unto its own material, entropic nature?[128] For it is the physical body which maintains all these things. But rather believe on our Lord Jesus Christ, whom we, His anointed, do preach, that your hope may be in Him and in Him ye may have life worlds without end, that He may become your fellow traveler in this land of error, and may be to you a harbor in this troublous sea.[129] And He shall be to you a fountain springing up in this

127 1 Samuel 15:22 (KJV): "And Samuel said, Hath the Lord as great delight in burnt offerings and sacrifices, as in obeying the voice of the Lord? Behold, to obey is better than sacrifice, and to hearken than the fat of rams."

128 1 John 2:17 (KJV): "And the world passeth away, and the lust thereof: but he that doeth the will of God abideth forever."

129 Calming the storm is one of the miracles of Jesus in the Gospels, reported in Matthew 8:23–27, Mark 4:35–41, and Luke 8:22–25. Jesus also walks on the water, rescuing Peter in the

thirsty land and a chamber filled of food in this place of them that hunger, and a rest unto your souls, yea, and a physician for your bodies."

Chapter 36: A Repentant People

Then the multitude of them that were gathered together hearing these things wept, and said unto me, "O man of God, the god whom thou preaches of, we dare not say that we are His, for the works which we have done are alien unto Him and not pleasing to Him; but if He will have compassion on us and pity us and save us, overlooking our former deeds, and will set us free from the evils which we committed being in error, and not impute them unto us nor make remembrance of our former sins, we will become His servants and will accomplish His will unto the end."

And I answered them and said, "He reckons not against you, neither taketh account of the sins which ye committed being in error, but overlooks your transgressions which ye have done in ignorance."[130]

Chapter 37: The Colt

And while I yet stood in the highway and spoke with the multitude, a she ass' colt came and stood before me. Wherefore, I did comment that, "It is not without the direction of God that this colt has come hither."

But unto the colt I said, "O colt that by the grace of our Lord there shall be given unto thee speech before these multitudes who are standing here;[131] and do thou say whatsoever thou wilt, that they may believe in the God of truth whom we preach."

---

process, in Matthew 14:22-36; Mark 6:45-56; and John 6:16-24. All Biblical references in the King James version.

130 The following is a revelation given by Jesus the Christ to the Mormon prophetess Annalee Skarin as recorded in her Book of Books (1972), *https://herenowforever.com/wp-content/uploads/2019/09/THE-BOOK-OF-BOOKS-BY-ANNALEE-SKARIN.pdf*, page 144 (Accessed 5 December 2022): "Yes, he that repenteth (which means to turn and travel that inward path of purification) and exerciseth FAITH and bringeth forth good works, and prayeth continually without ceasing unto such is given to know the mysteries of God. Yea, unto such it shall be given to reveal things which have never been revealed; yea, and it shall be given unto such to bring thousands of souls unto repentance." And those who keep the higher laws "Shall receive WISDOM and GREAT TREASURES OF KNOWLEDGE, EVEN HIDDEN TREASURES!"

131 Numbers 22:28 (KJV): "And the LORD opened the mouth of the ass, and she said unto Balaam, What have I done unto thee, that thou hast smitten me these three times?"

And the mouth of the colt was opened, and it spoke by the power of our Lord and said to me:

"Thou twin of Christ, apostle of the Most-High God and initiate in the hidden word of Christ who receives His secret oracles, fellow worker with the Son of God, who being free hast become a bondman, and being sold hast brought many into liberty. Thou kinsman of the great race that hath condemned the enemy and redeemed his own, that hast become an occasion of life unto man in the land of the Indians; for thou hast come here, even against thine own will, unto men that were in error, and by thy appearing and thy divine words they are now turning unto the God of truth which sent thee: mount and sit upon me and repose thyself until thou enter into the city."

To this I looked up into the heavens and spoke to the Lord:

"O Jesus, the Anointed One of the Most-High God, He that understands the perfect mercy in the tranquility and quiet that only now is spoken of among the masses; O hidden rest, that art manifested by thy working, Savior of us all and nourisher, keeping us and resting in alien bodies; O Savior of our souls, spring that is sweet and unfailing; fountain secure and clear and never polluted; defender and helper in the fight of thine own servants, turning away and scaring the enemy from us, He that fights in many battles for us and makes us conquerors in all; our true and undefeated champion of righteousness; our holy and victorious captain: glorious and giving unto Thine own a joy that will never pass away, and a relief wherein is none affliction;[132] good shepherd that gives thyself for thine own sheep, and hast vanquished the wolf and redeemed Thine own lambs and led them into a good pasture:[133] we glorify and praise Thee and Thine invisible Father and Thine Holy Ghost, as well as the Celestial Mother of all creation."

Chapter 38: Conversation with the Colt

And after I had said these things, all the multitude looked upon me, expecting to hear what I would answer to the colt. And I stood a long

132 Revelation 21:4 (KJV): "And God shall wipe away all tears from their eyes; and there shall be no more death, neither sorrow, nor crying, neither shall there be any more pain: for the former things are passed away."

133 John 10:14-15 (KJV): "I am the good shepherd, and know my sheep, and am known of mine. As the Father knoweth me, even so know I the Father: and I lay down my life for the sheep."

time astonished and turned to address the colt thusly, "Of whom art thou and to whom dost thou belong, for marvelous are the things that are shown forth by thy mouth, and amazing and such as are hidden from the many?"

And the colt answered and said: "I am of that stock that served Balaam,[134] and thy lord also and teacher sat upon one that appertained unto me by my species. And I also have now been sent to give you rest by thy sitting upon me, that I may be confirmed in a portion of faith that I shall surely receive for my service and ministrations unto thee; that such blessing shall never be taken from me. Of this mystery and myself, I am weak and helpless, but it is the angel possessing my spirit which moves me to speak with you and assist you."

Understanding the situation, I said to this helpful colt, "Yes, He is able who granted thee this gift through the visitation of one of his holy angels, to cause it to be fulfilled unto the end in thee and in them that belong unto thee by your species."

But I could not find a place in my heart to justify sitting upon this colt. Nevertheless, the colt besought and entreated me that it might be blessed of me through my allowing his ministering unto me. Then, after due reflection, I mounted him and sat upon him and we moved down the road together. Then the multitude followed me, some going before and some following after, with all of them running and all the while desiring to see us through to the end of our journey. They all wanted to know what would happen with the remarkable colt after I would dismiss him, whether the possessing angel[135] would depart and the colt would then return to his normal condition.

Chapter 39: Transmigration of the Soul

But when I came near to the city gates, I dismounted from the colt, saying, "Depart, and be thou kept safe where thou wert."

---

134 Op cit.

135 Angels are fundamentally spirit beings. Whether good or evil, they can temporarily possess a physical body, animal or human, and utilize it as a medium for manifesting on the Earth plane, by the command of another spiritual being higher in authority or, in the case of a human being, at their specific request.

And straightway the colt fell to the ground at my feet and died. And all they that were present were sorry and petitioned me, "Bring him to life and raise him up."

Saddened as I was, I answered and said unto them, "Be assured that I indeed am able to raise him by the power and in the name of Jesus Christ; but it is not expedient for me to do this, for He that gave him speech that he might talk was able to cause that he should not die; and I raise him not, not as being unable, but because this is that which is expedient and profitable for him."

"How so?" questioned those in the assemblage.

Then I recalled the words that my brother Jesus had taught me upon his return from the high mountains of this land, from a kingdom further to the east and north. I am referring to those words pertaining to the doctrine of reincarnation. Wherefore, I declared unto this people:

"Fear not, dear ones, for it is true what your sages have told you, that being that the soul, or spirit, if you will, of any living creature, whether human or animal, is possessed of a divine, immortal nature. Following the death of the material body, and based upon one's actions carried out in their prior life, whether for good or evil, a new body may be assumed, being either animal, human or angelic (spiritual). This good colt has redeemed himself by transcending those desires which trapped him in an animal body, and he is now ready to go on and regain a human form.

"There is an order to the process of reincarnation, this cycle of death and rebirth, and by our actions carried out in the material world, we determine the conditions of our subsequent birth."

Then Gad, the prince and disciple of the Lord Jesus, remarked, "The Apostle Thomas is correct, for even the gods must undergo this cycle of death and rebirth. Look at the sacred accounts of Lord Vishnu if you need further proof.[136] Even in the loka[137] of the spiritual hierarchy, he went through varied dasavataras[138] before he ever achieved a state of perpetual peace and happiness in the self-realization of his own godhood, thereby overcoming all desires of the material cosmos."

136 For a Christian parallel, see Matthew, Chapter 11, in the King James version, where Jesus explains that John the Baptist was more than a prophet, but even Elias of the Old Testament returned to Earth.

137 This is a Hindu reference to a "celestial realm."

138 This is a Hindu reference to "various incarnations passing through animal, human and superhuman forms."

"Yes, dear ones," I added, "This life is all maya.[139] The death of this colt is no cause for alarm. For there never was a time his soul did not exist, nor your soul, for that matter. Nor in the future, will this colt's soul, or yours, cease to be.[140] Be not bewildered; and know that the body which you now inhabit will one day become as a worn-out garment, one that you will be happy to shed, to be rid of. Then, if you be found walking in the path of righteousness, you shall, as this colt, don new vestments fitting royalty and continue your progress into the eternity of worlds."

Then I bade them that were present to dig a trench and bury the colt's body; and they did as I so commanded them.

Chapter 40: A Woman Tormented

And so it came to pass that I, Thomas, an apostle of the Lord Jesus, entered into the city and all the multitude followed me. And I thought to go unto the parents of the young man whom I had made alive after he was slain by the serpent, for they earnestly besought me to come unto them and enter into their house.

But a very beautiful woman suddenly uttered an exceeding loud cry, saying:

"O Herald of the new god that art come into India, and servant of that holy and only good God; for by thee is he preached, the Savior of the souls that come unto him, and by thee are healed the bodies of them that are tormented by the enemy, and thou art he that is become an occasion of life unto all that turn unto Him: command me to be brought before thee that I may tell thee what hath befallen me, and peradventure of thee I may have hope, and these that stand by thee may be more confident in the God whom thou preaches. For I am not a little tormented by the adversary now this five years' time."

---

139 This is a Hindu reference to "illusion."

140 The ambassador from Fifth Dimensional Venus, Omnec Onec, explained that, "Soul entered the lowest plane to begin the experience which one day would lead to becoming a conscious coworker with the Supreme Deity. We know it as the physical universe, where Soul picked up the physical sheath or body which was needed to survive here and begin Its experiences. "In the beginning, when you first entered the physical plane, you were not immediately a human being in form. For Soul to have every possible experience, which everyone must have in order to be perfected, you need to experience every state of consciousness that the physical world has to offer..." The Venus ambassador then goes on to explain the soul's condition through varied states of eternal progression. See Omnec Onec, The Venusian Trilogy.

Chapter 41: Freedom Sought from the Evil One

The tormented woman continued to explain her unfortunate situation to me:

"One day as I came out from the bath, there met me a man troubled and disturbed, and his voice and speech seemed to me exceeding faint and dim; and he stood before me and said, 'I and thou will be in one love and we will have intercourse together as a man with his wife.'

"And I answered him, explaining that, 'I have never had intercourse with any man, for I refused to marry; and how shall I yield myself to thee that would have intercourse with me in an adulterous manner?'

"And having so said, I passed on, and I said to my handmaid that was with me, 'Did you see that youth and his shamelessness, how boldly he spoke with me?'

"But she said to me: 'I saw an old man speaking to thee.'

"And when I was in mine house and had dined, my soul suggested unto me some suspicion and especially because he was seen of me in two forms; and having this in my mind I fell asleep. He came, therefore, in that night and was joined unto me in his foul intercourse. And when it was day, I saw him and fled from him, and on the night following he came and abused me; and now as you see me, I have spent five years being troubled by him; and he hath not departed from me. But I know and am persuaded that both devils and spirits and destroyers are subject unto thee and are filled with trembling at thy prayers. Pray thou, therefore for me, and drive away from me the devil that ever troubles me, that I also may be set free and be gathered unto the nature that is mine from the beginning, and receive the grace that hath been given unto my kindred."[141]

Chapter 42: Spiritual Confrontation

And then I said to the wicked one that possessed and troubled her:

"O evil that cannot be restrained! O shamelessness of the enemy! O envious one that art never at rest! O hideous one that subdues the comely! O thou of many forms! As he will he appears, but his essence

141 Matthew 10:1 (KJV): "And when he had called unto him his twelve disciples, he gave them power against unclean spirits, to cast them out, and to heal all manner of sickness and all manner of disease."

cannot be changed. O the crafty and faithless one! O the bitter tree whose fruits are like unto him! O the devil that overcomes them that are alien to him! O the deceit that employs impudence! O the wickedness that creeps like a serpent, and that is of his kindred!"

And after speaking thusly, the malicious one came and stood before me, no other seeing him save the woman and I; and with an exceeding loud voice did this evil being declare unto us:

"What have we to do with thee, thou apostle of the Most-High God! What have we to do with thee, thou servant of Jesus Christ? What have we to do with thee, thou counsellor of the Holy Son of God? Wherefore wilt thou destroy us, whereas our time is not yet come? Wherefore wilt thou take away our power, for unto this hour we had hope and time remaining to us. What have we to do with thee? Thou hast power over thine own, and we over ours. Wherefore, wilt thou act tyrannously against us, when thou thyself teaches others not to act tyrannously? Wherefore, dost thou crave other men's goods and not suffice thyself with thine own? Wherefore art thou made like unto the Son of God, which hath done us wrong, for thou truly bare a resemblance of Him altogether, as if thou wert born of Him? For we had thought to have brought Him under the yoke, such as we have the rest, but he turned and made us subject unto Him; for we knew Him not; but he deceived us with His form of all uncomeliness and his poverty and his neediness; for seeing Him to be such, we thought that He was a man wearing flesh, and knew not that it is He that giveth life unto men. And He gave us power over our own, and that we should not in this present time leave them but have our walk in them; but thou would get more than thy due and that which was given thee, and afflict us altogether."

Chapter 43: Devil Departs

And having said this, the devil wept, adding, "I leave thee now, my fairest consort, whom long since I found and rested in thee; I forsake thee, my sure sister, my beloved in whom I was well pleased. What I shall do I know not, or on whom I shall call that he may hear me and help me. I know what I will do: I will depart unto some place where the report of this apostle hath not been heard, and peradventure I shall call some substitute, 'my beloved.'"

And he lifted up his voice and concluded his remarks to the now liberated woman:

"Abide in peace for thou hast taken refuge with one greater than I; but I will depart and seek for one like thee. And if I find her not, I will return unto thee again: for I know that whilst thou art near unto this man thou hast a refuge in him; but when he departs, thou wilt be such as thou were before he appeared, and him thou wilt forget, and I shall have opportunity and confidence; but now I fear the name of Him that hath guided this apostle unto thee and saved you from my power."[142]

And having so said, the devil vanished out of sight; only when he departed fire and smoke were seen there in close proximity to the apostle and the woman, and all that stood there were astonished by the phenomenon.

Chapter 44: Prayer to Jesus on Behalf of the Assembled

Then I redeemed the time to explain the situation to those assembled, saying, "This devil hath clearly betrayed the motivations which are endemic to his own nature, wherein also he shall be consumed, for verily the fire shall destroy him utterly and the smoke of it shall be scattered abroad."

I continued with a prayer to Jesus on behalf of the assembled ones:

"Jesus, we, the assembled, know that thou art He that hast shown unto us many mysteries; and that thou didst call me apart from all my fellows and inspired me with your great words. Jesus, you have imparted to me this vast knowledge; yet I am unable at times to fully speak of these things with others, that they might adequately comprehend. Jesus, you are a man that was slain, certified dead and buried! Jesus, as a god among gods, in your capacity as a savior to all Israel, even the world, you quickened the dead to return unto us, and healed the sick! Jesus, you came among us from the celestial realms to live as a poor man; yet you have satisfied the needs of all who have hungered, those seeking after your presence. Jesus, as a poor wayfaring man of grief, you have sought a place of rest from the weariness of this world; but all the while, you have been seen walking on the waves like an immortal god.

142 Luke 8:2 (KJV): "And certain women, which had been healed of evil spirits and infirmities, Mary called Magdalene, out of whom went seven devils…."

"Jesus Most High, your voice arises in perfect mercy as that of the Savior of all. In your right hand is found the light, overthrowing the evil one in his own nature, and gathering all his nature into one place; thou of many forms, that art the Only Begotten, Firstborn of Many Brethren and divine manifestation of the Most-High God, a man that until now has been greatly despised. Jesus, you are the Christ that neglects not his people. Hear us, therefore, when we call upon you; for you have become an occasion of life unto all mankind, that for us was judged and shut up in prison. But even though all are found to be in bonds, physical and spiritual, you are redeeming thine own from the error of the evil one. I beseech thee for these that stand here and believe on thee, for they entreat thee to obtain thy gifts, having good hope in thy help, and having their refuge in thy greatness. They hold their hearing ready to listen unto the words that are spoken by us. Let thy peace come and tabernacle in them to redeem and renew them from their former deeds, and let them put off the old man with his deeds, and put on the new that now is proclaimed unto them by me."

Chapter 45: Thomas' Blessing Upon the Assembly

And then I said:

"Come, O perfect compassion; Come O communion of the Father of Lights; Come, She that knows the mysteries of Him who is chosen; Come, She that hath part in all the combats of the noble champion (athlete); Come, the silence that reveals the great things of the eternal realms; Come, She that manifests the hidden things and makes the unspeakable things plain, the Holy Dove that bears illumination and wisdom on her wings; Come, the Hidden Mother, Come, She that is manifest in Her deeds and giveth joy and rest unto them that are joined unto Her: Come and communicate with us in this common meal which we celebrate in Thy name and in the love feast wherein we are gathered together at thy calling."

And having spoken this, I marked out the sign of the true cross upon the bread, and brake it, and began to distribute it. At first, I gave the elements of the communion unto the newly liberated woman, saying, "This shall be unto thee for a remission of sins and the hope in Christ of the eternal resurrection."

Following the ministration unto her, I gave unto all the others which had received the true seal of their faith in Jesus the Christ,[143] declaring unto the recipients, "Let this sanctified bread and wine be unto you for life and rest, and not for judgement and vengeance."
And all the people proclaimed, "Amen!"

Chapter 46: Unworthy Partaking of Common Meal

Now there was a certain youth who had wrought an abominable deed, and he came near and attempted to partake of the common meal: but his two hands withered up, so that he could not put the morsels of bread into his mouth. And they that were there saw him and told me what had befallen; and I then called him and said unto him, "Tell me, my child, and be not ashamed, what was it that thou didst and came hither, for the meal of the Lord hath convicted thee? For this gift which passes among many doth rather heal them that with faith and love draw near thereto, but unto thee it hath withered away; and that which is come to pass hath not befallen without some effectual cause."

And the youth, being convicted by the bread of the Lord, came and fell down at my feet, saying, "I have done an evil deed, yet I thought to

143 The true sign of initiation into the Christian assembly is having been baptized by immersion for the remission of sins and the hope of the resurrection in the name of the Father, the Son and the Holy Ghost. The words "baptism" and "immersion" are synonymous. Immersion is the meaning of the New Testament Greek word transliterated into the English word "baptism;" and it means "an act of immersion," a "plunging" or a "dipping." A form of the word occurs in John 13:26-27, wherein Jesus "dips" or "baptizes" the morsel of bread that He then gives to Judas Iscariot. Given this original meaning of the word "baptism," it is impossible to speak of a baptism by sprinkling or pouring. However, even if we knew nothing about the original Greek word for "baptism," we could determine the mode of baptism by observing that both Philip and the Eunuch went down into the water for the baptism described in Acts 8:38; and that baptism is portrayed as a burial in Romans 6:1-11. If people attempt to administer "baptism" by pouring or sprinkling, they fail. Therefore, even if we knew nothing about the original Greek terms, we could tell that baptism must be done for the purpose of obtaining the remission of sins by observing the following, plain passages:

Acts 22:16. "Now why do you delay? Get up and be baptized, and wash away your sins, calling on His name."

1 Peter 3:21. "Baptism now saves you—not the removal of dirt from the flesh, but an appeal to God for a good conscience—through the resurrection of Jesus Christ."

Galatians 3:27. "For all of you who were baptized into Christ have clothed yourselves with Christ."

From these passages we note that a person has not had his sins washed away until that one has been baptized; and that individual has not been saved until he or she has been baptized; and as until such takes place, that one is still considered to be outside of Christ.

do somewhat good. I was enamored of a woman that dwelleth at an inn without the city, and she also loved me; and when I heard of thee, and of the living god of whom you proclaim, and I believed in your message, I came and received of thee the seal with the rest; for thou did say, 'Whosoever shall partake in sexual sin, he shall not have life with the God whom I preach.'

"Whereas that I loved her much, however, I entreated her and would have persuaded her to become my consort in chastity and pure conversation, until such time that we could be properly united in the bonds of matrimony, but she would not. When, therefore, she consented not, I took a sword and slew her, for I could not endure to see her proceed in sin and have sexual intercourse with another man to whom she is not lawfully married."

Chapter 47: Apostle Moved to Help

When I heard this young man's account, I said, "O how this insane desire has brought you so low unto shamelessness! O unrestrained lust, how hast thou stirred up this man to do this! O work of the serpent, how art thou enraged against thine own!"

Then I bade that water be brought unto me in a basin; and when the water was brought, I said, "Come, ye waters from the living waters, that were sent unto us, the true from the true, the rest that was sent unto us from the rest, the power of salvation that cometh from that power which conquers all things and subdues them unto its own will: come and dwell in these waters, that the gift of the Holy Ghost may be perfectly consummated in them."

And then I spoke unto the youth, "Go, wash thy hands in these waters." And when the youth had washed them, they were restored; and at that point, I inquired of him, "Believe thou in our Lord Jesus Christ that he is able to do all things?"

And the young man answered, "Though I be the least, yet I believe. But I committed this deed thinking that I was doing somewhat good: for I besought her as I told thee, but she would not obey me, to keep herself chaste."

Chapter 48: Thomas' Prayer for Divine Assistance

And then I spoke to the young man thusly, "Come, let us go unto the inn where thou didst commit this deed."

And the youth went before me in the way, and when we came to the inn, we found the woman lying dead, just as the young man said we would. And when I beheld her, I felt sorrow, for she was a comely girl. And I commanded her body to be brought into the midst of the inn: and they laid her on a bed and brought her forth and set her down in the midst of the court of the inn. And then I laid my hands upon her and began to pray:

"Jesus, who always shows Thyself unto us; for this is Thy will, that we should at all times seek Thee, and Thyself hast given us this power, to ask and to receive, and hast not only permitted this, but hast taught us to pray: Who art not seen of our bodily eyes, but art never hidden from the eyes of our soul, and in thine aspect art concealed, but in Thy works art manifested unto us: and in Thy many acts we have known Thee so far as we are able, and Thyself hast given us Thy gifts without measure, saying: 'Ask and it shall be given unto you, seek and ye shall find, knock and it shall be opened unto you;' we beseech Thee, therefore, having the fear (suspicion) of our sins; and we ask of thee, not riches, not gold, not silver, not possessions, not aught else of the things which come of the earth and return again unto the earth; but this we ask of Thee and entreat, that in Thine holy name thou would raise up the woman that lieth here, by Thy power, to the glory and faith of them that stand by."

Chapter 49: Second Chance for the Woman

And I instructed the youth, "Stretch thy mind towards our Lord," at the same time that I signed him with the cross, having sealed him with the mark of forgiveness. Then I continued speaking with the young man, "Go and take hold on her hand and say unto her: 'I with my hands slew thee with iron, and with my hands in the faith of Jesus I raise thee up.'"

Therefore, the youth went to her and stood by her, saying, "I have believed in Thee, Christ Jesus." And he looked unto me, Judas Thomas, the apostle of our Lord, and petitioned me, "Pray for me that my Lord may come to my help, whom I also call upon."

And he laid his hands upon her hands and said, "Come, Lord Jesus Christ: unto her grant Thou life and unto me the earnest of faith in Thee."

And straightway as he drew her hands she sprang up and sat up, looking upon the great company that stood by. And she saw the apostle also standing over against her, and leaving the bed she leapt forth and fell at his feet and caught hold on his raiment, saying, "I beseech thee, my lord, where is that other that was with thee, who left me not to remain in that fearful and cruel place, but delivered me unto thee, saying: 'Take thou this woman, that she may be made perfect, and hereafter be gathered into her place?'"

Chapter 50: Fate of the Wicked

In response, I asked her, "Relate unto us where thou hast been."

And she answered, "Dost thou who was with me and unto whom I was delivered desire to hear?"

"Yes," I replied, "please go on."

Still being somewhat shaken, she nevertheless continued with her account:

"There was a man that took hold of me who was dreadful to look upon, altogether clad in a shiny black raiment. He took me away to a place wherein were many vast chasms from which were emitted a great stench, having, as it were, the odor of sulfur. And he caused me to look into every pit, and I saw in the first pit a flaming fire, and there were also wheels of fire that spun round there, all with the souls of human beings hanged upon them; and these were dashed continually against each other until they were torn asunder and reduced to ashes. Similar functions were carried out in the other fiery pits. There was very great crying and howling in the pits, and there was none to deliver these wretched souls from their decreed destruction.[144]

144 The reader's attention is invited to Matthew 25:46 (KJV), that explains the nature of eternal punishment decreed for the wicked: "These shall go away into everlasting punishment; but the righteous unto life eternal." In the original Greek, this scripture more accurately reads "cutting-off" instead of "punishment," whereby the righteous go to life while the wicked ones go on to the "cutting off from life," or death. A further clarification of this doctrine is found in 2 Thessalonians 1:9 (KJV), wherein the Apostle Paul points out that the wicked ones shall suffer eternal ruin. See also Revelation 20:13 (KJV): "The sea gave up the dead which were in it; and death and hell delivered up the dead which were in them: and they were judged every man according to their works. And death and hell were cast into the lake of fire." Living righteously was a constant

"And then an angelic maiden approached me, and declared, 'These souls are of your fellow human beings, and when the number of their appointed days was accomplished on the surface of your world, they were delivered unto the second death, for their sins against God and their fellow beings were too great to merit any further chance for redemption.'"[145]

Chapter 51: Encounter with Jesus in the Well of Souls

The woman continued her account of a journey through the underworld:

---

theme in Thomas' writings, insofar as his fellow apostle Paul emphasized the same mode of thinking when he declared in Romans 6:23 (KJV): "The wages of sin is death."

145 Helena P. Blavatsky (1831-1890), the co-founder of the Theosophical Society, writes in her classic work, Isis Unveiled (New York: Theosophical Society, 1877), the following two paragraphs that bring much to bear upon the doctrine of the annihilation of the wicked souls:

"We have shown elsewhere that the Secret Doctrine does not concede immortality to all men alike. If the human soul has neglected during its lifetime to receive illumination from the Divine Spirit, our personal God, then it becomes difficult for the gross and sensual man to survive his physical death for a great length of time. No more than the mishappen monster can live long after its physical birth, can the soul, once it has become too material, exist after its birth into the spiritual world. The viability of the astral form is so feeble that the particles cannot cohere firmly once it is slipped out of the unyielding capsule of the external body. Its particles, gradually obeying the disorganizing attraction of universal space, finally fly asunder beyond the possibility of regeneration. Upon the occurrence of such a catastrophe, the individual ceases to exist; his glorious augoeides (i.e., Known since the classical era of Greek and Roman history as the luminous body, evidence of the higher self or ascended spiritual aspect. -R. Keller) has left him. During the intermediary period between his bodily death and the disintegration of the astral form, the latter, bound by magnetic attraction to its ghastly corpse, prowls about and sucks vitality from susceptible victims. The man, having shut out of himself every ray of the divine light, is lost in darkness and therefore clings to the earth and the earthy.

"No astral form, even that of a pure, good and virtuous man, is immortal in the strictest sense; 'from elements it was formed- to elements it must return.' But while the soul of the wicked vanishes and is absorbed without redemption, that of every other person, even moderately pure, simply changes its ethereal particles for still more ethereal ones; and while there remains in it a spark of the Divine, the individual man, or rather his personal ego, cannot die. 'After death,' says Proclus (i.e., a Greek neo-Platonist philosopher of the early Byzantine Empire, born 412 A.D. and died 485 A.D. -R. Keller), 'the soul (the spirit) continueth to linger in the aerial body (astral form), till it is entirely purified from all angry and voluptuous passions.... then doth it put off by a second dying the aerial body as it did the earthly one. Whereupon the ancients say that there is a celestial body always joined with the soul, which is immortal, luminous and starlike.'

I might add here that the Apostle Paul affirmed this doctrine of the celestial body, spoken of by Proclus, in 1 Corinthians 15:40 (KJV): "There are also celestial bodies, and bodies terrestrial: but the glory of the celestial is one, and the glory of the terrestrial is another."

"And then this maiden, one of the angels that kept guard of the souls which were in the dark caverns awaiting their final disposition, said unto the man in black that had taken me:

"'Give her unto us that we may bring her in unto the rest until the time cometh for her to be delivered unto the fiery pit.'

"But he answered them, 'I give her not unto you, for I fear Him that delivered her to me: for I was not charged to leave her here, but I take her back with me until I shall receive an order concerning her.'

"And then this man that looked like you took me and brought me unto another place where there was a cave of large, bright, multi-colored crystals, wherein were many souls awaiting their chance for a rebirth, to begin anew a life with promise, returning to the material plane as a baby. It was, in essence, a well of souls.

"And He, the angel that was like unto thee in his appearance, took me and delivered me to thee, saying thus to thee, "Take her, for she is one of the sheep that have gone astray." And I was taken by thee, and now am I before thee. I beseech thee, therefore, and supplicate that I may not depart unto those places of punishment which I have seen."

I calmly replied, "You have been allowed to see these things that you might return to the material plane and issue a voice of warning to your brothers and sisters yet inhabiting the world above."

Chapter 52: Turning to God in Repentance

I, Judas Thomas, an apostle of the Lord Jesus, then declared:

"Ye have heard what this woman hath related: If ye turn not unto this God whom I preach and abstain from your former works of sin and wicked deeds which ye committed, there are dire consequences awaiting you in the worlds to come. Believe therefore on Christ Jesus, and He will forgive you the sins ye have committed hitherto, and will cleanse you from all your bodily lusts that abide on the Earth, and will heal you of all your trespasses which follow you and depart with you and are found upon you. Put off, therefore, every one of you the old person, and put on the new,[146] and forsake your former walk and conversation; and let them that stole steal no more, but live by honest laboring and working; and let the adulterous cease from fornication, lest they deliver

146 Ephesians 4:24 (KJV): "And that ye put on the new man, which after God is created in righteousness and true holiness."

themselves unto judgment; for adultery is before God exceedingly evil beyond other sins. And put away from you all covetousness and lying and drunkenness and slandering, and render not evil for evil: for all these things are strange and alien unto the God who is preached by me. But rather, dear ones, walk ye in faith and meekness and holiness and hope, wherein God delights, that ye may become his own, expecting of Him the gifts which some few now only do receive."

Chapter 53: Ongoing Work of the Ministry

All the people therefore believed and gave their souls obediently unto the living God and Christ Jesus, rejoicing in the blessed works of the Most-High God and in His holy service. And they brought much money for the service of the widows: for I had them gathered together in the cities; and unto all of them I sent provision by my appointed deacons, both clothes and nourishment. And I ceased not preaching and speaking to them and showing that this is Jesus Christ whom the scriptures proclaimed, the One that came to this world and was crucified, and raised the third day from the dead. And next I showed them plainly, beginning from the Hebrew prophets, the things concerning the Christ, that it was necessary that He should come, and that in Him should be accomplished all things that were foretold of Him in the Hebrew scriptures. And as the word of the Lord went forth into all the cities and countries, all that had sickness or them that were oppressed by unclean spirits were brought to me and the deacons, and some they laid in the way whereby I and the deacons should pass, and we healed them all by the power of the Lord. Then all that were healed by the Lord's anointed said with one accord, "Glory be to Thee, Jesus, who hast granted us all alike healing through thy servant and apostle Thomas. And now being whole and rejoicing, we beseech Thee that we may be of thy flock, and be numbered among Thy sheep; receive us therefore, Lord, and impute not unto us our transgressions and our former faults which we committed, being in ignorance."

Chapter 54: "Glory be to the Firstborn!"

And then I said:

"Glory be to the Only Begotten of the Father! Glory be to the First-born of many brethren! Glory be to Thee, the defender and helper of them that come unto Thy refuge, that sleeps not, and awakens them that are asleep, thereby giving life to them that lie in death! O God Jesus Christ, Son of the Living God, Redeemer and Helper, refuge and rest of all that are weary that labor in Thy vineyard, giver of healing to them that for Thy name's sake bear the burden and heat of the day: we give thanks for the gifts that are given us of Thee and granted us by Thy help and Thy dispensation that cometh unto us from Thee."

Chapter 55: Universal Kinship in Christ Jesus

Continuing with my supplication unto Jesus, I further prayed:

"Perfect Thou therefore these things in us unto the end that we may have the boldness that is in Thee. Look upon us. For Thy sake have we forsaken our homes and our parents, and for Thy sake have we gladly and willingly become strangers. Look upon us, Lord, for we have forsaken our own possessions for Thy sake, that we might gain of thee the possession that cannot be taken away.[147] Look upon us, Lord, for we have forsaken them that belong unto us by race, that we might be joined unto Thy universal kinship.[148] Look upon us, Lord, that have forsaken our fathers and mothers and fosters, that we might behold thy Father, and be satisfied with His divine food, the spiritual nourishment of His word. Look upon us, Lord. For thy sake have we forsaken our bodily consorts and our earthly fruits, that we might be partakers in that enduring and true fellowship, and bring forth true fruits, whose nature is from above, which no man can take from us; for we understand that it is You with whom we shall abide and Who, in turn, shall abide with us."

147 Acts 2:44 (KJV): "Now all who believed were together, and had all things in common…." This early type of communalism among the early Christians should not be confused with contemporary systems of autocratically-imposed communism. According to the late Rev. Dr. Frank E. Stranges (1927-2008) of Van Nuys, California, the saints of the primitive church came together in a voluntary association.

148 Galatians 3:28 (KJV): "There is neither Jew nor Greek, there is neither bond nor free, there is neither male nor female: for ye are all one in Christ Jesus."

Chapter 56: King Misdaeus' Captain

Now while I was proclaiming throughout all India the word of God, a certain captain of King Misdaeus in the south of this vast country came to me and said:

"I have heard of thee that you take no reward of anyone, but even that thou hast, you give to them that need. For if thou didst receive rewards, I would have sent thee a great sum, and would not have come myself; for the king does nothing without me: for I have much substance and am rich, even one of the richest men of India. And I have never done wrong to any; but the contrary hath befallen me. I have a wife, and of her I had a daughter and I am well affectioned toward her, and taking no other woman to wife. Now it chanced that there was a wedding in our city, and they that made the marriage feast were well beloved of me: they came in therefore and bade me to it, bidding also my wife and our daughter. Forasmuch then as they were my good friends I could not refuse: I sent her therefore, though she desired not to go, and with them I sent also many servants. Therefore, they departed, both she and our daughter, decked with many ornaments."

Chapter 57: Wife and Daughter Assaulted

The captain of the king continued:

"And when it was evening and the time was come to depart from the wedding, I sent lamps and torches to meet them: and I stood in the street to espy when she should come and I should see her with my daughter. And as I stood in wait, I heard a sound of lamentation. 'Woe for her!' was heard out of every mouth.

"And my servants with their clothes rent came to me and told me what was done. 'We saw,' said they, 'a man and a boy with him. And the man laid his hand upon thy wife, and the boy upon thy daughter: and they fled from them: and we smote them with our swords, wounding them slightly, but our swords fell to the ground. And the same hour the women fell down, gnashing their teeth and beating their heads upon the earth; and seeing this, we came to tell you of it.'

"And when I heard this of my servants, I rent my clothes and smote my face with my hands, and becoming like one mad I ran along the street, and came and found them cast in the market-place; and I took them and brought them to my house, and after a long space they awaked and stood up, and sat down."

Chapter 58: Traumatized Wife and Daughter

The captain continued:

"I began therefore to inquire of my wife: 'What is it that hath befallen thee?'

"And she said to me: 'Don't you know what thou hast done unto me? I prayed thee that I might not go to the wedding, because I was not of good health in my body; and as I went on the way and came near to the aqueduct wherein the water flows, I saw a dark-skinned man standing over against me nodding at me with his head, and a boy like unto him standing by him; and I said to our daughter, 'Look at those two hideous men, whose teeth are like milk and their lips like soot.'

"And we left them and went towards the aqueduct; and when it was sunset and we departed from the wedding, as we passed by with the young men and drew near the aqueduct, my daughter saw them first, and was affrighted and fled towards me; and after her I also beheld them coming against us: and the servants that were with us fled from them and they struck us, and cast down both me and my daughter. And when she had told me these things, the devils came upon them again and threw them down: and from that hour they are not able to come forth, but are shut up in a smaller room enclosed in a larger one: and on their account, I suffer much, and am distressed: for the devils throw them down wheresoever they find them, and strip them naked. I beseech and supplicate thee before God, help me and have pity on me, for it is now three years that a table hath not been set in my house, and my wife and my daughter have not sat at a table: and especially for mine unhappy daughter, which hath not seen any good at all in this world."

Chapter 59: Proclamation of Faith

And after hearing these things from the captain, I was greatly grieved for him, and said unto him, "Believe thou that Jesus will heal them?"

And the captain said, "Yea."

And I replied, "Commit thyself then unto Jesus, and He will heal them and procure them succor."

Then the captain answered, "Show me him, that I may entreat him and believe in him."

And I explained that: "He appears not unto these bodily eyes, but is found by the eyes of the mind."

The captain, therefore lifted up his voice and said, "I believe thee, Jesus, and entreat and supplicate thee, help my little faith which I have in thee!"

Upon the captain's proclamation of faith, I commanded the deacon Xenophon to assemble all the brethren; and when the whole multitude was gathered, I stood in their midst and said:

Chapter 60: Apostle's Sermon

"Children and brethren that have believed on the Lord, abide in this faith, preaching Jesus who was proclaimed unto you by me, to bring you hope in Him; and forsake Him not; and He will not forsake you. While ye sleep in this slumber that weighs down the sleepers, He, sleeping not, keeps watch over you; and when ye sail and are in peril and none can help, He walking upon the waters supports and aids. For I am now departing from you, and it seems not if I shall again see you according to the flesh. Be ye not, therefore, like unto the people of Israel, who losing sight of their pastors for an hour, stumbled. But I leave unto you Xenophon the deacon in my stead; for he also, like myself proclaims Jesus.

"Neither Xenophon nor I, of our own power, are able to save your souls, but Jesus only; for I also am a man clothed with a body, a son of man like one of you; for neither have I riches as it is found with some, which also convict them that possess them, being wholly useless, and left behind upon the earth, whence also they came, and they bear away with them the transgressions and blemishes of sins which befall men by their means. And scantly are rich men found in almsgiving; but the merciful and lowly in heart, these shall inherit the kingdom of God: for it is not beauty that endures with men, for they that trust in it, when age cometh upon them, shall suddenly be put to shame: all things therefore have their time. In their season are they loved and hated. Let your hope then be in Jesus Christ the Son of God, which is always loved, and always desired: and be mindful of us, as we of you: for we too, if we fulfil not the burden of the commandments are not worthy to be preachers of this name, and hereafter shall we pay the price of our own head."

Chapter 61: Blessing of Peace and the Holy Spirit

And I prayed with them and continued with them a long time in prayer and supplication, and committing them unto the Lord, I said, "O Lord that rules over every soul that is in the body; Lord, Father of the souls that have their hope in Thee and expect Thy mercies: that redeems from error the men that are Thine own and sets free from bondage and corruption Thy subjects that come unto Thy refuge: Be Thou in the flock of Xenophon and anoint it with holy oil, and heal it of sores, and preserve it from the ravening wolves."

And I laid my hands on them and said, "The peace of the Lord shall be upon you and His Most Holy Spirit shall journey with us througout all these lands."

Chapter 62: Captain to Drive the Chariot

Having blessed the people, I therefore went forth to depart on the way. But the people, not wanting to see me go from their country, stayed with me along the road for a time, weeping and adjuring me to always keep them in remembrance in my prayers and to not forget them as I toiled in the work of the ministry. I went up then and sat upon the chariot, leaving all the brethren, and the captain came and woke up the driver, saying, "I entreat and pray that I may become worthy to sit beneath his feet, and I will be his driver upon this way, that he also may become my guide in that way whereby few there be that go."

Chapter 63: In Need of Roadside Assistance

And when they had journeyed about two miles, I begged of the captain and made him arise and caused him to sit by me, suffering the driver to sit back in his own place. And as we went along the road, it came to pass that the beasts were wearied with the great heat and could not be stirred at all. And the captain was greatly vexed and wholly cast down, and thought to run on his own feet and bring other beasts for the use of the chariot; but I said to him, "Let not thine heart be troubled nor affrighted, but believe on Jesus Christ whom I have proclaimed unto thee, and thou shalt see great wonders."

And I looked and saw a herd of wild asses feeding by the wayside, and said to the captain, "If thou hast believed on Christ Jesus, go unto that herd of wild asses and say, 'Judas Thomas the apostle of Christ, the new God, saith unto you: Let four of you come, of whom we require your services.'"

Chapter 64: Animals Called to Service

And the captain went in fear, for they were many; and as he went, they came to meet him; and when they were near, he said unto them, "Judas Thomas, the apostle of the new God, commands you: Let four of you come, of whom we have need."

And when the wild asses heard it, they ran with one accord and came to him; and when they came, they did approach him with in a respectful and even a reverent manner. And I, Judas Thomas, the apostle of our Lord, lifted up my voice in praise and said:

"Glorious art thou, God of truth and Lord of all natures, for Thou didst will with Thy will, and make all Thy works and finish all Thy creatures, and bring them to the rule of their nature, and lay upon them all Thy fear that they might be subject to Thy command. And Thy will trod the path from Thy secrecy to manifestation, and was caring for every soul that Thou didst make, and was spoken of by the mouth of all the prophets, in all visions and sounds and voices; but Israel did not obey because of their evil inclination. And Thou, because Thou art Lord of all, hast a care for the creatures, so that Thou spreads over us thy mercy in Him who came by Thy will and put on the body, Thy creature, which Thou didst will and form according to Thy glorious wisdom. He whom Thou didst appoint in Thy secrecy and establish in Thy manifestation, to Him Thou hast given the name of Son, He who was Thy will, the power of Thy thought; so that Ye are by various names, the Father and the Son and the Spirit, for the sake of the government of Thy creatures, for the nourishing of all natures, and Ye are One in glory and power and will; and Ye are divided without being separated, and are One though divided, and all subsists in Thee and is subject to Thee, because all is Thine and Thou art in all. And I rely upon Thee, Lord, and by Thy command have subjected these dumb beasts, that thou might show Thy ministering power upon us and upon them because it is needful, and that Thy name might be glorified in us and in the beasts that cannot speak."

And then I, Judas Thomas, said unto the asses, "Peace be unto you. Yoke ye four of you in the stead of these beasts that have come to a stand."

And every one of them came and pressed to be yoked: there were then four stronger than the rest, which also were yoked. And the rest, some went before and some followed. And when they had journeyed a little way, I dismissed the colts, saying, "I say unto you, the inhabitants of the desert, depart unto your pastures, for if I had had need of all, ye would all have gone with me; but now go unto your place wherein ye dwell." And they departed quietly until they were no more seen.

Chapter 65: At the Captain's Door

Now as I, the captain and the driver went on, the wild asses drew the chariot quietly and evenly, lest they should disturb us in some way. And when they came near to the city gate they turned aside and stood still before the doors of the captain's house. And the captain said: It is not possible for me to relate what hath happened, but when I complete my adventure, I will tell it. The whole city therefore came to see the wild asses under the yoke; and they had heard also the report of the apostle coming to visit them. Therefore, I asked the captain, "Where is thy dwelling, and whither dost thou bring us?"

And he said to me, "Thou thyself knows that we stand before the doors, and these which by thy commandment are come with thee know it better than I."

Chapter 66: Praying for the Assembled

And having so said, the captain came down from the chariot. I, therefore, still standing in the chariot, redeemed the time and began to pray to the Lord Jesus on behalf of all those assembled:

"Jesus Christ, that art blasphemed by the ignorance of Thee in this country; Jesus, the report of Whom is strange in this city; Jesus, that sent on before the apostles in every country and in every city, and that all are found worthy and glorified in Thee; Jesus, that didst take a form and become as a man, and wert seen of all us that thou might not separate us from Thine own love: Thou, Lord, art He that gave Thyself for us, and with Thy blood hast purchased us and gained us as a possession of great price: and what have we to give Thee, Lord, in exchange for Thy life which Thou gave for us? Now we understand that those who should entreat of Thee shall live on into the eternities."

Chapter 67: Exorcism Begins

And when I had thus spoken, many assembled from every quarter to see me, the apostle of the new God. And again, I said, "Why stand we idle? Jesus, Lord, the hour is come: what wilt Thou have done? Command therefore all that be fulfilled which needs to be done."

Now the captain's wife and her daughter were sore borne down by the devils, so that they of the house thought they would rise up no more: for they suffered them not to partake of aught, but cast them down upon their beds recognizing no man until that day when the apostle came thither. And then I, being that apostle, said unto one of the wild asses that were yoked on the right hand, "Enter thou within the gate, and stand there and call the devils and say to them: Judas Thomas, the apostle and disciple of Jesus Christ, saith unto you: 'Come forth hither: for on your account am I sent and unto them that pertain to you by race, to destroy you and chase you unto your place, until the time of the end come and ye go down into the depths of outer darkness to await your appointed time of destruction."

Chapter 68: An Animal Empowered

And that wild ass went in, with a great multitude following him, and said:

"Unto you I speak,[149] the enemies of Jesus that is called Christ: unto you I speak that shut your eyes lest ye see the light: unto you I speak, children of Gehenna (the grave) and of destruction, of him that ceases not from evil until now, that always renews his workings and the things

149 God can empower any nonhuman being, or even inanimate objects, to speak on His behalf when required. The reader's attention is invited to Jesus' words in Luke 19:40 (KJV): "And he answered and said unto them, I tell you that, if these should hold their peace, the stones would immediately cry out."

that befit his being: unto you I speak, most shameless, that shall perish by your own hands. And what I shall say of your destruction and end, and what I shall tell, I know not. For there are many things and innumerable to the hearing: and greater are your doings than the torment and annihilation that is reserved for you. But unto thee I speak, devil, and to thy son that follows with thee: for at this time am I sent against you. And wherefore should I make many words concerning your nature and root, which yourselves know and are not ashamed? But Judas Thomas, the apostle of Christ Jesus, saith unto you, 'He that by much love and affection is sent hither: Before all this multitude that stands here, come forth and tell me of what race ye are.'"

Chapter 69: Surmising Origin of the Devils

And straightway the woman came forth with her daughter, both like dead persons and dishonored in aspect. And I, Judas Thomas, the apostle of the Lord Jesus, beholding them was grieved, especially for the girl,[150] and saith unto the devils, "God forbid that for you there should be sparing or propitiation, for ye know not to spare nor to have pity: but in the name of Jesus, depart from them and stand by their side."

And when I had so said, the women fell down and became as dead; for they neither had breath nor uttered speech: but the devil answered with a loud voice and said, "Art thou come hither again, thou that derides our nature and race? And now have thou come again, that thou may blot out our devices? And as I take it, thou would not suffer us to be upon the earth at all: but this at this time thou canst not accomplish."

And I surmised that this devil was he that had been driven out from that other woman.

Chapter 70: Spiritual Warfare

And the devil said:

150 Luke 17:2 (KJV): "It were better for him that a millstone were hanged about his neck, and he (be) cast into the sea, than that he should offend one of these little ones." This is the eternal destiny of those who assail or oppress the children, i.e., to suffer the "second death" previously described by Thomas in Chapter L.

"I beseech thee, give me leave to depart even whither thou wilt, and dwell there and take commandment from thee, and I will not fear the ruler that hath authority over me. For like as thou art come to preach good tidings, so I also am come to destroy; and like as, if thou fulfil not the will of Him that sent thee, He will bring punishment upon thy head, so I also if I do not the will of him that sent me, before the season and time appointed, shall be sent unto mine own nature; and like as thy Christ helps thee in that thou does, so also my father helps me in that I do; and like as for thee He prepares vessels worthy of thine inhabiting, so also for me he seeks out vessels whereby I may accomplish his deeds; and like as He nourishes and provides for his subjects, so also for me he prepares chastisements and torments, with them with whom I dwell. And like as for a recompense of thy working He giveth thee eternal life, so also unto me he giveth for a reward of my works eternal destruction; and like as thou art refreshed by thy prayer and thy good works and spiritual thanksgivings, so I also am refreshed by murders and adulteries and sacrifices made with wine upon altars; and like as thou convert men unto eternal life, so I also pervert them that obey me unto eternal destruction and torment: and thou receive thine own and I mine."[151]

Chapter 71: Departing the "Habitation of the Human Beings"

And when the devil had said these things and yet more, I said, "Jesus commands thee and thy son, by me, to enter no more into the habitation of humans: but go ye forth and depart and dwell wholly apart from the habitation of the human beings."

And the devils said unto him, "Thou hast laid on us a harsh commandment: but what wilt thou do unto them that now are concealed from thee? For as you are well aware, they that have wrought all the images rejoice in them more than thee: and many of them do the more part worship, and perform their will, sacrificing to them and bringing them food, by libations and by wine and water and offering with oblations."

---

151 The Apostle Paul described such spiritual warfare, as engaged in by Christians, in Ephesians 6:12 (KJV): "For we wrestle not against flesh and blood, but against principalities, against powers, against the rulers of the darkness of this world, against spiritual wickedness in high places."

And I replied, "Have no doubts. They also shall now be abolished, with their works."

And suddenly the devils vanished away; but the women lay cast upon the ground, as if they were dead, and without speech.

Chapter 72: Apostle Admonished to Action

And the wild asses stood together and parted not one from another; but he to whom speech was given by the power of the Lord – while all men kept silence, and looked to see what they would do – the wild ass said unto me:

"Why stand thou idle, O apostle, anointed of the Most-High God, who looks that thou shouldest ask of Him the best of learning? Wherefore then tarry thou in asking Him, and He would give thee? Why delay thou, good disciple? For lo, thy teacher desires to show by thy hands His mighty works. Why stand thou still, O herald of the Hidden One? Thy Lord wills to manifest through thee His unspeakable things, which He reserves for them that are worthy of Him, to hear them. Why rest thou, O doer of mighty works in the name of the Lord? Surely, thy Lord encourages thee and engenders boldness in thee. Fear not, therefore; for He will not forsake the soul that belongs unto thee by birth. Begin therefore to call upon Him and He will readily hearken to thee. Why stand thou marveling at all His acts and his workings? Surely, these are small things which he hath shown by thy means. And what wilt thou tell concerning His great gifts? Surely, even thou wilt not be sufficient to declare them all. And why marvel thou at His cures of the body which He worketh, especially when ye know that healing of His which is secure and lasting, which He bringeth forth by His own nature? And why look ye unto this temporal life, and hast no thought of that which is eternal?"

Chapter 73: Assembly Admonished

The beast of burden continued with an admonition for the assembly:

"But unto you the multitudes that stand by and look to see these that are cast down raised up, I say, believe in the apostle of Jesus Christ: believe the teacher of truth, believe him that shows you the truth, believe Jesus, believe on the Christ that was born, that the born may live by His life: who also was raised up through infancy, that perfection might appear by His manhood. He did teach His own disciples: for He is the teacher of the truth and makes men wise, those who were schooled through Him that through Him perfect wisdom might be known. He taught His disciple Judas Thomas that stands before you today, because He was the teacher of verity and the master of the wise. This Jesus Christ also offered the gift in the temple that he might show that His offering was sanctified. This is His apostle, the shower of truth, he who performs the will of Him that sent him. But there shall come false apostles and prophets of lawlessness, whose end shall be according to their deeds; preaching indeed and ordaining to flee from ungodliness, but themselves at all times detected in sins, clad indeed with sheep's clothing, but within, ravening wolves. Who suffice not themselves with one wife but corrupt many women; who, saying that they despise children, destroy many children, for whom they will pay the ultimate penalty; that content not themselves with their own possessions, but desire that all useless things should minister unto them only; professing to be His disciples; and with their mouth they utter one thing, but in their heart they think another; charging other men to beware of evil, but they themselves perform nothing that is good; who are accounted temperate, and charge other men to abstain from fornication, theft and covetousness, but in all these things do they themselves walk secretly, teaching other men not to do them."

Chapter 74: Thomas Lauds the Works of Jesus

And after the wild ass had declared all these things, all assembled turned their eyes toward me. And then I, Judas Thomas, declared unto the multitude:

"What I shall think concerning thy beauty, O Jesus, and what I shall tell of Thee, for I know not the fulness thereof, or rather I am not able, for I have no power to declare it, O Christ that art in rest, and the only wise one that alone knows the inward of the heart and understands the thoughts of all. Glory be to Thee, merciful and tranquil. Glory to Thee, wise word. Glory to Thy compassion that was born unto us. Glory to Thy mercy that was spread out over us. Glory to Thy greatness that was made small for us. Glory to Thy most high kingship that was humbled for us. Glory to Thy might which was enfeebled for us. Glory to thy Godhead that for us was seen in likeness of men. Glory to Thy manhood that died for us that it might make us live. Glory to Thy resurrection from the dead; for thereby rising and rest cometh unto our souls. Glory and praise to Thine ascending into the heavens; for thereby Thou hast shewed us the path of the height, and promised that we shall sit with Thee on Thy right hand and with Thee judge the twelve tribes of Israel. Thou art the heavenly word of the Father: thou art the hidden light of the understanding, shower of the way of truth, driver away of darkness, and blotter-out of error."

Chapter 75: Two Women Raised to Life

Having thus spoken, I stood over the women, saying, "My Lord and my God, I have no doubts concerning Thee, nor as one unbelieving do I call upon Thee, Ye Who is always our helper and succorer and raiser-up; Who breathes Thine own power into us and encourages us and gives confidence in love unto Thine own servants. I beseech Thee, let these souls be healed and rise up and become such as they were before they were smitten of the devils."

And when I thus spoke, the women turned and sat up. And I bade the captain that his servants should take them and bring them indoors and provide them with food, for they had not eaten in many days. And when they were gone in, I said unto the wild asses, "Follow me."

And they went after me until I had brought them without the gate. And when they had gone out, I said to them, "Depart in peace unto your pastures."

The wild asses therefore went away willingly; and I stood and took heed to them lest they should be hurt by any, until they had gone afar off and were no more seen. And then I returned into the house of the captain, with the multitude standing without.

Chapter 76: Wife of Charisius Seeks the Apostle

Now it came to pass that a certain woman, the wife of Charisius, that was next unto the king,[152] whose name was Mygdonia, came to see and

152 This phrase should be translated in the same context as it is presented in 2 Chronicles 28:7 (KJV): "And Zichri, a mighty man of Ephraim, slew Maaseiah the king's son, and Azrikam the governor of the house, and Elkanah that was next to the king." Wherefore, the position of El-

behold the new name and the new God who was being proclaimed, and the new apostle who had come to visit their country: and she was carried by her own servants; and because of the great crowd and the narrow way they were not able to bring her near unto him. And she sent unto her husband to send her more to minister to her; and they came and approached her, pressing upon the people and beating them to clear a path.

And I, the apostle Judas Thomas, saw it and said to them, "Wherefore overthrow ye them that come to hear the word, and are eager for it? Surely, ye desire to be near me but are far off, as it was said of the multitude that came unto the Lord: 'Having eyes ye see not, and having ears ye hear not.'"

And I, therefore, further exhorted the multitudes in the very words of Jesus, the Christ: "He that hath eyes to see and ears to hear, let him see and hear;[153] and: Come unto me, all ye that labor and are heavy laden, and I will give you rest."[154]

Chapter 77: Thomas Issues a Blessing and Admonition

And looking upon them that carried her, I said unto them:

"This blessing and this admonition I proclaim unto those among you that are heavily burdened now. Ye are they that carry burdens grievous to be borne, and are borne about by her command. And though ye are men, they lay on you loads as on brute beasts, for they that have authority over you think that ye are not men such as themselves, whether bond or free. For neither shall possessions profit the rich, nor poverty save the poor from judgement; nor have we received a commandment which we are not able to perform, nor hath he laid on us burdens grie-

kanah and Charisius would signify the man who was "second in command" in their particular kingdom. See the rendition of this scripture in the New Living Translation.

153 Matthew 13:15-17 (KJV): "For this people's heart is waxed gross, and their ears are dull of hearing, and their eyes they have closed; lest at any time they should see with their eyes and hear with their ears, and should understand with their heart, and should be converted, and I should heal them. But blessed are your eyes, for they see: and your ears, for they hear. For verily I say unto you, That many prophets and righteous men have desired to see those things which ye see, and have not seen them; and to hear those things which ye hear, and have not heard them."

154 Matthew 11:28-29 (KJV): "Come unto me, all ye that labor and are heavy laden, and I will give you rest. Take my yoke upon you, and learn of me; for I am meek and lowly in heart: and ye shall find rest unto your souls."

vous to be borne which we are not able to carry; nor building which men build; nor to hew stones and prepare houses, as your craftsmen do by their own knowledge. But this commandment have we received of the Lord, that that which pleases not us when it is done by another, this we should not inflict on any other."[155]

Chapter 78: Shun Evil; Strive for Holiness

After the multitude had seated themselves round about me, I began my sermon:

"Abstain therefore first from adultery, for this is the beginning of all evils, and next from theft, which enticed Judas Iscariot, and brought him unto hanging; and cease from covetousness, for as many as yield unto covetousness see not that which they do; and from vainglory and from all foul deeds, especially them of the body, whereby cometh eternal condemnation. For this is the chief city of all evils; and likewise, it bringeth them that hold their heads high in haughtiness unto tyranny, and draws them down unto the deep, and subdues them under its hands that they see not what they do; wherefore the things done of them are hidden from them.

"But do ye become well-pleasing unto God in all good things, in meekness and quietness: for these doth God spare, and grants eternal life and sets death at naught. And in gentleness which follows on all good things, and overcomes all enemies and alone receives the crown of victory: with gentleness and stretching out of the hand to the poor, and supplying the want of the needy, and distributing to them that are in necessity, especially them that walks in holiness. For this is chosen before God and leads unto eternal life: for this is before God the chief city of all good: for they that strive not in the course of Christ shall not obtain holiness.

"And holiness[156] did appear from God, doing away with fornication outside of marriage, overthrowing the enemy, well-pleasing unto God: for she is an invincible champion, having honor from God, glorified

155 The Apostle Thomas renders a paraphrase of the Golden Rule as stated by Jesus in Matthew 7:12 (KJV): "Therefore all things whatsoever ye would that men should do to you: do ye even so to them: for this is the law and the prophets."

156 Words derived from the feminine root qdš appear some 830 times in the Hebrew Bible. Its use in the Hebrew Bible evokes ideas of separation from the profane, and proximity to the Otherness of God, while in nonbiblical Semitic texts, recent interpretations of its meaning link

of many: she is an ambassador of peace, announcing peace: if any gain her he abides without care, pleasing the Lord, expecting the time of redemption: for she doeth nothing amiss, but giveth life and rest and joy unto all that gain her."

Chapter 79: Benefits of Meekness

And I, Judas Thomas, did continue with my sermon:

"But meekness hath overcome death and brought him under authority, meekness hath enslaved the enemy, for meekness is the good yoke: meekness fears not and opposes not the many: meekness is peace, joy and exaltation, the bringer of rest. Abide ye therefore in holiness and receive freedom from me, and be near unto meekness; for in these three heads is portrayed the Christ whom I proclaim unto you. Holiness is the temple of Christ, and he that dwelleth in her obtains of her for a habitation of rest. Remember that for forty days and forty nights He fasted, tasting nothing: and he that keeps her shall dwell in her as on a mountain. And meekness is his boast: for he said unto Peter our fellow apostle: 'Turn back thy sword and put it again into the sheath thereof: for if I had willed so to do, could I not have brought more than twelve legions of angels from My Heavenly Father?'"[157]

Chapter 80: Beseeching the Apostle

And after I had said these things in the hearing of all the multitude, they approached me, pressing upon one another: and the wife of Charisius, the king's kinsman, leapt out of her chair and cast herself on the ground before me, directly in front of my feet, and beseeching me and saying:

"O disciple of the living God, thou art come into a desert country, for we live in the desert; being like unto brute beasts in our conversation; but now shall we be saved by thy hands. I beseech thee, therefore,

---

it to ideas of consecration, belonging, and purification. In Jewish Aramaic, the language of the apostle Thomas, Qudšu was later used to refer to the holiness of God.

הְשֻׁדְק q'dusha feminine sanctity, purity, holiness; (Jewish ritual) Kedushah

157 Matthew 26:52 (KJV): "Then said Jesus unto him (Peter), Put up again thy sword into his place: for all they that take the sword shall perish with the sword."

take thought of me, and pray for me, that the compassion of the God of whom ye preach may come upon me, and I may become his dwelling place and be joined in prayer and hope and faith in Him; and I also may receive the seal and become a holy temple and He may dwell in me."

Chapter 81: Those Who Abide Forever

And then I said, "I do pray and entreat for you all, brethren, that believe on the Lord, and for you, sisters, that hope in Christ, that in all of you the word of God may tabernacle and have his tabernacle therein: for ye are given power over your own souls and can admit therein whomsoever ye desire."

And I began to say unto the woman:

"Mygdonia, rise up from the earth and compose thyself. Remove thy ornaments and let the light of thy good spirit shine through you. Also, thine expensive attire shall not profit thee nor the beauty of thy body, neither yet the fame of thy rank, nor the authority of this world, nor any fantasies that thou should entertain, for all of these cometh to naught; and the body waxes old and changes, and raiment wears out, and authority and nobility passes away, as do all the pleasures this material world has to offer. All of this becomes corrupted. But Jesus only and those who have come unto him in the hope of celestial glory do abide forever."

In this manner I did speak and further said unto the woman: "Hence, depart now in peace, and the Lord shall make thee worthy of His own mysteries."

But Lady Mygdonia replied, "I fear to go away, lest thou forsake me and depart unto another nation."

Therefore, I did assure her, "Even if I go, I shall not leave thee alone, but Jesus of His compassion will be with thee."

And she fell down in gratitude to me and did reverence unto the Lord Jesus, and then departed unto her house.

Chapter 82: Mygdonia at Home

Now Charisius, the kinsman of Misdaeus the king, bathed himself and returned and laid him down to dine. And he inquired concerning his wife, where she was; for she had not come out of her own chamber to meet him as she was wont. And her handmaids said to him, "She is not well."

And he entered quickly into her chamber and found her lying on the bed and veiled; and he unveiled her and kissed her, saying, "Wherefore art thou sorrowful today?"

And she said, "I am not well."

And he said unto her, "Wherefore then didst thou leave thy house and didst go and listen unto vain speeches and look upon works of sorcery? Rise up now and dine with me, for I cannot dine without thee."

But she said to him, "Today I decline it, for I am sore afraid."

Chapter 83: Mygdonia Alienated from Spouse

And when Charisius heard this of Mygdonia, he would not go forth to dinner, but bade his servants bring the food to her chamber, that he might dine with her there. And when then they brought it in, he desired her to dine with him, but she excused herself. And since she would not dine with him, Charisius dined alone, saying unto her, "On thine account I refused to dine with Misdaeus the king, and thou, are thou still not willing to dine with me?"

But she said, "It is because I am not well."

Charisius therefore rose up as he was wont, and would sleep with her. But she said, "Did I not tell thee that for today I refused it?"

Chapter 84: Charisius' Dream

When he heard that he went to another bed and slept; and awaking out of sleep he said:

"My lady Mygdonia, hearken to the dream which I have seen. I saw myself lie at meat near to Misdaeus the king, and a dish of all sorts was set before us. And I saw an eagle come down from heaven and carry off from before me and the king two partridges, which he set against his heart; and once again he came over us and flew about above us, and the king bade a bow to be brought to him; and the eagle again caught away from before us a pigeon and a dove, and the king shot an arrow at him, and it passed through him from one side to the other and hurt him not; and he being unscathed rose up into his own nest. And I awoke, and

I am full of fear and sore vexed, because I had tasted of the partridge, and he suffered me not to put it to my mouth again."

And Mygdonia said unto him, "Charisius, thy dream is good; for thou every day eats partridges, but this eagle had not tasted of a partridge until now."

Chapter 85: Charisius Befuddled

And when it was morning Charisius went and dressed himself and shod his right foot with his left shoe; and he stopped, and said to Mygdonia, "What then is this matter with me? For look, the dream and this action of mine!"

But Mygdonia said to him, "And this also is not evil, but seems to me very good; for from an unlucky act there will be a change unto thee for the better."

And he washed his hands and went to salute Misdaeus the king.

Chapter 86: Charisius a "Hard Man"

And Mygdonia rose up early and went to my encampment to salute me; and she found me discoursing with the captain and all the multitude, and I was advising them and speaking of the woman which had received the Lord in her soul, whose wife she was; and the captain said of her, "She is the wife of Charisius the kinsman of Misdaeus the king. And her husband is a hard man, and in everything that he saith to the king, even he obeys him. And he will not suffer her to continue in this mind which she hath promised; for often-times hath he praised her before the king, saying that there is none other like her in love: all things therefore that thou sayeth unto her are strange unto her."

And then I replied, "If verily and surely the Lord hath risen upon her soul and she hath received the seed that was cast on her, she will have no care of this temporal life, nor fear death, neither will Charisius be able to harm her at all: for greater is He whom she hath received into her soul, if she hast received Him indeed."

Chapter 87: Mygdonia Visits the Camp of the Apostle

And Mygdonia hearing this said unto me, "In truth, my lord, I have received the seed of thy words, and I will bear fruit like unto such seed."

And then I, Judas Thomas, the apostle of our Lord Jesus, replied, "Our souls give praise and thanks unto Thee, O Lord, for they are Thine: our bodies give thanks unto Thee, which Thou hast accounted worthy to become the dwelling-place of Thy heavenly gift."

And I said also to them that stood by:

"Blessed are the holy, whose souls have never condemned them, for they have gained them and are not divided against themselves: blessed are the elect spirits of the pure, and they that have received the heavenly crown whole from overcoming the wicked spirit of the age; blessed are the bodies of the holy, for they have been made worthy to become temples of God, that Christ may dwell in them: blessed are ye, for ye have power to forgive sins: blessed are ye if ye lose not that which is committed unto you, but rejoicing and departing bear it away with you: blessed are ye the holy, for unto you it is given to ask and receive: blessed are ye meek for you hath God counted worthy to become heirs of the heavenly kingdom. Blessed are ye meek, for ye are they that have overcome the enemy: blessed are ye meek, for ye shall see the face of the Lord. Blessed are ye that hunger for the Lord's sake, for you is rest laid up, and your souls rejoice from henceforth. Blessed are ye that are quiet in spirit and wait upon the Lord to be set free from sin and from the exchange of clean and unclean beasts."[158]

And after I had said these things in the hearing of all the multitude, Mygdonia was all the more confirmed in the faith and glory and greatness of Christ.

158 Compare to the Sermon on the Mount given by the Lord Jesus Christ in Matthew Chapters 5, 6 and 7 (KJV). Like Jesus in the Sermon on the Mount, Thomas here espouses moral sayings providing sure guidance for the sanctified walk of the Christian through life in this age of iniquity.

Chapter 88: Fidelity to the Gospel

But Charisius the kinsman and friend of Misdaeus the king came to his breakfast and found not his wife in the house; and he inquired of all that were in his house, "Whither is your mistress gone?"

And one of them answered and said, "She is gone unto that stranger." And when he heard this of his servant, he was wroth with the other servants because they had not straightway told him what was done; and he sat down and waited for her.

And when it was evening and she was come into the house he said to her, "Where were you?"

And she answered and said, "With the physician."

And he said, "Is that stranger a physician?"

And she said, "Yea, he is a physician of souls; for most physicians do heal bodies that are dissolved, but he tends to the souls that are not destroyed, mending them and setting them on the path that leads to the one true God, and not to the thousands of worthless idols our people have been fruitlessly serving for all of this time past."[159]

---

159 Mygdonia recognizes that the Holy Spirit has impressed visions upon her spouse that he must allow her to pursue spiritual truth with the Apostle Thomas. She is waiting to see if Charisius will, indeed, change the course of his life and disavow the worship of idols, after the manner of the Indians, and repent and follow her in the way of Christ, whence they can resume a normal course of marital relations.

The gist of Ezra Chapter 9 in the Old Testament is the prophet's confessing the sins of the returned Jewish exiles when he learned that many of them had intermarried with pagan peoples and were practicing some of their abominations.

Yahweh, through the voice of his prophet in Israel, made the following statement in Ezra 10:11 (KJV): "Make confession to the Lord, the God of your fathers and do His will. Separate yourselves from the peoples of the land and from the foreign wives." Clearly, the same held true for the foreign husbands of Israelite wives, who continued in paganism and worshipped the strange gods of foreign lands, practicing all manner of idolatry.

Upon taking note of Ezra's deep sorrow over this situation, one of the Israelite men who had taken a foreign wife, Shecaniah, acknowledged his sin and proposed that the Jews divorce their pagan wives and disown the children born to these unions. The prophet Ezra approved of Shecaniah's proposal and had all of the Jewish men married to pagan wives take such an oath and made sure that they followed through on it.

While there appears to be some contradiction here with the words of the apostle Paul to the church at Corinth as noted in 1 Corinthians 7:12-16 (KJV), keep in mind that Paul did say that he was speaking only his own opinion, and not necessarily that of the Lord, and that while unbelieving spouses should be given a chance to come around, if they leave of their own accord, then let it be so, as the Christ-believing partner is no longer "enslaved." There is always a myriad of circumstances that one must take into account in marital and family situations involving conflicts that arise between believers in Christ and pagan spouses.

Charisius, hearing this, was very angry in his mind with Mygdonia because of her attraction to me in my commission as an apostle, but he answered her nothing, for he was afraid; for she was above him both in wealth and birth: but he departed to dinner, and she went into her chamber. And he said to the servants, "Call her to dinner."

But she would not come.

Chapter 89: Charisius Doubts the Apostle

And when he heard that she would not come out of her chamber, he went in and said unto her, "Wherefore wilt thou not dine with me and perchance not sleep with me as the wont is? Yea, concerning this I have the greater suspicion, for I have heard that that sorcerer and deceiver teaches that a man should not live with his wife, and that which nature requires and the gods hath ordained he overthrows."

When Charisius said these things, Mygdonia kept silence. He saith to her again:

"My lady and consort Mygdonia, be not led astray by deceitful and vain words, nor by the works of sorcery which I have heard that this man performs in the name of the Father, Son, and Holy Ghost; for it was never yet heard in the world that any raised the dead, and, as I hear, it is reported of this man that he raises dead men. And for that he neither eats nor drinks. Therefore, think not that for righteousness' sake he neither eats nor drinks, but this he doth because he possesses naught, for what should he do which hath not even his daily bread? And he hath one garment because he is poor, and as for his not receiving aught of any and knowing in himself that he doth not verily heal any man, he continues in this deception."

Chapter 90: Mygdonia Prays for Strength

And when Charisius so said, Mygdonia was silent as any stone, but she prayed, asking when it should be day, that she might go to the apostle of Christ. And he withdrew from her and went to dinner heavy in mind, for he thought to sleep with her according to the wont. And when he was gone out, she bowed her knees and prayed, saying, "Lord God and Master, merciful Father, my Savior Christ, do thou give me strength to overcome the shamelessness of Charisius, and grant me to keep the holiness wherein thou shall delight, that I also may by it find eternal life."

And when she had so prayed, she laid herself on her bed and veiled herself.

Chapter 91: Mygdonia Flees from Charisius

But Charisius, having dined, came upon her, and she cried out, saying, "Thou hast no more any room by me; for my Lord Jesus is greater than thou. He Who is with me rests in me."

And he laughed and said, "Ye would do well to mock that sorcerer, and to deride him who saith, 'Ye have no life with God unless ye purify yourselves.'"

And when he had so said he essayed to sleep with her, but she endured it not and cried out bitterly and said, "I call upon Thee, Lord Jesus, forsake me not; for with Thee have I made my refuge when I learned that Thou art He that seeks out them that are veiled in ignorance and saves them that are held in error. And now I entreat Thee whose report I have heard and believed; come Thou to my help and save me from the shamelessness of Charisius, that his foulness may not get the upper hand of me."

At that, she fled from Charisius naked; and as she went out from him, she pulled down the curtain of the bedchamber and wrapped it about her; and went to her nurse, and slept there with her.

Chapter 92: Charisius Blames the Apostle

But Charisius was in heaviness all night, and smote his face with his hands, and he was minded to go that very hour and tell the king concerning the injustice that was perpetrated upon him by the apostle, but he considered with himself, saying:

"If the great heaviness which is upon me compels me to go now unto the king, who will bring me in to him? For I know that my abuse hath overthrown me from my high looks and my vainglory and majesty, and hath cast me down into this vileness and separated my dear Mygonia from me. Yea, if the king himself stood before the doors at this hour, I could not have gone out and answered him. But I will wait until dawn, and I know that whatsoever I ask of the king, he will grant it me: and

I will tell him of the madness of this stranger, how that it tyrannously casts down the great and illustrious into the depth. For it is not this that grieves me, that I am deprived of her companying, but for her am I grieved, because her greatness of soul is humbled: being an honorable lady in whom none of her house ever found fault; and yet she hath fled away naked, running out of her own bedchamber, and I know not whither she is gone; and it may be that she is gone mad by the means of that sorcerer, and in her madness hath gone forth into the marketplace to seek him; for there is nothing that appeals unto her lovable except him and the things that are spoken by him."

Chapter 93: Seeks King's Help Against Apostle and Captain

Then Charisius began to lament and say:
"Woe to me, O my consort, and to thee besides! Alas, I am too quickly bereaved of thee. Woe is me, my most dear one, for thou of my race: neither son nor daughter have I had of thee that I might find rest in them; neither hast thou yet dwelt with me a full year, and an evil eye hath caught thee from me. Would that the violence of death had taken thee, and I should yet have reckoned myself among kings and nobles: but that I should suffer this at the hands of a stranger. And lo, this sorcerer is like a runaway slave to mine ill fortune and the sorrow of my unhappy soul! Let there be no impediment for me until I destroy him and avenge this night, and may I not be well-pleasing before Misdaeus the king if he avenges me not with the head of this stranger. I will also tell him of Siphor the captain who hath been the occasion of this. For by his means did the stranger appear here, and lodges at his house; and many there be that go in and come out whom he teaches a new doctrine; saying that none can live if he quit not all his substance and become a renouncer like himself; and he strives to make many partakers with him."

Chapter 94: Thomas and Siphor in Danger

And as Charisius thought on these things, the day dawned: and he put on a mean habit, and shod himself, and went downcast and in heaviness to salute the king. And when the king saw him, he inquired, "Wherefore art thou sorrowful, and comes to my presence in such garb of lamentation? And I see that thy countenance is changed."

And Charisius said unto the king:

"I have a new thing to tell thee and a new desolation which Siphor hath brought into India, even a certain Hebrew, a sorcerer, whom he hath sitting in his house and who departs not from him: and many are there that go in to him: whom also he teaches of a new God, and lays on them new laws such as never yet were heard, saying: It is impossible for you to enter into that eternal life which I proclaim unto you, unless ye rid you of your wives, and likewise the wives of their husbands. And it chanced that mine unlucky wife also went to him and became a hearer of his words, and she believed them, and in the middle of the night she forsook me and ran unto the stranger. But send thou for both Siphor and that sorcerer that is hid with him, and visit destruction upon their heads, lest all that are of our nation perish of this cult."

Chapter 95: Siphor Stands Before the King

And when King Misdaeus his friend heard this he saith to him, "Be not grieved nor heavy, for I will send for him and avenge thee, and thou shalt have thy wife again, and the others that cannot I will avenge."

And the king went forth and sat on the judgement seat, and when he was situated, he commanded Siphor the captain to be called. They went therefore unto his house and found him sitting on my right hand and Mygdonia at my feet, hearkening to me with all the multitude. And they that were sent from the king said unto Siphor, "Sit thou here listening to vain words, and Misdaeus the king in his wrath thinketh to destroy thee because of this sorcerer and deceiver whom thou hast brought into thine house?"

And Siphor hearing it was cast down, not because of the king's threat against him, but for me, the apostle, because the king was disposed contrary to me. And he said to me, "I am grieved concerning thee: for I told thee at the first that that woman is the wife of Charisius the king's friend and kinsman, and he will not suffer her to perform that she hath promised, and all that he asks of the king he grants him."

But I said unto Siphor: Fear nothing, but believe in Jesus that pleads for us all,[160] for unto his refuge are we gathered together." And Siphor, hearing that, put his garment about him and went unto Misdaeus the king.

Chapter 96: Apostle Comforts Mygdonia

And then I, the apostle of the Lord Jesus, inquired of Mygdonia, "What was the cause that thy husband was wroth with thee and devised this against us?"

And she said, "Because I gave not myself up unto his corruption; for he had desired last night to subdue me and subject me unto that passion which he serves: and He to whom I have committed my soul delivered me out of his hands; and I fled away from him naked, and slept with my nurse: but that which befell him I know not, wherefore he hath contrived this."

I replied, "These things will not hurt us; but believe thou on Jesus, and He shall overthrow the wrath of Charisius and his madness and his impulse; and He shall be a companion unto thee in the fearful way, and He shall guide thee into His kingdom, and shall bring thee unto eternal life giving thee that confidence which passes not away nor changes."[161]

Chapter 97: Siphor's Defense

Now Siphor stood before the king, and he inquired of him, "Who is that sorcerer and whence doth he come? And what does he teach whom thou hast lurking in thine house?"

And Siphor answered the king, "Thou art not ignorant, O king, what trouble and grief I, with my friends had concerning my wife, whom thou doth know of and many others remember, and concerning my daughter, whom I value more than all my possessions, what a time and trial I suffered; for I became a laughing-stock and a curse in all our

160 We are greatly blessed in having a great High Priest in the Lord Jesus Christ, one who ever lives to make intercession for us. John describes him as our "Advocate with the Father" (1 John 2:1-2). Jesus understands our weaknesses without himself being weak. There is no one closer to God than His Son, the Lord Jesus Christ.

161 Deuteronomy 31:6 (KJV): Be strong and courageous, do not be afraid or tremble at them, for the LORD your God is the one who goes with you. He will not fail you or forsake you.

country. And I heard the report of this man and went to him and entreated him, and took him and brought him hither. And as I came by the way I saw wonderful and amazing things: and here also many did hear the wild ass and concerning that devil whom he drove out, and healed my wife and daughter, and now are they whole; and he asked no reward but requires faith and holiness, that men should become partakers with him in that which he doeth: and this he teaches to worship and fear only one God, the ruler of all things,[162] and Jesus Christ His Son, that they may have eternal life. And that which he eats is bread and salt, and his drink is water from evening unto evening, and he makes many prayers; and whatsoever he asks of his God, He giveth him. And what he teaches is that this God is holy and mighty, and that Christ is living and makes alive; wherefore also He charges them that are there present to come unto Him in holiness and purity and love and faith."

Chapter 98: King Dispatches Soldiers

And when King Misdaeus heard these things of Siphor he sent many soldiers unto the house of Siphor the captain, to bring me, Thomas the apostle, and all others that were found there. And they that were sent entered in and found me teaching much people, with Mygdonia sitting at my feet. And when they beheld the great multitude that were about me, they feared, and departed to their king and said, "We durst not say aught unto him, for there was a great multitude about him, and Mygdonia sitting at his feet was listening to the things that were spoken by him."

And when King Misdaeus and Charisius heard these things, Charisius leaped out from before the king and drew much people with him and said, "I will bring him, O king, and Mygdonia whose understanding he hath taken away." And he came to the house of Siphor the captain, greatly disturbed, and found him me teaching: but Mygdonia he found not, for she had withdrawn herself unto her house, having learnt that it had been told her husband that she was there.

162 Deuteronomy 6:4 (KJV): "Hear, O Israel: The LORD our God is one LORD:"

Chapter 99: Apostle Thomas Arrested

And Charisius said unto me, "Up, thou wicked one and destroyer and enemy of mine house: for me thy sorcery harms not, for I will visit thy sorcery on thine head."

And when he so said, I, Thomas, looked upon him and said unto him, "Thy threats shall return upon thee, for me thou wilt not harm any whit: for greater than thee and thy king and all your army is the Lord Jesus Christ in whom I have my trust."

And Chalisius took a turban of one of his slaves, unraveled it and cast it about my neck, saying, "Seize him and bring him away; let me see if his God is able to deliver him out of my hands." And then the soldiers took me into their custody and led me away to the court of King Misdaeus.

And I stood before the king, and the king said to me, "Tell me who thou art and by what power thou art doing these things." But I kept silence. And the king commanded his officers that I should be scourged with one hundred and twenty-eight blows, and bound, and be cast into the prison. And they bound me and led me away. And the king and Charisius considered how they should put me to death, for many in the multitude actually worshipped me as a god, while others considered me a divine messenger.

In my estimation, the king and Charisius were planning on charging me with being a "deceiver of the people and reviling the good name of King Misdaeus."

Chapter 100: Psalm of the Soul

And as I prayed, all the prisoners looked upon me, and besought me to pray for them: and when I had prayed and was set down, I began to utter a psalm in this wise:

When I was a little child, and dwelling in my father's palace,
I enjoyed the wealth and luxuries of my nourishers;

Our home was in the East,
and from there my parents equipped me and sent me forth.

And of the wealth of our treasury

they took abundantly,

Equipping me for my journey;
those items which I myself could carry,

Gold of Beth-Ellaya, and silver of Gazak the Great, And rubies of India,
and agates from Kushan,

And they girded me with steel,
which can even crush iron.

And they took off from me the glittering robe,
which in their affection they made for me,

And the purple toga,
which was measured and woven to my stature.

And they made a compact with me,
and wrote it in my heart, that it might not be forgotten:

“If ye go down into Egypt,
and bring the one pearl,

Which is in the midst of the sea
around the loud-breathing serpent,

Thou shalt put on thy glittering robe
and thy toga, with which thou art contented;

And with thy brother, who is next to us in authority,
thou shalt be heir in our kingdom.”

Therefore, I did depart from the East and went down,
being led by two guardians,

For the way was dangerous and difficult,
and I was very young to travel it.

I passed through the borders of Maishan,

the meeting-place of the merchants of the East,

And I reached the land of Babel,
entering through the walls of Sarbug.

Then I went down into Egypt,
and my companions parted from me.

I went straight to the serpent,
staying in the vicinity of his abode,

Waiting till he should lumber and sleep,
that I could take my pearl from him.

Being alone in this strange land,
I dressed as the locals;

So as not to attract undue attention,
yet I would seem an alien unto my own people.

One of my people, a free-born man,
and Oriental, I saw there,

A youth fair and loveable,
the son of oil-sellers;

And he came and attached himself to me,
and I made him my intimate friend.

An associate with whom I shared my merchandise.
I warned him against the Egyptians,

"Stay clear of those who are unclean among them,"
is what I admonished my friend.

And I dressed in their dress,
that they might not hold me in abhorrence,

Because I was come from abroad in order to take the pearl,
I feared lest I should arouse the serpent against me.

But in one way or another,
the locals found out that I was not their countryman.

And they dealt with me treacherously,
and gave me nothing but their food to eat.

In time, I forgot that I was a son of kings,
and I served their king;

and I forgot the pearl,
for which my parents had sent me.

And because of the burden of their oppressions,
I lay in a deep sleep.

But all these things that befell me
my parents perceived that something was wrong and grieved for me;

And a proclamation was made in our kingdom,
that all should come to the gates of our kingdom,

Kings and princes of Parthia,
and all the nobles of the East.

And they devised a plan on my behalf,
that I might not be left in Egypt;

And they wrote to me a letter,
and every noble signed his name to it:

"From thy Father, the King of Kings,
and thy mother, the mistress of the East,

and from thy brother, our second in authority,
to thee our son, who art in Egypt, greetings!

Call to mind that thou art a son of kings!
Consider the condition of your slavery, and whom ye now serve!

Remember the pearl,
for which ye were sent to Egypt!

Think of thy robe;
and remember thy splendid toga,

Which thou shalt wear and with which thou shalt be adorned,
when thy name hath been read out in the list of the valiant,

Along with the name of thy brother, our viceroy,
who shall reign with you."

My letter bore a royal seal,
which my father sealed with his own right hand,

to keep it from the wicked ones, the children of Babel,
and from the savage demons of Sarbug.

It was flown to me by an eagle,
the king of all birds.

It flew to me and alit beside me,
and began to screech.

At its voice and the sound of its rustling,
I started and arose from my sleep.

I took up the letter from its talons and kissed it,
and I began and read it;

And according to what was traced on my heart
were the words of my letter.

I remembered that I was a son of royal parents,
and my noble birth asserted itself.

I remembered the pearl,
for which I had been sent to Egypt,

And when I went to confront the serpent,

my soothing voice began to calm and charm it.

I hushed him asleep and lulled him into slumber,
for the name of my father I declared over him,

As well as the name of my brother, the second in power,
and the name of my mother, the Queen of the East.

And I snatched away the pearl,
and turned to go back to the house of my father.

And the filthy and unclean dress of Babylonish Egypt I stripped off,
and left it in their country;

And I took my way straight to come
to the light of our home in the East.

On the road home, I encountered a beautiful young girl with golden tresses,
whose words of hope encouraged me and lifted me up.

She was an oracle,
Guiding me to the light.

Her royal, white silken garment
Gave a bright light before me.

And with her voice and guidance,
she also encouraged me to speed along.

I went forth and passed by the gates at Sarbug;
I left Babel on my left hand;

And I came to the great Maisan,
to the haven of merchants, which sits on the shore of the sea.

And my bright robe, which I had stripped off,
and the toga that was wrapped with it,

From Rantha and Reken,
my parents had sent thither,

By the hand of their treasurers,
who in their truth could be trusted therewith.

And because I remembered not its manner of fashion,
for in my childhood I had left it in the house of my father,

All of a sudden, when I received it,
the garment I held up in front of a mirror.

And when I imagined myself wearing it,
I saw two glorious beings.

The two shared a likeness unto myself,
both regally dressed.

And the treasurers too, with their money and wealth
who brought the garment to me, I saw in a like manner.

While two beings, they shared but one likeness,
yet the one sign of the king was written on them both,

On the hands of them who restored to me
my trust and my wealth,

My decorated robe, which
was adorned with glorious colors.

With gold and beryl
and rubies and agates,

And sardonyxes, varied in color.
And it was skillfully worked, to be sure;

And with diamond clasps
were all its seams fastened;

And the image of the King of Kings

was embroidered and depicted in full all over it,

And like the stone of the sapphire, too,
its hues were varied.

And in the process of donning it,
I felt the instincts of knowledge stirring within me.

And I was compelled to speak,
and uttered with a majestic voice:

"I am active in deeds,
reared in righteousness before my father;

And I perceive of myself,
that my stature grows according to my diligence in the appointed labors."

With the beauty of its varied colors, I adorned myself,
and I wrapped myself wholly in my toga of brilliant hues.

I clothed myself with it, and went up to the gate
of salutation and prostration;

I bowed my head
and worshipped the majesty of my father;

For I had kept his commandments,
and he, too, had done what he promised.

And at the gate of his palace
I mingled with his royal ones.

And my brother rejoiced in me and received me;
and I was with him in his kingdom at last,

And with the voice of angels
all the king's servants did praise us.

And my brother promised that

I should go with him;

And with my offering and my pearl,
we, the heirs of the kingdom, should present ourselves to our father.

And here ends the Psalm of Judas Thomas, the Apostle,[163] which I sang in prison.

Upon hearing the Psalm of the Apostle, all the prisoners perceived that Judas Thomas was an angel, an emissary of the One True God. All rejoiced and gave thanks for the presence of Judas Thomas among them, and for his beautiful words of light and love.

Chapter 101: Charisius Returns Home

And Charisius went home glad, thinking that his wife would be with him, and that she had become such as she was before, even before she heard the divine word and believed on Jesus. And he went, and found her with her hair disheveled and her clothes rent; and when he saw her in this condition, he said unto her, "My lady Mygdonia, why doth this cruel disease keep hold on thee? And wherefore hast thou done this? I am thine husband from thy virginity, and both the gods and the law grant me to have rule over thee. What is this great madness of thine, that thou art become a derision in all our nation? But put thou away the care that cometh of that sorcerer; and I will remove his face from among us, that thou mayest see him no more."

163 Compare the moral of Judas Thomas' Psalm to that of Jesus' theme in Luke 15:11-32 (KJV), the Parable of the Prodigal's Son. Those whose self-esteem is based on worldly standards of accomplishment, appearance, and possessions is prideful, focuses on self, and doesn't add value to your life. Overall, it minimizes your potential for growth and influence. On the other hand, self-image based upon the value God has placed on you is Christ-centered and goes far beyond what you can dream or imagine. The lesson of Judas Thomas and his brother Jesus is that if you are a believer who wants to be a leader, you must live as someone valued by God, created in His image (Genesis 1:26). Keeping in mind that one is a redeemed Christian, a daughter or son of God, they should thus walk uprightly, "worthy of the calling" to which they were called (Ephesians 4:1). The Apostle Paul, in his fourth chapter of Ephesians, aptly explains how the Christian can follow through on this.

Chapter 102: Charisius Laments His Situation

But Mygdonia, when she heard the words of her husband, gave herself up unto grief, groaning and lamenting; and Charisius spoke again:

"Have I then so much wronged the gods that they have afflicted me with such a disease? What is my great offence that they have cast me into such humiliation? I beseech thee, Mvgdonia: Tangle my soul no more with the pitiful sight of thee and thy mean appearance and afflict not mine heart with care for thee. I am Charisius, thine husband, whom all the nation honors and fears. What must I do? I know not whither to turn. What am I to think? shall I keep silence and endure? Yet who can be patient when men take his treasure? And who can endure to lose thy sweet ways? And what is there for me? For thy beauty is ever before me, and the fragrance of thee is in my nostrils, and thy bright face is fixed in my eyes. They are taking away my soul, and the fair body which I rejoiced to see they are destroying, and that sharpest of eyes they are blinding and cutting off my right hand: my joy is turning to grief and my life to death, and the light of it is being covered with darkness. Let no man of you, my kindred, henceforth look on me; for from you no help hath come to me, nor will I hereafter worship the gods of the east that have enwrapped me in such calamities, nor pray to them anymore, nor sacrifice to them, for I am bereaved of my spouse. And what else should I ask of them? For all my glory is taken away, yet am I a prince and next unto the king in power; but Mygdonia hath set me at naught, and taken away all these things. Thus, I am reduced to crying out my lamentations!"

Chapter 103: So Great a Loss for Charisius

And while Charisius sobbed, Mygdonia sat silent and looking upon the ground; again he came unto her and said:

"My lady Mygdonia, most desired of me, remember that out of all the women that are in India I chose and took thee as the most beautiful, though I might have joined to myself in marriage many more beautiful: but yet I lie, Mygdonia, for even by the gods it would not have been possible to find another like thee in the land of India; but woe is me always, for thou wilt not even answer me a word: but if thou wilt, revile me, so that I may only be vouchsafed a word from thee. Look at me, for I am surely more attractive than that sorcerer: but thou art my wealth and honor: and all men know that there is none like me: and thou art of my race and kindred; and lo, he taketh thee away from me."

Chapter 104: Charisius Negotiates with Mygdonia

And when Charisius had so said, Mygdonia saith unto him:

"He whom I love is better than thee and thy substance: for thy substance is of earth and returns unto the earth; but he whom I love is of heaven and will take me with him unto heaven. Thy wealth shall pass away, and thy beauty shall vanish, and thy robes, and thy many works: and thou shalt be alone, naked, with thy transgressions. Call not to my remembrance thy deeds unto me, for I pray the Lord that I may forget thee, so as to remember no more those former pleasures and the custom of the body; which shall pass away as a shadow, but Jesus only endures forever, and the souls which hope in Him. Jesus himself shall quit me of the shameful deeds which I did with thee."

And when Charisius heard this, he turned him to sleep, vexed in soul, saying to her:

"Consider it by thyself all this night: and if thou wilt be with me such as thou were before, and not visit that sorcerer again, I will do all according to thy mind, and if thou wilt remove thine affection from him, I will take him out of the prison and let him go and remove into another country, and I will not vex thee, for I know that you esteem the stranger. And not with you first did this matter apparently come about, for many other women also hath he deceived; and they have awoken sober and returned to themselves. Do not thou then make naught of my words and cause me to be a reproach among the Indians."

Chapter 105: Mygdonia Seeks the Apostle

And Charisius having thus spoken went to sleep; but she took ten denarii and went secretly to give them to the jailers that she might enter into my place of detention. But on the way, a stranger came and met her, and she saw him and was afraid, for she thought that he was one of the rulers bearing a torch: for a great light went before him. And she said to herself as she fled, "I fear that I have lost thee, O my unhappy soul; for I shall not again see Judas Thomas, the apostle of Jesus, the Living God, and not yet have I received the holy seal."

And she fled and ran into a narrow place and there hid herself, saying, "I would rather choose to be living among the poor ones, whom it is possible to persuade, or even to be killed,[164] than to fall into the hand of this mighty ruler, who will despise spiritual gifts."

Chapter 106: Stranger Revealed

And while Mygdonia thought thus with herself, I, Judas Thomas, came and stood over her, and she saw me and was afraid, and fell down and became lifeless with terror. But I stood by her and took her by the hand and said unto her:

"Fear not, Mygdonia, for it is I, Judas Thomas. Know now that Jesus will not leave thee, neither will the Lord unto whom thou hast committed thy soul overlook thee. His compassionate rest will not forsake thee: He that is kind will not forsake thee, for His kindness' sake, nor He that is good for His goodness' sake. Rise up then from the earth, thou that art become wholly above it: look on the light, for the Lord abandons not them that love Him to walk in darkness. Behold Him that travels with His servants, that He is unto them a defender in perils."

And Mygdonia arose and looked on me and said, "Whither went thou, my lord? And who is the one who secured your release out of prison to behold the Sun?"

And I answered unto her, "My Lord Jesus is mightier than all powers and all kings and rulers.[165] There is none like unto Him."

Chapter 107: Mygdonia Visits Her Nurse

And Mygdonia said, "Give me the seal of Jesus Christ and I shall receive the gift at thy hands before thou depart out of life."

And she took me with her and entered into the court and aroused her nurse, saying unto her, "Narcia, my mother and nurse, all thy service and refreshment thou hast done for me from my childhood until my present age are vain, and for them I owe thee thanks which are

164 Matthew 10:28 (KJV): "And fear not them which kill the body, but are not able to kill the soul: but rather fear him which is able to destroy both soul and body in hell."

165 The title of "King of Kings" is applied twice to the Lord Jesus Christ in the Book of Revelation in verses 17:14 and 19:16. -R. K.

temporal; do for me now also a favor, that thou may forever receive a recompense from Him that giveth great gifts."

And Narcia in answer saith, "What wilt thou, my daughter Mygdonia, and what is to be done for thy pleasure? For the honors which thou didst promise me before, the stranger hath not suffered thee to accomplish, and thou hast made me a reproach among all the nation. And now what is this new thing that you are commanding me?"

And Mygdonia saith:

"Become thou partaker with me in eternal life, that I may receive of thee perfect nurture: take bread and bring it me, and wine mingled with water, and spare my freedom, taking compassion on me as a freeborn woman of India."

And the nurse said, "I will bring thee many loaves, and for water flagons of wine, and fulfil thy desire."

But she saith to the nurse, "Flagons I desire not, nor the many loaves: but this only, bring wine mingled with water and one loaf, and oil, even so much as would be found in small lamp."

Chapter 108: Baptism of Mygdonia

And when Narcia had brought these things, Mygdonia stood before me with her head bare; and I took the oil and poured it on her head, saying, "Thou holy oil given unto us for sanctification, secret mystery whereby the cross was shown unto us, thou art the straightener of the crooked limbs, thou art the humbler that softens all the works of the hard-hearted ones, thou art it that shows the hidden treasures, thou art the sprout of goodness; let thy power come, let it be established upon thy servant Mygdonia, and heal thou her by this freedom."

And when the oil was poured upon her head, I bade her nurse unclothe her and gird a linen cloth about her; and there was there a fountain of water upon which I went up, and baptized Mygdonia in the name of the Father and the Son and the Holy Ghost. And when she was baptized and clad, I broke bread and took a cup of water and made her a partaker in the body of Christ and the cup of the Son of God, and said, "Thou hast received thy seal, get for thyself eternal life."

And immediately there was heard from above a voice saying, "Yea, amen."

And when Narcia heard that voice, she was amazed, and besought me that she also might receive the seal; and I gave it her and said, "Let the care of the Lord be about thee as about the rest. As with Mygdonia, ye shall find welcome now in the Assembly of the Church of the First-born."

Chapter 109: Thomas Returns to Prison on His Own Accord

And having done these things, I returned unto the prison, and found the doors open and the guards still sleeping. Beholding this amazing sight, I said, "Who is like Thee, O God, who withholds not Thy loving affection and care from any who is like Thee, the Merciful, the same Who hast delivered Thy creatures out of evil! Life that hath subdued death, rest that hath ended toil. Glory be to the Only Begotten of the Father! Glory to the Compassionate that was sent forth of His heart!"

And when he had said thus, the guards waked and beheld all the doors open, and the prisoners still asleep, and said in themselves, "Did not we fasten the doors? And, how are they now open, and the prisoners yet within?"

Chapter 110: Charisius Confronts His Wife

But at the dawn Charisius went unto Mygdonia and her nurse and found them praying and saying:

"O new God that by the stranger hast come hither unto us, hidden God of the dwellers in India; God that hast shown thy glory by thine apostle Thomas, God whose report we have heard and believed on Thee; God, unto whom we are come to be saved; God, who for love of man and for pity didst come down unto our littleness; God who didst seek us out when we knew Thee not; God that dwellest in the heights and from whom the depths are not hid: turn Thou away from us the madness of Charisius."

And Charisius hearing that, said to Mygdonia:

"Now you call me evil and mad and foul! But if I had not borne with thy disobedience, and given thee liberty, thou would not have called on God against me and made mention of my name before God. But believe me, Mygdonia, that in that sorcerer there is no profit; and what he promises to perform he cannot: but I will perform before thy sight all that I promise, that thou mayest believe, and bear with my words and be to me as thou were before this sorcerer came along."

Chapter 111: Mygdonia Bemoans Her Earthly Marriage

And Charisius came near and besought her again, saying, "If thou wilt be persuaded of me, I shall henceforth have no grief; remember that day when thou didst meet me first; tell the truth: was I more beautiful unto thee at that time, or Jesus at this?"

And Mygdonia said:

"That time required its own, and this time also; that was the time of the beginning, but this of the end; that was the time of temporal life, this of eternal; that of pleasure that passes away, but this of pleasure that abides forever; that, of day and night, this of day without night. Thou saw that marriage that was passing, but now this marriage will continue forever; that was a partnership of corruption, but this of eternal life; those groomsmen and maids were men and women of time, but these abide unto the end. That marriage was sanctioned by the authorities of this Earth; but this new one is founded upon the bridge of fire upon which only the holy may stand, full of grace and free of the corruption of this world; that bride-chamber is taken down again, but this remains always; that bed was strown with sheets that fade, but this with love and faith. Thou art a bridegroom that passes away and changes with circumstance, but Jesus is a true bridegroom, enduring forever, being immortal; that dowry was of money and robes that grow old, but this is of living words which never pass away."

Chapter 112: King Misdaeus Sends for the Apostle

And when Charisius heard the words of his wife, he went unto the king and told him all; and the king commanded for me, Judas Thomas, to be brought, that he might judge me and destroy me. But Charisius said, "Have patience a little, O king, and first persuade the man making him afraid, that he may persuade Mygdonia to be unto me as formerly."

And Misdaeus sent and fetched me, the apostle of Christ, and all the prisoners were grieved because I departed from them, for they yearned after me, saying, "Even the comfort which we had have they taken away from us."

Chapter 113: Thomas Defends His Teachings

And Misdaeus inquired of me, Judas Thomas, "Wherefore teaches thou this new doctrine, which both gods and men hate, and which hath nothing of profit?"

And I answered with a question, "What evil do I teach?"

And Misdaeus answered, "Thou teaches, saying that men cannot live holy and approved lives except with the God with whom ye proclaim."

To which I said: "Thou sayest true, O king: This I do teach. For tell me, art thou not wroth with thy soldiers if they wait on thee in filthy garments? If then, thou, being a king on Earth, request thy subjects to be circumspect in their doings, are ye wroth and said ye that I teach ill when I say that they who serve my king must be holy and pure and free from all grief and care of children and unprofitable riches and vain trouble? For indeed, thou would have thy subjects follow thy conversation and thy manners, and thou punish them if they despise thy commandments: how much more must they that believe on Him serve my God with much reverence and cleanness and security, and be quit of all idolatry, adultery and prodigality and theft and drunkenness and belly-service and foul deeds?"

Chapter 114: Thomas Refuses to Dissuade Mygdonia

And Misdaeus, hearing these things, said, "Lo, I let thee go. Go then and persuade Mygdonia, the wife of Charisius, not to desire to depart from him."

Therefore, I said unto him, "Delay not if thou hast something to do for her. For if she hath rightly received what she hath learned, neither iron nor fire nor aught else stronger than these will avail to hurt or to root out him that is held in her soul."

Then the king saith unto me, "Some poisons do dissolve other poisons, and an antidote cures the bites of the viper; and thou, if thou wilt, canst give a solvent of those diseases, and make peace and concord betwixt this couple: for by so doing, thou wilt spare thyself, for not yet art thou sated with life; and know thou that if thou do not persuade her, I will catch thee away out of this life which is desirable unto all men."

And I replied, "This life hath been given as a loan, and this time is one that changes; but that life whereof I teach is incorruptible; and beauty and youth that are seen shall in a little cease to be."

The king saith to me, "Very well, then. I have counselled thee for the best; but ye surely know the course to take in thine own affairs."

Chapter 115: Charisius Asks Thomas to Change His Mind

And as I, Judas Thomas, the appointed apostle of my brother Jesus, went forth from before the king, Charisius came to me and entreated me, saying:

"I beseech thee, O man: I have not sinned against thee or any other at any time, nor against the gods; wherefore hast thou stirred up this great calamity against me? And for what cause hast thou brought such disturbance upon my house? And what profit hast thou of it? But if you think to gain somewhat, tell me the gain, what it is, and I will procure it for thee without labor. To what end dost thou make me mad, and cast thyself into destruction? For if thou persuade her not, I will both dispatch thee and finally take myself out of life. But if, as thou sayest, after our departing hence, that there is life and death, and also condemnation and victory and a place of judgement, then will I also go in thither to be judged with thee: and if that God whom ye preach is just and awards punishment justly, I know that I shall gain my cause against thee; for thou hast injured me, having suffered no wrong at my hands: for indeed, even here I am able to avenge myself on thee and bring upon thee all that thou hast done unto me. Therefore, be thou persuaded, and come home with me and persuade Mygdonia to be with me as she was at first, before she beheld thee."

And I replied, "Believe me, my child, that if men loved God as much as they love one another, they would ask of him all things and receive them, and none would do them violence. Also, there would be no task asked by the Lord Jesus Christ that these believers would not do for the promulgation of His glory."

Chapter 116: Mygdonia Willingly Follows Thomas

And as I said this, we came unto the house of Charisius and found Mygdonia sitting and Narcia, her nurse attendant, standing by her, and her hand supporting her cheek. And Mygdonia was saying:

"Let the remainder of the days of my life be cut off from me, and all the hours become as one hour, and let me depart out of life that I may go the sooner and behold that Beautiful One, whose report I have heard, even that Living One and giver of life unto them that believe on Him, where is not day and night, nor light and darkness, nor good and evil, nor poor and rich, nor male and female, nor free and bond, nor proud that puts under subjection the humble."[166]

And as she spoke, I stood by her, and forthwith she rose up and did me reverence. Then Charisius said unto him, "See how she fears and honors thee and all that thou shalt bid her she will do willingly?"

Chapter 117: Charisius Decides on Course of Action

And I said unto Mygdonia, "My daughter Mygdonia, insofar as ye are not of the House of Israel, and that your life may go well with you, obey that which Charisius saith, should you find it in your heart to continue in your marriage with him.[167] Nevertheless, ye are free in Christ, an agent unto yourself in this matter."

---

166 That God shows no distinction between various peoples here on Earth, please see Romans 10:12, Colossians 3:11 and Galatians 3:28. -R. K.

167 Ephesians 5:22-24 (KJV): "Wives, submit yourselves unto your own husbands, as unto the Lord. For the husband is the head of the wife, even as Christ is the head of the church: and he is the savior of the body. Therefore, as the church is subject unto Christ, so let the wives be to their own husbands in everything." Clearly, Thomas understood that as a new Christian, Mygdonia was free in Christ to either submit to her husband's patriarchal authority, thereby leaving the door open to possibly convert him in the future, or to free herself of his pagan influence by divorcing or leaving Charisius. See 1 Corinthians 7:12-16 (KJV): "If any brother hath a wife that believeth not, and she be pleased to dwell with him, let him not put her away. And the woman which hath an husband that believeth not, and if he be pleased to dwell with her, let her not leave him. For the unbelieving husband is sanctified by the wife, and the unbelieving wife is sanctified by the husband: else were your children unclean; but now are they holy. But if the unbelieving depart, let him depart. A brother or a sister is not under bondage in such cases: but God hath called us to peace. For what knowest thou, O wife, whether thou shalt save thy husband? or how knowest thou, O man, whether thou shalt save thy wife?" At the beginning of this scripture, the Apostle Paul does remark that this is only his opinion, whereby the Christian is free to decide for his or herself the viability of continuing in a relationship with an unbelieving spouse. It seems that Thomas shared these sentiments as expressed by Paul.

And Mygdonia saith: "If thou were not able to name the deed in word will thou compel me to endure the act? For I have heard of thee that this life is of no profit, and this relief is for a time, and these possessions are transitory. And again, thou said that whoso renounces this life shall receive the life eternal, and whoso hates the light of day and night shall behold a light that is not overtaken, that whoso despises this money shall find other and eternal money. But now thou sayeth these things because thou art in fear. Who that hath done somewhat and is praised for the work now changes it? Ye who has built a tower straightway now overthrows it from the foundation? Ye who digs a spring of water in a thirsty land and straightway fills it in? Ye who finds a treasure and uses it not?"

And Charisius heard it and said, "I will not imitate you, neither will I hasten to destroy you; nor though I may so do, will I put bonds about thee; and I will not suffer thee to speak with this sorcerer; and if thou obey me, well, but if not, I know what I must do."

Chapter 118: Trepidation in the Preaching Work

And I went out of Charisius' house and departed unto the house of Siphor and lodged there with him. And Siphor said, "I will prepare for you a dwelling place to live and a hall wherein ye may continue to teach."

And Siphor did as he had said he would and declared, "I and my wife and daughter will dwell henceforth in holiness, and in one affection. I beseech thee that we may receive of thee the seal, and become worshippers of the true God and numbered among his sheep and lambs."

And I, Judas Thomas, said, "Due to the precarious circumstances that I find myself in, I am afraid to speak that which I really think: yet I know somewhat, and what I know it is not possible for me to utter at this time."

Chapter 119: Baptism of Siphor and His Family

Then I explained that this baptism is for the remission of sins:

"Once baptized, the heavens open above us and light is shed forth round about, bringing on the new birth in Christ Jesus. The Holy Ghost descends and mingles with the physical body. You arise from the water a new individual washed clean of sin. The Hidden One can now reveal Himself through your works of righteousness carried out among the inhabitants of this world. Glory to Thee, the Unseen Power that is in baptism! Glory to Thee that renews both spirit and body unto life eternal!"

Following these words, I poured oil over their heads and said, "Glory be to Thee, the Love of Compassion! Glory to Thee, the blessed name of Christ! Glory to Thee, the Power established in Christ!" Then I immediately walked with them down into the river and baptized them there in the name of the Father and the Son and the Holy Ghost.

Chapter 120: Common Meal Shared with Siphor and His Family

And when they were baptized and clad again in dry clothing, I set bread on the table and blessed it, and said:

"Bread of Life, that whosoever eats of it abides incorruptible: Bread that fills the hungry souls with the blessing thereof: Thou art Him that decrees for us to receive a gift, that Thou mayest become unto us the remission of sins, and that they who partake of Thee may become immortal: we invoke upon thee the name of the Divine Mother, of the unspeakable mystery of the hidden powers and authorities; and we search the unspeakable mystery whereby we invoke upon Thee the name of Jesus."

And then I declared, "Let the powers of blessing come, and be established in this bread, that all the souls which partake of it may be washed from their sins." And I broke the bread and gave it unto Siphor and his wife and daughter.

Chapter 121: King Tells of Charisius' Fate

Now Misdaeus the king, when he had let Judas go, dined and went home, and told his wife what had befallen Charisius their kinsman, saying:

"See what hath come to pass to that unhappy man, and thou thyself knows, my sister Tertia, that a man hath none better than his own wife on whom he relies; but it chanced that his wife went unto that sorcerer of whom thou hast heard that he is come to the land of the Indians, and fell into his charms and is parted now from her own husband; and he knows not what he should do. And when I would have destroyed the malefactor, but he would not have it. But do thou go and counsel her to incline unto her husband, and forsake the words of that sorcerer."

Chapter 122: Tertia Challenges Mygdonia

And as soon as she arose Tertia went to the house of Charisius, her husband's kinsman, and found Mygdonia lying upon the ground in humiliation; and ashes and sackcloth were spread under her. And Mygdonia was praying that the Lord would forgive her of her former sins and that she might soon depart out of this life. And Tertia said unto her, "Mygdonia, my dear sister and companion, what is this foolishness? What is the disease that hath overtaken thee? Why do you continue in the deeds of the insane? Know thyself and come back unto thine own way, come near unto thy many kinfolks, and spare thy true husband Charisius, and do not things unbefitting a free-woman."

Mygdonia saith unto her: "O Tertia, thou hast not yet heard the preacher of life: not yet hath he touched thine ears, not yet hast thou tasted the medicine of life nor art freed from corruptible mourning. Thou art standing in the life of time, and the everlasting life and salvation thou know not, and ye perceive not the incorruptible fellowship. Ye stand clad in robes that grow old and desire not those that are eternal, and art proud of this beauty which vanishes and hast no thought of the holiness of thy soul; and art rich in a multitude of servants; yet thou hast not freed thine own soul from servitude; and prides thyself in the glory that cometh of many, but redeems not thyself from the condemnation of death."

Chapter 123: Tertia Inquires of Jesus

And when Tertia heard this of Mygdonia she said, "I pray thee, sister, bring me unto that stranger that teaches these great things that I also may go and hear him, and be taught to worship the God whom he preaches, and become partaker of his prayers, and a sharer in all that thou hast told me of."

And Mygdonia saith to her, “He is in the house of Siphor the captain; for he is become the occasion of life unto all them that are being saved in India.”

And hearing that, Tertia went quickly to Siphor’s house, that she might see the new apostle that was come thither. And when she entered in, I, Judas Thomas, the Apostle of the Lord Jesus, said unto her:

“What art thou come to see- a man that is a stranger and poor and contemptible and needy, having neither riches nor substance? Yet one thing I possess which neither kings nor rulers can take away, that neither perishes not, is Jesus the Savior of all mankind, the Son of the Living God, who hath given life unto all that believe on him and take refuge with him and are known to be of the number of his servants.”

Then Tertia inquired of me, “May I become a partaker of this life which ye have promised that all they shall receive who come together unto the Assembly of God?”

And I replied:

“The treasury of the Holy King is opened wide, and they which worthily partake of the good things that are therein do rest, and resting do reign: but first, no man cometh unto Him that is unclean and vile: for He knows our inmost hearts and the depths of our thought, and it is not possible for any to escape Him. Thou, then, if verily thou believe in him, shalt be made worthy of his mysteries; and He will magnify thee and enrich thee, and make thee to be an heir of his kingdom.”

Chapter 124: Tertia Follows the Apostle, Too

And Tertia, having heard this, returned home rejoicing, and found her husband awaiting her, not having dined. And when Misdaeus saw her, he said, “Whence is it that thine entering in today is more beautiful? And wherefore art thou come walking, which seems unlike free-born women like thee?”

And Tertia saith unto him:

“I owe thee the greatest of thanks for that thou didst send me unto Mygdonia, for I went and heard of a new life, and I saw the new apostle of the God that giveth life unto them that believe on Him and fulfil His commandments; I ought, therefore, myself to recompense thee for this favor and admonition with good advice; for thou shalt be a great king in heaven if thou obey me and fear the God that is preached by the stranger, and keep thyself holy unto the living God. For this kingdom passes away, and thy comfort will be turned into affliction: but go thou to that man, and believe him, and thou shalt live unto the end."

And when Misdaeus heard these things of his wife, he smote his face with his hands and rent his clothes and said, "May the soul of Charisius find no rest, for he hath hurt me to the soul; and may he have no hope, for he hath taken away my hope." And he went out greatly vexed.

Chapter 125: King Rues Charisius' Mention of Thomas

And the king found Charisius his kinsman in the market-place, and said unto him:

"Why hast thou cast me into hell to be another companion like unto thyself? Why hast thou emptied and defrauded me to gain nothing? Why hast thou hurt me and profited thyself not at all? Why hast thou slain me and thyself not lived? Why hast thou wronged me and thyself not got justice? Why didst thou not suffer me to destroy that sorcerer before he corrupted my house with his wickedness?"

And he kept hold upon Charisius, upbraiding him for introducing the messenger of the Christian cult into his kingdom. And Charisius saith: "Why, what hath befallen thee?"

Misdaeus said: "Now he hath bewitched Tertia." And they went both of them unto the house of Siphor the captain, and found me sitting and teaching. And all they that were there rose up before the king, but I arose not. And Misdaeus perceived that it was me, and took hold of the seat and overset it, and took up the seat with both his hands and smote my head so that he wounded it, and delivered me to his soldiers, saying, "Drag him with violence that his shame may be manifest unto all men." And the king's guards dragged me off and took me to the place where Misdaeus would judge me, and there stood, held in custody by the guards of Misdaeus, awaiting his arrival.

Chapter 126: Thomas Admonishes Iuzanes the Prince

And Iuzanes, the son of Misdaeus the King, came unto the soldiers and said, "Give me that man, Judas Thomas, that I may speak with him until the king cometh." And they gave him up, and Iuzanes the Prince brought him in where the king gave judgement. And Iuzanes said, "Do you know that I am the son of Misdaeus the king, and I have power to say unto the king what I will, and he will suffer thee to live? Tell me then, who is thy God, and what power dost thou claim and glory in it? For if it be some power or art of magic, tell it to me and teach me, and I will let thee go."

Then I replied to Iuzanes:

"Yes, this I know. Thou art the son of Misdacus the king who is king for a time, but I am the servant of Jesus Christ the eternal king, and thou hast power to say to thy father to save whom thou wilt in the temporal life wherein men continue not, which thou and thy father grant, but I beseech my Lord and intercede for men, and he giveth them a new life which is altogether enduring. And ye boast of thyself possessions and servants and robes and luxury and unclean chamberings, but I boast myself of poverty and philosophy and humility and endurance of sufferings and prayer and the fellowship of the Holy Ghost and of my brethren that are worthy of God: and I boast myself of eternal life. And ye rely on the arm of flesh for refuge with a man like unto thyself and one not able to save his own soul from judgement and death, but I rely upon the living God, upon the Savior of kings and princes, who is the judge of all men. And ye indeed, today perchance are, and tomorrow are no more, but I have taken refuge with him that abides forever and knows all our seasons and times. And if thou wilt become the servant of this God thou shalt soon do so, too; but show that thou wilt be a servant worthy of Him hereby: first by holiness made manifest through living a pure life, which is the originator of all good things, and then by fellowship with this God whom I preach, and philosophy and simplicity and love and faith in the everlasting life to be found in Him, and the unity of the communion of His saints."

Chapter 127: Miracle Rescues Thomas from Torture

And the young prince was persuaded by the Lord and sought occasion how he might let me escape from the clutches of his father. But while he thought thereon, the king came, and the soldiers took me and led me forth. And Iuzanes went forth with me and stood beside me. And when the king was ready, he bade me be brought in, with my hands bound behind me; and I was brought into the midst and stood there.

And the king saith, "Tell me who thou art and by what power ye do these things."

And I said to him, "I am a man like thee, and by the power of Jesus Christ I do these things."

And Misdaeus, seeming quite frustrated, declared, "Tell me the truth before I destroy thee."

And I replied, "Thou hast no power against me, as ye suppose; and thou wilt not hurt me at all."

And now the king was angered by my words, and commanded his soldiers to heat iron plates and set me upon them barefoot; and as the soldiers took off my sandals, I said, "The wisdom of God is better than the wisdom of men. Thou Lord and King, do thou take counsel against them and forgive their thoughtless aggressions against me, your servant; and let Thy goodness resist his wrath." And they brought the plates which were like fire, and set me upon them; and straightway water sprang up abundantly from the ground, breaking through the very floor insomuch that the plates were swallowed up in it; and they that held me let me go and withdrew themselves in fear.

Chapter 128: Thomas Prays for His Persecutor

And the king seeing the abundance of water pleaded with me, "As His Apostle, ask thy God that He deliver me from this death, that I perish not in the flood."

And then I prayed:

"Thou that didst bind this element and gather it into one place, and sending forth this earthquake into this remote land; that didst bring disorder into order, that grants mighty works and great wonders by the hands of Judas thy servant; that hast mercy on my soul, that I may always receive of thy illumination; that gives wages unto them that have labored; thou savior of my soul, restoring it unto its own nature that it may have no fellowship with hurtful things; that hast always been the occasion of life: do thou restrain this element that it lift not up itself to destroy; for there are some of them that stand here who shall believe on thee and live."

And when I had thus prayed, the water was swallowed up little by little, and the place became dry again. And after Misdaeus beheld this wonder, he commanded me to be taken temporarily into custody in the prison, at least until such time as he could determine what should be done with me.

Chapter 129: Thomas Yearns to Be with Jesus Again

And as I, Judas Thomas, was led away to the prison they all followed me, and Iuzanes the king's son walked at my right hand, and Siphor at the left. And I entered into the prison and sat down, and Iuzanes and Siphor did as well; and I persuaded his wife and his daughter to sit down, for they also were come in to hear the words of life. For they knew that Misdaeus, despite the miracle that saved me and my prayer for the king, would slay me because of the excess of his anger. And then I began to say: O Liberator of my soul from the bondage of the many, because I gave myself to do the work for which Thou has sent me; behold, I rejoice and exult, knowing that the times are fulfilled for me to enter in and receive of Thee my rest. Lo, I am to be set free from the cares that are on this world. Lo, I fulfil mine hope and receive truth. Lo, I am set free from sorrow and put on joy alone. Lo, I become careless and griefless and dwell in rest. Lo, I am set free from bondage and am called unto liberty. Lo, I have served times and seasons, and I am lifted up above times and seasons. Lo, I receive my wages from my recompense who giveth without reckoning abundantly because his wealth is sufficient for the gift. Lo, and of my raiment, on and off put I, and I shall not put it on again. Lo, I sleep and awake, and I shall not more go to sleep. Lo, I die and live again, and I shall no more taste of death. Lo, they rejoice and expect me, that I may come and be with their kindred and be set as a flower in their crown. And lo, I reign in the kingdom whereon I set my hope, even from hence; lo, the rebellious fall before me, for I have escaped them. Lo, the peace of the Lord Jesus hath come unto me, whereunto all are gathered.

Chapter 130: Thomas' Revelation Inspires a Vision of the Christ

And as I spoke in this manner, all that were there hearkened, supposing that in that hour I would depart out of this life. And again, I exhorted all there, saying:

"Believe on the Physician who cures all illnesses, both seen and unseen, and on the Savior of the souls that need help from Him. This is the free-born son of kings; this the physician of his creatures; this is He, the one that was reproached of his own slaves; this is the Father of the heights and the Lord of nature and the Judge of all. Father of nature and Lord of the heights and the Supreme Judge, He came of the greatest, the only-begotten son of the deep; and he was called the son of God when the power of God became manifest through Him in the material world. His mother Mary and he was known as the son of Joseph the carpenter: he whose littleness we beheld with the eyes of our body, but his greatness we received by faith, and saw it in his works whose human body we felt also with our hands, and His divine aspect we saw transfigured with our eyes, but his heavenly semblance on the mount we were not able to see: He that made the rulers stumble and did violence unto death: He, the Truth that lieth not, that at the last paid the tribute for Himself and His disciples."

Upon hearing these words, the young prince and the others in my cell beheld an awesome vision of the divine presence of the Lord Jesus Christ. Iuzanes testified that he saw that the rulers of this world quaked before the Christ. Having beheld this great power and glory, Iuzanes and the others feared for the fate of the king and any of those in India who strove against the work to which I, the apostle, was called. Then the prince bare witness as to the holy and majestic presence of the Christ, who He was and from whence He came. For before the prince knew not the truth, because he was born in a land alien from truth, being filled with misguided ones falsely worshipping gods of wood and stone.

Iuzanes testified of his faith in the Lord Jesus Christ when he declared that, "He who has authority over the world, to include all of the pleasures found therein, along with all the possessions and comfort that goes with them, rejected these things and told his subjects to turn away from them as well, that we should not partake of them. I cannot speak for the rest of my house, but personally I will not use them. Rather, I shall follow the example of the Lord's apostle, Judas Thomas, and devote my time and energy to the service of the poor and all in need of assistance."

Chapter 131: Thomas Teaches His Friends to Pray

Following this marvelous vision of the prince, I arose and prayed thus, "Our Father, which art in heaven: hallowed be Thy name: Thy kingdom come: Thy will be done, as in heaven so upon Earth. Give us this day our sustenance, and forgive us our debts as we also have forgiven our debtors. And lead us not into temptation, but deliver us from the evil one."[168]

Chapter 132: Thomas Prays for the Lord Jesus' Intervention

Then I continued in prayer, beseeching the aide of my brother from the celestial realms:

"My Lord and God, hope and confidence and teacher, Thou hast taught me to pray thus, behold, I pray this prayer and fulfil Thy commandment: be Thou with me unto the end; Thou art He that from childhood hast sown life in me and kept me from corruption; Thou art He that hast brought me unto the poverty of this world, and exhorted me unto the true riches; thou art He that hast made me known unto myself and showed me that I am thine; and I have kept myself pure from woman for the period of my appointed ministry, that that which Thou requires of me be not found in defilement.

"My mouth ceases not to praise Thee, neither am I able to conceive the care and providence which hath been about me from Thee which Thou hast had for me. For I desired to gain riches, but Thou by a vision didst show me that they are full of loss and injury to them that gain them and I believed Thy showing, and continued in the poverty of the world until Thou, the true riches wert revealed unto me, who didst fill both me and the rest that were worthy of Thee with Thine own riches and set free thine own from care and anxiety. I have therefore fulfilled Thy commandments, O Lord, and accomplished Thy will, and become poor and needy and a stranger and a bondman and set at naught and a prisoner and hungry and thirsty and naked and unshod, and I have toiled for Thy sake, that my confidence might not perish and my hope that is in Thee might not be confounded and my much labor might not be in vain and my weariness not be counted for nothing: let not

168 Matthew 6:9-13 (KJV): Jesus reveals the "Lord's Prayer."

my prayers and my continual fasting perish, and my great zeal toward Thee; let not my seed of wheat be changed for tares out of Thy land, Let not the enemy carry it away and mingle his own tares therewith; for Thy land verily receives not his tares, neither indeed can they be laid up in Thine houses.

"I have planted Thy vine in the earth, it hath sent down its roots into the depth and its growth is spread out in the height, and the fruits of it are stretched forth upon the earth, and they that are worthy of Thee are made glad by them, whom also Thou hast gained. The money which Thou hast from me I laid down upon in savings; this, when thou require it, restore unto me with usury, as Thou hast promised. With Thy one mind have I traded and have made ten, Ye hast added more to me beside that I had, as Thou didst covenant. I have forgiven my debtor what was owed to me, require Thou it not at my hands. I was bidden to the supper and I came: and I refused the land and the yoke of oxen and the wife, that I might not for their sake be rejected; I was bidden to the wedding, and I put on white raiment, that I might be worthy of it and not be bound hand and foot and cast into the outer darkness. My lamp with its bright light expects the master coming from the marriage, that it may receive him, and may I not see it dimmed because the oil is spent. Mine eyes, O Christ, look upon Thee, and mine heart exults with joy because I have fulfilled Thy will and perfected Thy commandments; that I may be likened unto that watchful and careful servant who in his eagerness neglects not to keep vigil. I have not slumbered idly in keeping Thy commandments; for all the night have I laboured to keep mine house from robbers, lest it be broken through.

"My loins have I girt close with truth and bound my shoes on my feet, that I may never see them gaping: mine hands have I put unto the yoked plough and have not turned away backward, lest my furrows go crooked. The plough-land is become white and the harvest is come, that I may receive my wages. My garment that grows old I have worn out, and the labor that hath brought me unto rest have I accomplished. I have kept the first watch and the second and the third, that I may behold Thy face and adore Thine holy brightness. I have rooted out the worst, delipidated structures, and left them desolate upon earth, that I may be filled full from thy treasures; and all my substance have I sold, that I may gain Thee the pearl. The moist spring that was in me have I dried up, that I may live and rest beside Thine inexhaustible spring whose living waters grant perpetual life. Him that was inward have I made outward and the outward have I made inward, and all Thy fullness hath been fulfilled in me. I have not returned unto the things that are behind, but have gone forward unto the things that are before, that I become not a reproach. The dead man have I quickened, and the living one have I overcome, and that which was lacking have I filled up, that I may receive the crown of victory, and the power of Christ may be accomplished in me. I have received the reproach of this world, but give thou me the return and the recompense in Thy celestial realm on high.

"Let not the powers and the officers perceive me, and let them not have any thought concerning me; let not the publicans and exactors ply their calling upon me; let not the evil cry out against me that am valiant and humble, and when I am borne upward let them not rise up to stand before me, by Thy power, O Jesus, my brother and Lord, which surrounds me as a crown: for they do flee and hide themselves, they cannot look on Thee. Do Thou then grant me, Lord, that I may pass by in quietness and joy and peace, and pass over and stand before the judge, and let not the devil, that accuser of the saints, look upon me; let his eyes be blinded by Thy light which Thou hast made to dwell in me, effectively closing up thou up his mouth: for he hath found nothing against me."

Chapter 133: Manifestation of the Christ

And I said again unto them that were about me:

"Believe now in the Firstborn of All Creation, of Whom I am of but one of His servants and Whose life I preach and whose message I proclaim. Children, believe in the Savior of them that have labored in His service: for my soul already flourishes because my time is near to be received of Him; for He, being beautiful, draws me on always to speak concerning his beauty, what it is though I be not able and suffice not to speak it worthily."

Then an orb of intense light filled the room and a voice emerged from that light, saying:

"Judas Thomas, thou art my beloved brother and valiant disciple. I have been, and will forever be, that light that illumines your walk through this life in this lone and dreary world, until such time as I receive you into the kingdom of the Father of Lights, the Father to us all. The poverty you have endured will soon come to an end; and any perceived defects will be overlooked, for great will be your reward. You have done well, my good and faithful brother in the light. When you see me next, I come to receive thee forevermore and to escort thee into your mansion in Barbelo,[169] one of the heavenly worlds I have spoken of, the one in closest proximity to the Father of Lights."

All in the room heard the voice in their own language, falling down to the floor and prostrating themselves before the Living Light, the manifestation of the Christ.

Chapter 134: Iuzanes Wants Thomas to Heal His Ill Wife

And Iuzanes the young prince besought me, saying:

"I pray thee, O man, apostle of God, suffer me to go, and I will persuade the jailer to permit thee to come home with me, that by thee I may receive the seal, and become thy minister and a keeper of the commandments of the God whom you preach. For indeed, formerly I walked in those things which thou taught, until my father compelled me and joined me unto a wife by the name of Mnesara; for I am in my one-and-twentieth year, and have now been seven years married. And before I was joined in marriage, I knew no other woman, wherefore also I was accounted useless of my father; nor have I ever had son or daughter of this wife; and also my wife herself hath lived with me in chastity all this time, and today, if she had been in health, and had listened to thee, I know well that both of us should have been content and she would have received eternal life; but she is in peril and afflicted with much illness; I will therefore persuade the keeper that he promise to come with me, for I live by myself: and thou shalt also heal that unhappy one."

And I, Judas Thomas, the Apostle of the Most-High, hearing this, said to Iuzanes, "If you believe that you shall see the marvels of God, as such He will carry out on behalf of His servants."

169 Realm of the "Self-Generated Ones" or Aeons, the First Emanations of the Divine in the material universe. -R. K.

Chapter 135: Christians Locked Up in Royal Compound

And as I was speaking to Iuzanes, Tertia and Mvgdonia and Narcia stood at the door of the prison, and between them they had given 363 staters of silver to the jailer and entered into the cell block to visit with me; and found Iuzanes and Siphor and his wife and daughter, and all the prisoners sitting and hearing the words of the Lord Jesus Christ that I was preaching. And when they stood by me, I said to them, "Who hath suffered you to come unto us? And who opened unto you the sealed door that ye came forth?"

Tertia said, "Now the king had locked us up in the palace compound, but didst not thou speak to us from behind the sealed door and tell us to come into the prison that we might take our brethren that were there, and then should the Lord show forth his glory in us? And when we came near the door, I know not how, it was unsealed and thou had greeted us and remained with us for a while to comfort us, yet parted from us and hid thyself and came hither ahead of us. Thus, we came here immediately and we gave money therefore to the keepers and came in and lo, we are here praying thee that we may persuade thee and let thee escape until the king's wrath against thee shall cease."

"How did the king lock you up?" I inquired.

Chapter 136: Details of the Escape

And she continued, somewhat puzzled:

"Don't you know? After all, you never left us for the space of one hour after we walked out of the open door of our compound. But if you want to hear about again, hear. The king Misdaeus sent for me and said unto me, 'Not yet hath that sorcerer prevailed over thee, for, as I hear, he bewitches men with oil and water and bread, and hath not yet bewitched thee; but obey thou me, for if not, I will imprison thee and wear thee out, and him I will destroy; for I know that if he hath not yet given thee oil and water and bread, he hath not prevailed to get and exercise power over you.'

"And I said unto him: Over my body thou hast authority, and do thou all that thou wilt; but my soul I will not let perish with thee. And hearing that he shut me up in a chamber beneath his dining hall in the compound: and Charisius brought Mygdonia and shut her up with me:

and thou liberated and didst bring us even hither; but give thou us the seal quickly, that the hope of Misdaeus who wants to kill you may be cut off."

Chapter 137: The Liberator Revealed

And when I heard this, I said, "Glory be to thee, O Jesus of many forms, glory to thee that appears in the guise of our poor manhood: glory to thee that encourages us and makes us strong and gives grace and consoles and stands by us in all perils, and strengthens our weakness." And as I said this, the jailer came and said, "Put out the lamps, lest any accuse you unto the king."

And then they extinguished the lamps, and turned to sleep; but I spoke unto the Lord, "It is the time now, O Jesus, for thee to make haste; for, lo the children of darkness have engulfed us in their own darkness; do thou therefore enlighten us with the light of thy nature." And on a sudden, the whole prison was light as the day; and while all they that were in the prison slept a deep sleep, they only that had believed in the Lord continued awake.

Chapter 138: Mnesara Guided by a Boy

Upon hearing this, I said to Iuzanes, "Go thou before and make ready the things for our need."

Iuzanes inquired, "And who will open me the doors of the prison? As of now, the jailers shut them and are gone to sleep."

And I replied, "Believe in Jesus, and thou shalt find the doors open." And when he went forth and departed from them, all the rest followed after him. And as Iuzanes was gone on before, Mnesara his wife met him coming unto the prison. As it was dark outside, they did not immediately recognize one another.

But after they recognized each other, Iuzanes said unto her, "Whither walks thou, especially at so late an hour? And how were you able to rise up?"

And she said, "This youth laid his hand on me and raised me up, and in a dream, he said that I should go with him where the stranger sits, that the perfection of my body might be made perfect."

Iuzanes saith to her, "What youth is with thee?"

And she said, "Can't you see that is here on my right hand, leading me by the hand?"

Chapter 139: Jesus Working Behind the Scenes

And while they were speaking together thus, I, along with Siphor and his wife and daughter and Tertia and Mygdonia and Narcia, came unto Iuzanes' house. And Mnesara the wife of Iuzanes, upon seeing me, did reverence and said, "Art thou come that saves us from the sore disease? Thou art he whom I saw in the night delivering unto me this youth to bring me to the prison. But thy goodness suffered me not to grow weary, but thou thyself art come unto me."

And saying this, she turned about and saw the youth no more; and finding him not, she saith to me, "I am not able to walk alone: for the youth whom thou gavest me is not here."

And then I assured her that, "Jesus will henceforth lead thee." And thereafter she came running unto him. And when they entered into the house of Iuzanes, the son of Misdaeus the king, though it was yet night, a great golden light shined and was shed about them.

Chapter 140: Baptismal Prayer

And then I began to pray and to speak thus:

"O companion and defender and hope of the weak and confidence of the poor: refuge and lodging of the weary: voice that came forth of the height: comforter dwelling in the midst: port and harbor of them that pass through the regions of the rulers: physician that heals without payment: who among men was crucified for many: Who didst go down into the realm of the dead with great might: the sight of whom the princes of death endured not; and Thou came up with great glory, and gathering all them that fled unto thee didst prepare a way, and in thy footsteps all they journeyed whom thou didst redeem; and Thou brought them into thine own fold and didst join them with thy sheep: son of mercy, the son that for love of man was sent unto us from the perfect world of Barbelo, that is above, the Lord of all pure possessions that serves thy servants that they may live: that fills creation with thine own riches: the poor, that was in need and didst hunger forty days: that satisfies thirsty souls with Thine own good things; be Thou with Iuzanes the son of Misdaeus and with Tertia and Mnesara, and gather them into Thy fold and mingle them with Thy number. Be unto them a guide in the land of error: be unto them a physician in the land of sickness: be unto them a rest in the land of the weary: sanctify them in a polluted land: be their physician both of bodies and souls: make them holy temples of Thee, and let thine Holy Spirit dwell in them."

Chapter 141: Baptism of the New Christians

Having thus prayed over them, I said unto Mygdonia, "Unclothe thy sisters."

And she took off their clothes and girded them with girdles and brought them: but Iuzanes had first gone before, and they came after him; and I took oil in a cup of silver and prayed thus over it: "Fruit more beautiful than all other fruits, unto which none other whatsoever may be compared: altogether merciful: fervent with the force of the word: power of the tree which men putting upon them overcome their adversaries: crowner of the conquerors: help and joy of the sick: that didst announce unto men their salvation that shows light to them that are in darkness; whose leaf is bitter, but in thy most sweet fruit thou art fair, that art rough to the sight but soft to the taste; seeming to be weak, but in the greatness of thy strength able to bear the power that beholds all things."

Having thus prayed, I continued: O Jesus, that Thou would let Thine victorious might come and be established in this oil, like as it was established in the tree that was its kin, even Thine might at that time, whereof they that crucified Thee could not endure the word: let the gift also come whereby breathing upon Thine enemies Thou didst cause them to go backward and fall headlong and let it rest on this oil, whereupon we invoke Thine holy name."

And having thus said, I poured it first upon the head of Iuzanes and then upon the women's heads, saying, "In thy name, O Jesus Christ, let it be unto these souls for the remission of sins and for the turning back of the adversary and for the salvation of their souls." And I commanded Mygdonia to anoint them but I, myself, anointed Iuzanes. And having anointed them we led them down into the water in the name of the Father and the Son and the Holy Ghost.

Chapter 142: Mysterious Voice

And when they were come up, I took bread and a cup, and blessed it and said:

"Thine holy body which was crucified for us do we eat, and thy blood that was shed for us unto salvation do we drink; let therefore thy body be unto us salvation and thy blood for remission of sins. And for the gall which Thou didst drink for our sakes let the gall of the devil be removed from us: and for the vinegar which Thou hast drunk for us, let our weakness be made strong: and for the spitting which Thou didst receive for us, let us receive the dew of thy goodness: and by the reed wherewith they smote Thee for us, let us receive the perfect house: and whereas Thou received a crown of thorns for our sake, let us that have loved Thee put on a crown that fades not away; and for the linen cloth wherein Thou was wrapped, let us also be girt about with Thy power that is not vanquished and for the new tomb and the burial let us receive renewing of soul and body: and for that Thou didst rise up and revive, let us revive and live and stand before Thee in righteous judgement."

And I brake and shared the common meal unto Iuzanes and Tertia and Mnesara and the wife and daughter of Siphor and said: "Let these elements of the common meal be unto you for salvation and joy and health of your souls."

And they said: "Amen."

And a voice was heard, coming out of the air, as it were, and saying: "Amen. Fear ye not, but only believe."

Chapter 143: Parting Words for the Women

And after these marvelous things, I, Judas Thomas, departed to be imprisoned.

And Tertia with Mygdonia and Narcia also went to be imprisoned. And I said unto them, with the multitude of them that had believed being present:

"Daughters and sisters and fellow-servants which have believed in my Lord and God, ministers of my Jesus, hearken to me this day: for I do deliver my word unto you, and I shall no more speak with you in this flesh nor in this world; for I go up unto my Lord and God Jesus Christ, unto Him that sold me, unto that Lord that humbled himself even unto me the little, and brought me up unto eternal greatness, that vouchsafed to me to become His servant in truth and steadfastness: unto Him do I depart, knowing that the time is fulfilled, and the day appointed hath drawn near for me to go and receive my recompense from my Lord and God: for He that provides my recompense is righteous, Whom best knows me, how I ought to receive my reward; for He is not grudging nor envious, but is rich in His gifts; He is not miserly in that he giveth, for he hath confidence in His possessions which cannot fail."

Chapter 144: Look Forward for Jesus' Return

I, Judas Thomas, continued with my exhortations:

"I am not Jesus, but I am His servant: I am not Christ, but I am His minister; I am not the Son of God, but I pray to become worthy of God. Continue ye in the faith of Christ: continue in the hope of the Son of God: faint not at affliction, neither be divided in mind if ye see me mocked or that I am shut up in prison; or even that thou witness my execution; for I do accomplish His will. For if I had willed not to die, I know in Christ that I am able thereto: but this which is called death, is not death, but a setting free from the body; wherefore I receive gladly this setting free from the body, that I may depart and see Him that is beautiful and full of mercy, Him that is to be loved: for I have endured much toil in His service, and have labored for His grace that is come upon me, which departs not from me. Let not Satan, then, enter you by stealth and catch away your thoughts: let there be in you no place for him: for He is mighty whom ye have received."

Then, drawing attention to my own appearance, I continued, "Look for the coming of Christ, for He shall come and receive you, and this is how He shall appear, He Whom ye shall see, when He cometh, for I am his twin brother born but minutes after Him."

Chapter 145: Pessimism Prevails

When I had ended these sayings, we all went into the house, and I prayed, "Savior that didst suffer many things for us, let these doors be as they were and let seals be set on them." And then I left them and went to be imprisoned: and they wept and were in heaviness, for they were sore afraid that Misdaeus would have me killed.

Chapter 146: Prison Found Secure

And I found the keepers wrangling and saying, "Wherein have we sinned against this wizard, for by his art magic he hath opened the doors and would have had all the prisoners escape? But now let us go and report it unto the king, and tell him concerning his wife and his son."

And as they disputed thus, I held my peace. They rose up early, therefore, and went unto the king and said unto him, "Our lord and king, do thou take away that sorcerer and cause him to be shut up elsewhere, for we are not able to keep him; for except thy good fortune had kept the prison, all the condemned persons would have escaped, for now, this second time have we found the doors open: and see for thyself, also that thy wife, O king, and thy son and the rest depart not from him."

And the king, hearing that, went, and found the seals that were set on the doors whole; and he took note of the doors also, and said to the keepers: "Wherefore lie ye? For behold, the seals are whole. How said ye that Tertia and Mygdonia come unto him into the prison?"

And the keepers said, "We have told thee the truth."

Chapter 147: Jesus' Power Transcends Death

And Misdaeus the king went to the prison and took his seat, and sent for me, Judas Thomas, the apostle of the Lord Jesus Christ, and stripped me. Then he had me girded with a girdle, setting me before him and saith unto me, "Art thou bond or free?"

I replied that, "I am the bondsman of one only, over whom thou hast no authority."

And Misdaeus saith to me, "How didst thou run away and come into this country?"

And I explained, "I was sold hither by my master, that I might save many, and by thy hands depart out of this world."

And Misdaeus said, "Who then is thy lord? And what is his name? And of what country is he?"

And I answered, "My Lord is thy master and He is Lord of Heaven and Earth."

And Misdaeus queried, "What is his name? Perhaps I know of him."

And I said, "Thou canst not hear His true name at this time, for it of an angel: but the name that was given unto him is Jesus the Christ, which in my language signifies that He is the anointed one."

And Misdaeus saith unto me, "I have not made haste to destroy thee, but have had long patience with thee: but thou hast added unto thine evil deeds, and thy sorceries are dispersed abroad and heard of througout all the country: but this I do that thy sorceries may depart with thee, and our land be cleansed from them."

And I, Judas Thomas saith unto him:

"These sorceries that you accuse me of are not brought about by the power of any evil spirits; and I assure you that such will not cease in the land when I set forth hence, for I will continue to work on behalf of God's people from the other side of the veil. And you should know this very day that I and Jesus, my master, shall never forsake them that are here, believing as they are in His mighty power made manifest through the Holy Ghost."

Chapter 148: King Misdaeus' Order

When I, Judas Thomas the apostle, had said these things, Misdaeus considered how he should put me to death; for he was afraid because of the much people that were followers of me, for many also of the nobles and of them that were in authority believed on the message of hope that I delivered. He took me, therefore and went forth out of the city; and armed soldiers also went along. And the people supposed that the king desired to learn somewhat of me, and they stood still and gave heed. And when we had walked one mile, he delivered me unto four soldiers and an officer, and commanded them to take me into a high mountain and there pierce me with spears and put an end to my life, and afterwards return again to the city. And saying thus unto the soldiers, he himself also returned unto the city, thinking that he would finally be rid of me.

Chapter 149: Abiding Words

But the men ran after me, desiring to deliver me from death. And two soldiers went at my right hand and two on my left, holding spears, and the officer held my hand and supported me. And then I said:
"O the hidden mysteries which even until our departure that are accomplished in us! O riches of His glory, Him that will not suffer us to be swallowed up in this passion of the body! Four are they that cast me down, but one now draws me, for of one I am, and unto Him I go."

And being come up into the mountain unto the place where I was to be slain, I said unto them that held me, and to the rest, "Brethren, hearken unto me now at the last; for I am come to my departure out of the body. Let not then the eyes of your heart be blinded, nor your ears be made deaf. Believe on the God whom I preach, and be not guides unto yourselves in the hardness of your heart, but walk in all your liberty, and in the glory that is toward men, and the life that is toward God."

Chapter 150: Thomas Prays for the Work of the Ministry

And then I spoke unto Iuzanes:

"Thou son of the earthly king Misdaeus and minister to me, the apostle and minister of our Lord Jesus Christ: give unto the servants of Misdaeus their price that they may suffer me to go and pray." And Iuzanes persuaded the soldiers to let me go and pray. And then I departed for a corner of the prison grounds apart from the guards, knelt down in reverence to our Heavenly King Jesus, then rose up and stretched forth my hands unto the heavens, and voiced the following:

"My Lord and my God, and hope and redeemer and leader and guide in all countries, be Thou with all them that serve Thee, and guide me this day as I come unto Thee. Let not any take my soul which I have committed unto Thee: let not the publicans see me, and let not the exactors accuse me falsely. Let not the serpent see me, and let not the children of the dragon hiss at me. Behold, Lord, I have accomplished Thy work and perfected Thy commandment. I have become a bondman; therefore, today do I receive my freedom. Do Thou therefore give me this and perfect me: and this I say, not for that I doubt, but that they may hear for whom it is needful to hear, and to prepare the way for other messengers who shall surely follow in my stead; and this I ask in Thy holy name."

Chapter 151: Death of Thomas

And when I had thus prayed, I called out to where the guards were stationed and spoke unto them, "Come hither and accomplish the commandments of him that sent you." And the four came and pierced me with their spears; and as for the life to which I was called in this world, I fell down and died.

My spirit having now penetrated that veil that separates our world from the countless kingdoms of Jesus and His Heavenly Father, I watched events immediately unfold on Earth with my spiritual eyes, those new eyes that can see beyond the limits imposed on them while living in this terrestrial sphere. Yet none could see me, for I was as a ghost. And all the Saints that were with me in the prison compound remained there and wept; and later in the day some of the faithful ones brought beautiful robes and much and fair linen to wrap my body and bury it in a royal sepulchre wherein the former kings of these southern Indian lands were laid. None dared object to this at the insistence of Iuzanes, the prince whose voice would count for much in dissuading future opposition to the work of the ministry.

Chapter 152: Ministry of an Angel

But Siphor and Iuzanes would not go down to the city, but continued sitting by my corpse all the day. And then I condensed, as it were, those particles that formed my ethereal body into a more solid but still luminous form, the which I could and did appear unto these dear Indian friends. "Why sit ye here and keep watch over me?" I inquired of them, adding that, "Know ye now that I am not here in the material world, but I have gone up and received all that I was promised. But rise up and go down hence; for after a little time ye also shall be gathered unto me."

But Misdaeus and Charisius took away Mygdonia and Tertia and afflicted them sorely: howbeit they consented not unto their will. Therefore, I appeared unto them and said, "Be not deceived: Jesus the Holy, the Living God, shall quickly send help unto you." And Misdaeus and

Charisius, when they perceived that Mygdonia and Tertia obeyed them not, suffered them to live according to their own desire.

Now it came to pass after a long time that one of the children of Misdaeus the king was smitten by a devil, and no man could cure him, for the devil was exceeding fierce. And Misdaeus the king took thought and said, "I will go and open the sepulcher, and take a bone of the apostle of God and hang it upon my son and he shall be healed. But while Misdaeus thought upon this, I appeared to him and said unto him, "Thou believes not on a living man, and wilt thou believe on the dead? Yet fear not, for my Lord Jesus Christ hath compassion on Thee and shows pity on thee out of His goodness."

And he went and opened the sepulcher, but found not my body there, for one of the brethren had stolen it away and taken it unto Mesopotamia; but from that place where my bones been lain, Misdaeus took dust and put it about his son's neck, saying, "I now believe on thee, Jesus Christ, seeing the good that your disciples have demonstrated throughout the land. And I repent that I persecuted your Apostle and saints." And when he had placed some fragment of bone that he had recovered from the dust upon his son, the lad became whole, the devil having gone out of him.

Misdaeus the king therefore was also gathered among the brethren, and bowed his head under the hands of Siphor the priest; and Siphor said unto the brethren: Pray ye for Misdaeus the king, that he may obtain mercy of Jesus Christ, and that he may remember no more the evil against him perpetrated. They all therefore, with one accord rejoicing, made prayer for him; and the Lord that loveth men, the King of Kings and Lord of Lords, granted Misdaeus also to have hope in Him; and he was gathered with the multitude of them that had believed in Christ, glorifying the Father and the Son and the Holy Ghost, whose is power and adoration, now and forever and world without end.

And those Saints of India, constituting the Assembly of the Church of the Firstborn, gathered together and rejoiced in the grace of the Holy Ghost. It should be known that before I departed out of the material world to be with my dear brother Jesus in the Realms of Barbelo, a sphere of light in the center of a vast multitude of stars, that I did ordain Siphor a presbyter and Iuzanes a deacon in the assembly. This was right before I went up into the mountains to die. But I and my brother Jesus, the Lord, with a great love in our hearts for the people of these southern lands, did work with Siphor and Iuanes to prosper the Assembly and many were added unto the faith in accordance to their belief and the illumination revealed through the ministerial leaders by the power of the Holy Ghost.

It was to Siphor and Iuzanes that I did appear on many occasions to reveal these acts of my apostleship. It is my sincerest desire that these disciples of our Lord Jesus the Christ will accurately convey my words to all who read or hear them, just as I have spoken and delivered them unto these my servants, to whom they were entrusted. For these are the words that testify of Jesus and lead to life eternal. It is I, Judas Thomas, an apostle and now an angel of the Lord, who now bids you all peace in the one name that redeems and saves us all, on worlds without end, that of my dearest brother, Jesus the Christ. Amen.

Gospel of Mary Magdalene

Mary Magdalene appreciates Thomas' defense of her role as the sole female apostle in his gospel.

In the weeks following his resurrection, Jesus appeared to his disciples both individually and assembled together on numerous occasions, imparting to them a knowledge of the nature of the material world and also of the higher worlds in the spiritual realm of the Pleroma. I, Mary of Magdala, the only woman called by Jesus, the Holy One of Israel, to be numbered among his apostles, provide now my testament of his words and teachings for the edification of the saints in Jerusalem and scattered throughout the nations:

One evening, as the apostles were roasting some fish and breaking bread along the banks of the Jordan river, Jesus appeared in their midst, but assuming a much younger appearance. The apostles were praying and initially did not recognize that it was Jesus, when he entered their camp. Jesus laughed and said, "Fear not, friends. It is I, Jesus."

Peter was the first to recognize him, rise and welcome Jesus. "It is so good to see you again, Master," he said, embracing and kissing Jesus. Then the other apostles rose, embracing and kissing Jesus as well. The apostles then inquired of Jesus, "Master, where did you go and what did you do there, after you left us?"

"The Father of Lights regenerated my soul and carried me away to the celestial realm of Barbelo, where all stand immortal before Him. Barbelo is but one of the kingdoms of the Father far beyond the Sun and even the stars. It is populated with innumerable concourses of angels, to which I could see no end. These great ones are holy and perfected beings. Only those who have been purged of the impurities of the material realm can pass by the angelic sentries that guard the gates of Barbelo."

Then the apostles wanted to know how they could purge themselves of these material pollutions, and Jesus explained that, "One begins this process by setting aside their unbelief. Being thus quickened in the spirit, the seeker opens their spiritual eyes to the reality of the Flame of Truth that dwells in their heart. No longer relying on the arm of flesh, and having dispelled the darkness, this one henceforth finds themself among the ranks of the awakened.

"Those consumed by the darkness have never found the Flame of Truth that abides in every one who cometh into the world. These are the ones who have been blinded by their unbelief, ignorantly rejecting the Divine Light granted them from above. There are none so blind as those who will not see.

"Those who continue to stumble in the darkness do so because they love darkness rather than light. The minds of these pathetic, misdirected, blind ones are still focused on the lures of the material world. Having filled their minds with earthly wisdom and scholarly, mortal knowledge, their blindness has manifoldly increased as to those spiritual matters important to godliness. This blindness of mind was brought on themselves through their great wickedness of unbelief, whereby they cannot behold the things of the Spirit, but only the tangible, gross, physical things of the flesh, which is to say only those things to which their five weak mortal senses bear witness.

"No one can possibly turn their heart to God fully without discovering the Flame of Truth that dwells within them. That is the Flame that contains all power, truth and love that will heal the blindness of their mind. The Flame of Truth contains all that is required to cleanse and purify any individual, directing their life to a path of peace, power and fulfillment, thereby bringing about their redemption while securing a place for them in the celestial realms of the Father of Lights."

Upon hearing these wondrous teachings, Peter wanted to know if the material world would cease to exist when the Kingdom of the Father was established. In answer to Peter's inquiry, Jesus said, "All natures, formations and creatures owe their existence to being first called forth in the spiritual realms. All of these, no matter how diverse they outwardly appear, are intimately connected on the spiritual plane. Therefore, when the material world ceases to exist, all of these will return to their appropriate spiritual foundation."

Peter was grateful to the Master for the revelations of the eternal realms that he provided to him and the other apostles. Then Peter had another question for Jesus: "Please tell us, Master, what constitutes sin in the world?"

Jesus said, "There is no sin, per se, to be found in the natural order of the world. But when we stray from the illumined path by committing adultery or other actions contrary to the Decalogue, we retard our own spiritual progress. For this reason, it pleased the Father of Lights to send me to this world, to awaken you to the presence of His Flame of Truth that abides in your heart. I came into your midst to set a torch before you and reset your feet upon the illumined path.

"Those not finding the Flame of Truth have been buffeted by disturbances to their natural body. This is why they have experienced sickness and eventually death. But take courage, dear souls, for those abiding in the Spirit will live forever; and some of you that are here with me this day, much like Enoch of old, will be taken up bodily into the Kingdom of our Father.

"Those who have ears to hear, let them hear."

After the Blessed One had spoken these words, he further said his apostles, "Peace be with you. Receive my peace to yourselves. Beware that no one lead you astray, saying 'Lo here!' or 'Lo there!' for the Son of Man is within you. Follow after him! Those who seek him will find him. Go then; and preach the gospel of the Kingdom. Do not lay down any rules beyond that which I have appointed for you; and do not give a law like the lawgiver, lest you be constrained by it."

And when he had said this, Jesus departed from us, stepping, as it were, into a column of light that beamed down from the clouds, and disappearing therein. Then we all wept greatly, asking ourselves, "How shall we go forth unto the peoples of the nations and preach the gospel of the Kingdom of the Son of Man? Insofar as the gentiles did not spare the Master's life, how will they spare us?"

Then I stood up in the midst of the apostles, greeted them all and said to these, my brethren, "Do not weep and do not grieve, nor be irresolute, for His grace will be entirely with you, and protect you. But rather, let us praise His greatness; for he has prepared us, empowering us with His Spirit from above, to the accomplishment of mighty deeds." And after I had spoken these the His Spirit. The hearts of my brethren then turned to the Good and they began to discuss the words of the Savior.

Then Peter, speaking on behalf of the apostles, said to me, "Mary, dear sister, we know that the Master loved you above all women. Please tell us the words of Jesus which you remember, those words that you know and cherish, but which we have no knowledge of, the words that we have never heard him speak.

I answered Peter thusly: "Very well, Peter, what has been hidden from you and the brethren, I will now make known to you."

At first, I was hesitant to reveal these great truths, not that they are so much a secret, but of a sacred nature. But insofar as Peter and the apostles were his closest friends, I proceeded to tell them of the marvelous things taught me by my Beloved when we were together and alone, apart from them in the work of the ministry:

There were times when I…. I saw the Lord as if in a vision, similar in appearance to the way he just departed from us. The last time I encountered Jesus, I was standing outside his tomb, crying aloud in the brokenness of my heart. I feared looking at His corpse, knowing how the Roman crucifiers had so abused and tortured Him at the cross. But I found the needed courage, bent over and looked into the tomb.

I was dismayed, for I saw not his body there, but two angels, dressed in pure white garments and arrayed in light, seated where the body of the Master had lain. One angel stood up at the head and the other at the foot of the stone upon which His body had rested.

The angels wanted to know why I was crying.

The one at the head of the stone said, "The One Ye Seek informed us that we should be expecting you. Let your heart be calm and know that He lives; and that His love for you endures forever."

Then the angels bade me farewell and disappeared in a flash of light, in the twinkling of an eye."[170]

I then left the tomb, overcome by the intensity of the angelic encounter, but rejoicing in my heart to know that my Beloved yet lived. I was still crying, but with tears of happiness. At this point, however, I still wasn't sure if I was dreaming or not.

While I was walking through the garden and about to leave the grounds, the caretaker approached me. "Why are you crying, dear lady? Who is it that ye seek?" he asked me.

I said to the caretaker of the garden, "They have taken my Lord away and I have no idea where he can be found. Good sir, if you have taken him away, please let me know where you have put him, and I will go and get him."

Then the gentleman looked deep into my eyes and softly called me by name, "Mary."

Upon hearing my name spoken, it immediately dawned upon me that this was my Beloved Jesus. I cried out in my native tongue of Aramaic, 'Rabboni,' which means teacher, and moved to embrace Him. But Jesus stopped me, saying, "Do not touch me, for I have not yet ascended to my Father in the heavenly realms. But rather go to my brethren and inform them that I am ascending to My Father and your Father, to My God and your God."[171]

"Have I truly been so blessed as to see my Beloved in a vision this day?" I asked the seeming apparition.

To this question, Jesus replied, "Blessed are you, Mary, that you did not waver at the sight of me. For where the mind is, there is the treasure."

---

170 1 Corinthians 15:52 (KJV): "In a moment, in the twinkling of an eye, at the last trump: for the trumpet shall sound, and the dead shall be raised incorruptible, and we shall be changed."

171 For a parallel version, see John 20:11-18 (KJV).

I queried Him, "Lord, does the one who sees a vision while yet in this world view it through their physical or spiritual eyes?"

The Master replied, "In this world, a vision is beheld through neither the physical nor spiritual eyes, but rather through the mind's eye. The vision is but a living projection of light emanating from a spiritual reality. Your mind holds the key to bridging the physical and spiritual planes of existence. Thoughts are emanations from the spiritual realms that can be transformed into realities in the material world by the power of the mind. These include all natures, formations and creatures, great and small. These are the Aeons, the Emanations of the Father of Lights, the firstborn in the creation of the cosmos. Those awakened to the Truth understand that we all have a part in it, that we are all dependent upon one another and that our destinies are linked through the eternities."

I wanted to know why Jesus prohibited me from touching Him. The Master explained that for the time being, He was in a transitory state between the material world and the spiritual planes. But of His physical body that I remember, Jesus said, "While I lived with you, it served me as a garment. Where I am going, I will have no need of it. However, for appearance's sake, I have donned a new garment, but of a finer substance. That is why you did not immediately recognize me. When you come into the Kingdom, all shall be well with you as we both shall assume imperishable bodies of spirit."

When the Master lived in India, before He began his ministry among the House of Israel, He learned many great spiritual truths among the sages of that far country. From the knowledge passed on to Jesus from His teachers there, He told me that there are four powers working to assist the seeker of enlightenment that must be mastered while that one is still living in the material world.

Jesus said, "The first power is becoming acquainted with grief and suffering. Grief and suffering come from unfulfilled expectations in the material world. By keeping our desires fixated on the Kingdom and the righteousness of the Father, we shall be satisfied and grateful for all that we have; and great will be our eternal reward.

"The second power is putting an end to grief and suffering. Once aware of our grief and suffering, one must learn to praise and give thanks to the Father continually, whereby light and love will be generated out through you. And as you learn to generate light, the darkness will be banished from you and you yourself will be filled with the Light of Truth and comprehend all things! This is not accomplished by any outward demonstrating, but by learning to harken unto the Holy Spirit, that still small voice of Truth; and in following the divine instructions and fulfilling the celestial terms as delivered unto you. Then only is it possible to actually know the One Eternal God and to enjoy life eternal in the Father's Kingdom.

"The third power is becoming aware of our delusions of anger and attachment. These are based in an ignorance of the fact that everything in this material world is passing away; and that each soul in this world begins to die from the very day that they are born. Once one abandons their demands upon others and their desires for the things of the world, they are on the path that leads to gaining their celestial crown.

"And the fourth power is finding and following the path of accurate knowledge, the knowledge that leads to life eternal. Very few have attained the realization that love is the greatest of all elements; for it is a nonmaterial substance, the only remnant of the first, or spiritual creation. Love is also a boundless energy, an almighty power that manifests in all newly created life forms. Those that abide in love are already on the path that leads to the unseen worlds of light."

After relating these profound teachings of the Master to the apostles, I bore my testimony of Jesus and how he freed my soul of all that had previously bound it to the snares of this world. I testified as to the transient nature of the material world and its fetters of oblivion. I now attain to the eternities in the presence of my Beloved Jesus.

Remaining silent, I awaited a response from the brethren. Then Andrew, the younger brother of Peter, spoke up. "Say what you will about what she has said," declared the apostle, "but I do not believe that the Savior said this; for certainly these teachings are strange ideas."

Then Peter stood up, showing some partiality with Andrew, and declared to the brethren, "I do not recall a time that the Master spoke with a woman without our knowledge about such spiritual things, and not openly, at that. Are we to turn about and listen to her now? Did he prefer her to us? I am not sure what to make of this. But what think ye, dear brothers, for I value your opinions."

Being saddened by Peter's response, and wondering why he asked me about Jesus' teachings in the first place insofar as he seemed to be taking sides with Andrew, I said to the chief apostle, "My brother Peter, what do you think? Do you think that I made all of this up in my heart, or that I am lying about the Savior?"

Peter was stammering, looking for the words to say, when Levi (a.k.a. Matthew) said, "Peter, you have always been hot-tempered. Now I see that you are contending against this woman, treating her as if she were an adversary. But if the Savior found her worthy, who are you to reject her? Surely, the Savior knows her very well. This is why he loved her more than us. Rather, let us be ashamed and now put upon ourselves the mind of Christ, and preach His gospel, not laying down any other rule or other law beyond what the Savior has given us. Let us go forth and proclaim his words to the ends of the world, preaching the gospel to all peoples."

In the space of a few months, after Jesus had ascended to his celestial home, it was his mother Mary's uncle, Joseph of Arimathea, who took my children and I on a long journey to a wild country far to the north, where we found safety from the enemies of Jesus. It was this same Joseph who had kindly provided, along with Nicodemus, the tomb and memorial garden for Jesus. Joseph remained with us for twelve more years, until he died in his eighty-sixth year, a righteous man and servant of God since his youth.

About the Author

Dr. Raymond Keller "Cosmic Ray"

Through individual acts of kindness we transform the world.

Dr. Raymond A. Keller, II, international awards-winning, retired history professor and honorable military veteran of both the United States Navy and Army, is the author of the Venus Rising book series. Dr. Keller began his career as a writer back in the mid-1960s, as a reporter for the Bedford, Ohio, Times-Register newspaper and editor of the Bedford High School Fourth Estate newspaper. In the Navy, he was the feature editor of the Jet Journal, the official publication of the Miramar Naval Air Station in San Diego, California. And in the Army, he worked as a voice intercept operator in the Spanish language in Central America. Dr. Keller received his Master's degree from West Virginia University at Morgantown in 2004 in the Spanish language, with an emphasis on magical realism in Latin American literature. He received his doctoral degree from the same institution in 2011, focusing on various aspects of the Basque settlement of Venezuela. Dr. Keller has lived and worked in 45 different countries. His travels through the Middle East, his recent discovery of some Egyptian DNA through the 23 and Me website, his studies at the Community of Christ Graceland University Temple School in Independence, Missouri, as well as his firm belief in and experiences with continued revelation, inspired him to research and write these Gospels of Thomas and Mary Magdalene.

About the Illustrators

Dan Gorman

Dan Gorman is a trained Medical Illustrator with his Bachelor in Fine Arts in Medical Illustration from the Cleveland Institute of Art (1999). Dan began working as a Sketch Card Artist in 2010 and has since worked on over 150 Licensed Trading Card sets featuring properties that include but are not limited to Marvel, DC, Star Wars, Star Trek, Game of Thrones, Alien, The Lord of the Rings, Vampirella, Bettie Page, KISS, Rick & Morty, Steven Universe and AMC's The Walking Dead. In 2012, Dan began his career as a Comic Book penciler and has been published by Dark Horse (Grindhouse), AC Comics (FemForce), Empire Comics Lab (Cemetery Plots), Source Point Press (The Rejected, Kringle, Turkey Day) and Caliber Comics (Mississippi Zombie, Harvest of Horrors).

Dan is a member in good standing of the National Cartoonists Society and creates a weekly webcomic for the Akron Rubber Ducks (Cleveland Guardians Affiliate) baseball team called Rubber Ducks Tales which posts weekly to their Instagram Stories. Dan also helps run and promote several local Comicons and Pop Culture Cons, most notably the Akron Comicon. You can see more of Dan's work at https://dangormanart.com and be sure to follow him @GDanArtist on Twitter and Instagram!

Peter Holle

Peter Holle is an illustrator and children's book author. He lives in Hanover, Germany, and describes himself as a "nature-loving, self-confessed barefoot walker with deep ties to the spiritual worlds." He is fascinated by sacred geometry and numbers, as well as spiritual masterminds and brilliant people like Nikola Tesla. Peter is very imaginative and has been passionate about drawing people since childhood.

Through his friendly connection with the publisher of this book Anja Schäfer, a cooperation came about in 2022 for the German edition of Dr. Raymond Keller's book "Venus Rising", as Peter had offered his assistance with the German proofreading. Based on this wonderful cooperation and knowing Peter's talent for illustration, Ray and Anja asked him to draw a cover for the Gospels. The wonderful result of this inspired collaboration now adorns the cover of this book. To learn more about Peter and see a selection of his delightful children's illustrations, visit his website at *https://www.barfuss-junge.de*.

Publisher's Recommendations

Venus Rising Book Series by Dr. Raymond Keller

Dr. Raymond Keller "Cosmic Ray" and his Venus Rising Book Series

1. Venus Rising – A Concise History of the Second Planet, 2016
2. The Final Countdown: Rockets to Venus, 2018
3. Cosmic Rays Excellent Venus Adventure, 2018
4. The Vast Venus Conspiracy, 2021
5. Lady Columba Venus Revelations, 2021
6. Flying Saucers and the Venus Legacy, 2022
7. From Venus They Come, 2022

Book 1 to 7 published by Headline Books, WV, USA https://headlinebooks.com/ in cooperation with Dr. Raymond Keller.

The Book of Books by Annalee Skarin

https://herenowforever.com/wp-content/uploads/2019/09/THE-BOOK-OF-BOOKS-BY-ANNALEE-SKARIN.pdf

Omnec Onec – Messenger from Venus

The reader is also invited to check out Omnec Onec and her publications.

Omnec Onec was born on the astral level of the planet Venus and came to Earth with her own physical body in 1955. In the Ninetees, she became publicly known with her autobiography FROM VENUS I CAME. In this book, she portrays life on the astral level of Venus and describes why and how she was born there and why as a child she was given the opportunity to lower her vibrations, to manifest a physical body and to come to Earth at the age of seven in order to later in her life work as a spiritual teacher and fulfill her life cycles here on Earth.

Omnec Onec and Dr. Raymond Keller at the Mount Shasta Summer Conference 2023. In the background an illustration of the Temple City Teutonia on the astral Venus.

From Venus I Came
In her autobiography, Omnec tells about her first years of life on the astral Venus, explains why and how she came to Earth and what mission she has to fulfill here. This book is a unique document of its kind about the fabulous world of the astral. Being a sister planet to Earth, Venus has already gone through a similar process of transformation into a higher frequency plane as the Earth and its inhabitants are currently going through.

The history of Venus, delivered through Omnec Onec, along with its spiritual teachings, are a gift of pure love and show how the transformation into an expanded consciousness can be mastered in accordance with the universal laws of the Supreme Deity.
New Release 2023, DISCUS Publishing
ISBN: 978-3-910804-09-8

Angels Don't Cry

Angels Don't Cry is the stunning sequel to Omnec Onec's autobiography "**From Venus I Came**". This book is about the earthly life of the Venusian. Difficult family circumstances, constant changes of location and a spiritually unawakened environment presented very challenging conditions for the conscious child from Venus. The telepathic and sometimes physical contact with her friends and relatives from Venus as well as the awareness of her mission gave Omnec the strength to endure this life and to master it in love. Slowly, Omnec's way to the public was paved and the fulfillment of her mission as an Ambassador of Venus took hold with the first publication of her life story by Lt. Col. Ret. Wendelle C. Stevens in 1991.
New Release 2023, DISCUS Publishing
ISBN: 978-3-910804-10-4

Handbook of Venusian Spirituality

A spiritual guide to mastering life from the perspective of the Soul

This little book contains the essence of the message with which the Venusians have been living for a long time in harmony with the laws of the Supreme Deity. Because of their compassion, unity consciousness and love for all that is, they are equipped with the keys to raise their frequency. As Earth is currently experiencing a dimensional ascension, we can benefit from the knowledge of our sister planet Venus, which has already undergone this transformation.
New Release 2023, DISCUS Publishing
ISBN: 978-3-910804-11-1

Simply Wisdom and Love – Venusian Spirituality
Omnec Onec and Anja Schäfer
The world as we know it is changing rapidly, the Transformation Process of the Earth is in progress. The current world system, in which a few powerful people control and manipulate others, is coming to an end.
Contents: The Unknown History of our Solar System and the ongoing Transformation of the Earth from Venusian perspective · "The True Story of Christ" · "A Venusian Letter" · Transcripts of Omnec's public appearances with Q&A · Project Omnec's Oasis.
Loving, wise, inspiring. This book is a light focus for the expansion of consciousness and gives a deep insight into the teachings of the Venusians.
DISCUS Publishing, 2016
ISBN: 978-3-9817441-0-1

Venus and I
Anja Schäfer
My Journey of Coming to Remembrance of my Soul Mission
— 25 years with Omnec Onec —
A Story about Initiations, the Transformation of the Earth, and Love
"This book describes the author's spiritual awakening process. Her refreshing and witty way of writing made me feel like I was along on her journey." Axel
Contents: Venus Ambassadors, Omnec Onec, Dr. Raymond Keller "Cosmic Ray", Phaistos Disc, Atlantis, Cyclic Time – Linear Time, Venus-Germany-Connection, Transformation and Future of the Earth, Ascension, Awakening, Artificial Timeline and Natural Timeline, Spiritual Practices, Levels of Consciousness, Journey of Soul, Twin Flames, Unconditional Love, Jo Conrad Interview with Omnec Onec.
"I am certain today that I have incarnated as one of the souls to break down encrusted structures and to help both myself and people to allow true, divine love to rise and to embody. We are here to help Mother Earth to ascend to a higher vibrational frequency and to end the age of darkness and ignorance." Anja Schäfer – *venus-spirit.com*
New Release 2023, DISCUS Publishing
ISBN: 978-3-910804-02-9

Contact

Dr. Raymond Keller "Cosmic Ray"

Email: *rkeller1@mix.wvu.edu*
https://venus-spirit.com/en/raymondkeller

Robert Potter

Author of this book's introduction, contactee of the Venusians, organizer of the Mount Shasta Summer Conferences
Email: *thepromiserevealed@gmail.com*
https://thepromiserevealed.net

Anja Schäfer

Publisher, Facilitator of the Venusians
Email: *contact@venus-spirit.com*
https://venus-spirit.com
https://discuspublishing.com
https://youtube.com@venus-spirit

Made in United States
Cleveland, OH
19 February 2025

14513907R00125